Hollywood's Earth Shattering Scandals: The infamous, villains, nymphomaniacs and shady character in motion pictures. Part 1. 4th Edition.

Showbiz, Entertainment and Cinema Stars obsession with Money, Drugs, Fame, Sex, Power, Gossip and Greed.

<u>**Check also**</u> **:** Hollywood's Most Horrible People, Stars, Times, and Scandals. Revised: From The Stars Who Slept With Kennedy To Lavender Marriages And The Casting Couch.

Capucine: "They (Hollywood's actors/actresses) fucked each other so much...women began to smell semen and men perfume..."

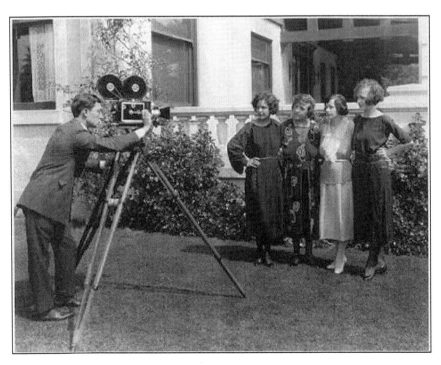

1920: Buster Keaton filming Norma, Peg, Natalie and Constance Talmadge. Natalie took him to the cleaners!

———

"In the early days of Hollywood, a film actor was even more disreputable than a stage performer."-*Buster Keaton*

1

"I'm only interested in two kinds of people, those who can entertain me and those who can advance my career."-**Ingrid Bergman**
Bergman's quote echoes what 99.99% of actors and actresses believe in! Their ego and greed are bigger and taller than the Empire State Building!

"Lionel Barrymore first played my grandfather, later my father, and finally, he played my husband. If he'd lived, I'm sure I'd have played his mother. That's the way it is in Hollywood. The men get younger and the women get older."-**Lillian Gish**

"To place in the limelight a great number of people (actresses and actors) who ordinarily would be chambermaids and chauffeurs, and give them unlimited power and wealth, is bound to produce disastrous results."-
Anita Loos (April 26, 1888 – August 18, 1981. She was an American screenwriter, playwright and author.)

Photo: Anita Loos

"Give those babes (Hollywood's actresses) the freedom and equality they are screaming for...and the first thing they will do...spread their legs."-**Clark Gable**

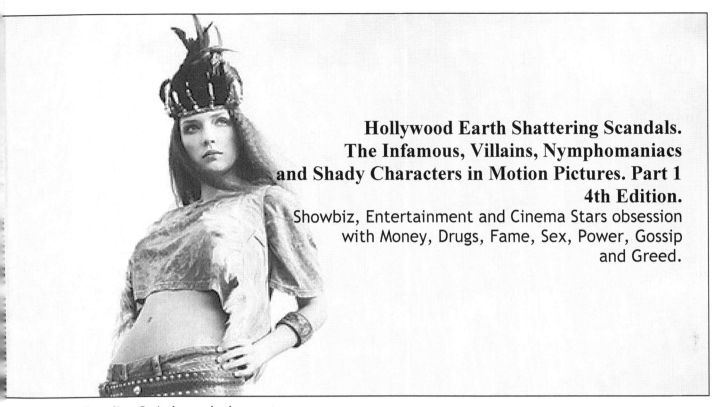

Hollywood Earth Shattering Scandals.
The Infamous, Villains, Nymphomaniacs and Shady Characters in Motion Pictures. Part 1
4th Edition.

Showbiz, Entertainment and Cinema Stars obsession with Money, Drugs, Fame, Sex, Power, Gossip and Greed.

Credits & Acknowledgment
References, sources, data, contributions:

13 Above
ABC News
Alex Johnson
Alternative Film Guide
Anita Page
Ann Sothern
AOL news
Arrested.com
Art & Style Magazine
Associated Contents
Bill Hewitt,
Blogtown
Bob Stewart
Brian Drive-in Theater
Cassandra Tate
Chasing the Frog
Claroscureaux
Classic Film Stars
CNN
Comcast
Cyber City Radio
Dahlia Site
Daily Express
Daily News
David Levin
David Stenn
David Wallechinsky

Dina-Marie Kulzer
Economic Expert
Extraordinary Thing.com
Gadling
Geoffrey Macnab
Gunsock
Hollywood Gossip
Hollywood Scandals
IMBD
International Herald Daily News
International News Agency
Irving Wallace
ITN
Jean Gabin
Jim Nolte
John Marriot
John O'Dowd
Joseph Harmes
Kat Giantis
KTLA-TV
La Femme Magazine
Lacey Rose
Lacy Conradt
Laura Orem
Lawrence Murray, Jr.
Leslie Coquette

Leslie Davis
Lewis Yablonsky
Linda Pomerleau
M.L. Costa
Matt; Homeless Tales)
MGM
MGN Ltd
MSN Entertainment
MSNBC
Mugshots.com
Ncole Cammorata
Ned Lannaman
Netscape Celebrity
Nickel in the Machine
OTB Media
Paramount Pictures
People's Almanach
Pop Eater
Prairie Ghosts
ProQuest Information and Learning Company
Rachel Bell
Richard Babcok
Robin Cross
Rolling Stone
Seeing Stars
Simone Signoret

Soshannah Rosenstein
Spout
Stacy Conrad
Star Ledger
Stars Illustrated Magazine
Stephanie Barish
Stephen Weissman
Stuff Entertainment
Sunshine and Shadow
Telegraph
The Desert Sun
The Independent
The Seattle Times
Tom Johansmeyer
Total Lawyers
Taylorogy
Troy Taylor
TV Party
Uk CIA
Vanity Fair
Vickey K.
Vinyl Zart
Voice of Reason
Who Dated Who
William Pop Crunch
Wpix

The message: Good people don't go near Hollywood.

"Hollywood, its stars and their lives are nothing more than piles of "merde" (Shit) covered with a thin layer of gold dust..."- *Simone Signoret*

"The desperate reality behind the glittering facade of Tinseltown's so-called Golden Age, a world of "cocaine-crazed comedies," "heroin heroines", "amoral extravagances", Hollywood wannabes, has-beens, cokeheads, burnouts, drunks, heroin addicts, rebels, sluts and losers."

"98% of the divas of Hollywood were "baptized" in the casting couch." *Jean Gabin*

"Hollywood's new ingénues lost their virginity either on the casting couch or in a star's dressing room." *a famous columnist*

"No sexual favors...no roles." *Anita Page*
In a 2004 interview with author Scott Feinberg, Anita Page said, that her refusal to meet demands for sexual favors by MGM head of production, Irving Thalberg, who was married to Norma Shearer, supported by Studio chief Louis B. Mayer, is what truly ended her career.

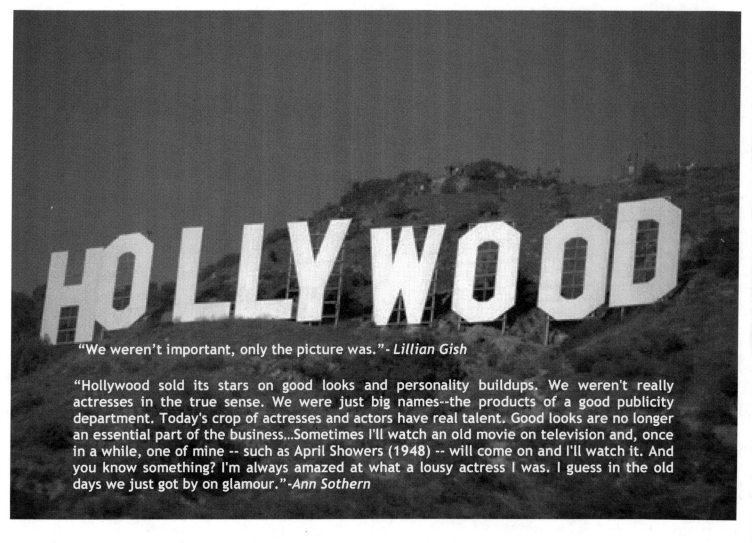

"We weren't important, only the picture was."- *Lillian Gish*

"Hollywood sold its stars on good looks and personality buildups. We weren't really actresses in the true sense. We were just big names--the products of a good publicity department. Today's crop of actresses and actors have real talent. Good looks are no longer an essential part of the business...Sometimes I'll watch an old movie on television and, once in a while, one of mine -- such as April Showers (1948) -- will come on and I'll watch it. And you know something? I'm always amazed at what a lousy actress I was. I guess in the old days we just got by on glamour."-*Ann Sothern*

"Any girl can be glamorous. All you have to do is stand still and look stupid."-*Louis B. Mayer*

Hollywood human tragedy:
When stars loose their stardom status and become unemployed and homeless.
A question was asked on the Internet: "Which is the worst scandal/tragedy that will someday happen in Hollywood?" And the best posted answer was: "They (all the celebs) going on welfare as the vehicle known as Hollywood, goes flat broke and those who are in the entertainment industry, (music ,movies, writers, make-up, hair, models, designers, etc... etc...) have no other way to make a living. And they have to get "real" jobs. "Would you like fries with that?" I can just see Justin Timberlake asking me that in McDonald's one day!"

Covers and book design:
Maximillien de Lafayette.
Senior Editor: Germaine Poitiers
Editor: Carol Lexter.

Researcher and senior contributor: Melinda Pomerleau.
Art Production: Solange Berthier and Fabiola Rossi.
A project of the Federation of American Musicians, Singers and Performing Artists Inc. (FAMSPA) New York

Published in 2009

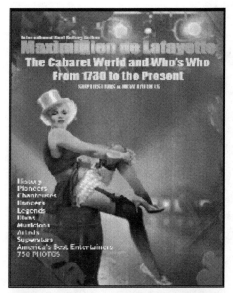

1- The Cabaret World and Who's Who From 1730 to the Present.
Superstars & New Talents: History, Pioneers, Chanteuses, Dancers, Legends, Divas, Musicians, Artists, America Best Entertainers.
(10 inches by 8 inches. 400 pages.)
Everything you wanted to know about Cabaret from day one to the present. Almost 280 years of events, shows, musicals, mega stars, new talents, the world's greatest divas, chanteuses, singers, performers, entertainers.
Stories about the private lives of legends never told before. Profiles and lists of America and the world best female and male singers. 750 rare, modern and vintage photos. The hidden world of the cabaret of Paris, Berlin, Hollywood and the dark alleys.

2- 400 Years Of Music, Entertainment And Showbiz.
From Pilgrims Psalm Chants and Spirituals, to Hollywood and Broadway: Golden Era, Vaudeville, Musicals, Cabaret, Pop, Jazz, Radio, TV, Divas, Stars. (10 inches by 8 inches. 400 pages.)
563 rare, modern, vintage photos & collectors' items. Chronological history of American music and songs from 1606 to present: Revolutionary war, post-colonial era, Afro-American music, Negro Spirituals, slaves songs, Gospel, Blues, Jazz, Folk, Rag time, Cakewalks, oldies, Rock & Roll, Standards. The early nostalgic days of radio entertainment, shows, celebrities, Vaudeville, Hollywood golden age, Las Vegas , Broadway, Paris, London.
Forgotten giants of American entertainment. Prettiest and legendary women in showbiz, movies, music, radio, stage, burlesque, theater. Explosive gossips of the era.
Greatest musicians & entertainers in history. Today's music/showbiz legends & greatest stars. Thousands of names, listings, profiles, biographies & entries.

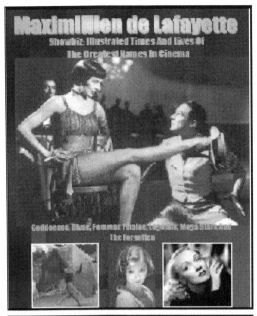

3- Showbiz: Illustrated Times and Lives of the Greatest Names in Cinema. (10 inches by 8 inches. 400 pages.)

Birth of cinema from 1867 to the present, Hollywood's golden age, the gangsters' days, German, French, Italian, British & American films and legends from a to z, Europe greatest divas and stunning beauties of showbiz, greedy superstars, Hollywood worst gossip, affairs & scandals, villains and villainesses of the silver screen on the set & behind closed doors, United States, and world's best drama and acting coaches & teachers, times and lives of the greatest stars of all time, bona fide femmes fatales from day one to the present. Hollywood's most beautiful stars/starlets, cinema terminology and dictionary, in depth study of world cinema and all genres.

In brief, cinema, Divas & Legends from A to Z, hundreds upon hundreds of rare, hard to find & vintage photos.

4-Hollywood's Earth Shattering Scandals: The infamous, villains, nymphomaniacs and shady character in motion pictures.

Includes: All Cartoon of scandals of the era...How bad Hollywood's stars were? All the infamous Cases. Sex scandals of early Hollywood. The MGM rape scandals. How studios tried to kill accusers before the trials. Divas and stars involvement with organized crime. The Mafia inside Hollywood's studios. The illegal children of the stars. Courts trials. All the divas who posed naked. Mega stars who gave sexual favors. Secret lives of homosexual and lesbian legends. The sites and locations of famous celebrity scandals, crimes, and accidents. Stars who killed themselves. And much more!

5- Hollywood Most Beautiful, Exclusive and Rarest

Photos Albums. (10 inches by 8 inches. 400 pages.)

The great and wonderful book on the nostalgia, glamour, extravaganza, and sophistication of the vanished world of early Hollywood, and glittering stars.

Hundreds upon hundreds of photos of the divas and mega stars (Females/Males) of the silver screen never seen before. A huge collection of rare, vintage studios & stars portraits, posters, and large pictures directly from stars & Hollywood vaults. Photos album of the stunning, greatest, famous and forgotten mega stars.

This is an illustrated book of their lives, styles, fashions, their homes, friends, way of life, entourage, gossip. Everything about Hollywood's extravaganza, glamour and golden era! Stills from the greatest 100 movies after 100 years of cinema. You will treasure it for years to come. Absolutely a must buy book.

9

6- Hollywood Past and Present (10 inches by 8 inches. 400 pages.)

One of the most beautiful books published in recent times, displaying 308 photos in colors and 80 in black & white, and a great number of huge full-page pictures. The perfect gift for the lovers of Hollywood's golden age, the magic of cinema, the fashion, sophistication and glamour of the divas and superstars of all time, past and present. Learn how they live, visit their mansions, hear their stories, discover their secrets and how they made it big time.

Also included: The glittering fashion and mesmerizing lifestyles of the biggest names in the business; today's most stunning actresses and sexiest men alive; America's majestic movie palaces; and lots of gorgeous film posters of the vanished era of the silver screen and epic movies. This is a collector item. A fabulous book of splendors, beauty and sparkling life of showbiz you will never see it again in your life, except in this book!

7 & 8- Film Noir, Femmes Fatales and Crime Movie Vintage Posters from Day One: Hollywood Studios Posters of the Silver Screen, Classic Period and the Gangsters Days.

A set of 4 books. This book is different from others, because, 1-Other books are limited to 1 poster per film. This book gets you acquainted with multiple posters for each film, issued at various dates, and/or for specific reasons. 2-American films shown abroad usually had regional posters published in foreign languages with a particular cache, quite different from the American edition. It is always interesting to learn how foreigners perceived the films, and presented them to their world's markets. This book gives you posters in both English and foreign titles. 3-This book gives you the opportunity to find out foreign artwork and special details given to those foreign posters. 4-Distinctive stills from the films are published next to the posters on separate pages, thus giving you a general idea about the mystique & cache of the film.

9, 10 & 11-Hollywood and Europe Greatest Black and White Films Stills and Cinema Legends Portraits. Book 1 and Book 2.

The first book of its kind, with its wealth of stills and rare "scene prints", never known to the public before. New light, and new discoveries are focused on what was going on between actors, actresses, directors and the set crew who produced these films' stills and scenes. Strong emphasis on the "behind the scene and the screen" stories, events and fascinating new "stuff and talks" surrounding the film, the still, the print, the actors and Hollywood studios. Hundreds upon hundreds of rare, vintage and collector's items photos and pictures, some published for the first time ever, coming directly from Hollywood vaults, studios, happy & "unhappy producers."

Many very large (full page size) photos are reproduced in their entire glory and mesmerizing black & white splendor.

The book is full of these incredible stills and prints that have created the mystique, nostalgia, beauty, magic and dream-world of Hollywood and its stars.

12-Hollywood's Most Horrible People, Stars, Times, and Scandals: From The Stars Who Slept With Kennedy To Lavender Marriages And The Casting Couch.

Published in 2007-2008

1- Biographical Encyclopedia of Singers, Musicians and Entertainers: Jazz, Pop, Standards and Cabaret (8 Volumes. 4,600 Pages. 10 inches by 8 inches.)

2- Best Musicians, Singers and Entertainment Personalities of the 19th, 20th And 21st Centuries. (970 Photos. 400 Pages. 12 inches by 8 inches.)

3- Showbiz, Pioneers, Best Entertainers and Musicians from 1606 to the Present. (800 Photos. 400 Pages. 12 inches by 8 inches.)

4- Entertainment Greats from the 1800's to the Present: Cinema Stage, Music, Divas, Legends. (1,500 Photos. 400 Pages. 12 inches by 8 inches.)

5- Entertainment: Divas, Cabaret, Jazz, Then and Now. (65 Photos. 740 Pages. 12 inches by 8 inches.)

6- Music, Showbiz and Entertainment (60 Photos. 400 Pages. 12 inches by 8 inches.)

7- World Who's Who in Jazz, Cabaret, Music and Entertainment. (10 Volumes. 7,000 Pages. 12 inches by 8 inches.)

Revised Hollywood Earth Shattering Scandals

The Infamous, Villains, Nymphomaniacs and Shady Characters in Motion Pictures. Part 1. 4th Edition.

Showbiz, Entertainment and Cinema Stars obsession with Money, Drugs, Fame, Sex, Power, Gossip and Greed.

Maximillien de Lafayette

Revised by
Germaine Poitiers
Contributor and Senior Researcher
Melinda Pomerleau

A PROJECT OF THE FEDERATION OF AMERICAN MUSICIANS, SINGERS AND PERFORMING ARTISTS (FAMSPA)
Website: www.federationofamericanmusicianssingersandperfomingartists.org

Times Square Press/Elite Associates International
New York   California   London   Paris   Tokyo

2010

Senior Researcher: Peggy North.
Photo Editor & Art Director: Daniel Iliescu.
Series Publication Editor: Dr. Erica Soderholm. Managing Editor: David Bloom.
Editor: Germaine Poitiers. Production Director: Shoshanna Rosenstein.
Data Base Editor: Carol Lexter.

DE LAFAYETTE WORLD MEDIA EDITORIAL STAFF, RESEARCHERS AND DATA PROCESSORS

www.delafayetteworldmedia.org

Table of Contents of Part 1 (Book 1)

Chapter 3: A juicy synopsis: From Hollywood's grapevine, and what it seems to be true!...71

Chapter 4: Hollywood's Biggest scandals: Suicides...140

Chapter 5: Hollywood's biggest scandals: Murders and crimes...170

Chapter 6: Hollywood's biggest scandals: Sex scandals...200

- Bill Murray...300
- Bo Bice...301
- Bob Marley...301
- Bobby Brown...301
- Bon Scott...301
- Brad Renfro...301
- Carlos Santana...301
- Charlie Sheen...301
- David Bowie...301
- David Faustino...301
- David Lee Roth...301
- Dawn Wells...302
- Dennis Hopper...302
- Dionne Warwick...302
- Don Henley...302
- Donovan...302
- Faith Evans...302
- Freddy Fender...302
- George Harrison...302
- Gregg Allman...302
- Haley Joel Osment...302
- James Brown...303
- Jason Cook...303
- Jennifer Capriati...303
- Jeremy London...303
- Jerry Garcia... 303
- John Lennon...303
- Kevin Gage...303
- Kimora Lee Simmons...303
- Lenny Bruce...303
- Linda McCartney...304
- Macaulay Culkin...304
- Matthew McConaughey...304
- Mischa Barton...304
- Neil Diamond...304
- Paul McCartney...304
- Peter Reubens...304
- Peter Tork...304
- Queen Latifah...304
- Ray Charles...304
- Sebastian Bach...304
- Steve-O...305
- Tony Curtis...305
- Tupac Shakur...305

*** *** ***

Section 2: Modern Hollywood. Scandals in Recent Years...306

Chapter 3: Stars'/Celebrities' Mug-Shots and Arrests...335
They are up to no good!

Chapter 4: Sex, and over-sex...361

Chapter 5: What they have said about each other...and themselves...381

Chapter 6: Homeless Stars and Legends...once upon a time...390

Chapter 7: Who were they before they became famous and arrogant?...394

*** *** ***

Introduction

"Hollywood's like Egypt. Full of crumbling pyramids. It'll never come back. It'll just keep on crumbling until finally the wind blows the last studio prop across the sands."-Attributed to David Selznick

*** *** ***

"Hollywood, its stars and their lives are nothing more than piles of "merde" (Shit) covered with a thin layer of gold dust..." once, said to me, Simone Signoret. Of course, Simone was referring to the 99% of Hollywood's stars and starlets, those who made it big time, and those who didn't. For we know, the remaining 1% has decent people like Henry Fonda, June Allison, Audrey Hepburn, Peter Ustinov, Ernest Borgnine, Helene Hayes, Joan Woodward, etc...

Jean Gabin once told me, almost 98% of the divas of Hollywood were "baptized" in the casting couch; a term invented circa 1940-1945, to mean "wherein actors and actresses exchanged sexual favors in order to be cast in a film or in a show production." In other words, the actress had to have sex with the casting director or the producer to get a job. This book has a strong emphasis on this subject.

Scandals and dirty stories about Hollywood's moguls, actors, actresses, producers, and studios' tycoons, exploded on the landscape of gossip, accusations, and in juicy tabloids, with a book called "Hollywood Babylon", written by former child actor and underground filmmaker Kenneth Anger. The book was first published in 1975, and colorfully depicted "the desperate reality behind the glittering facade of Tinseltown's so-called Golden Age, a world of "cocaine-crazed comedies," "heroin heroines", "amoral extravagances", Hollywood wannabes, has-beens, cokeheads, burnouts, drunks, heroin addicts, rebels, sluts and losers."

Well, this is one way to look at the birth of steamy stories about Hollywood's stars. But this is not totally correct, because, years before "Hollywood Babylon" was published, and the general public began to hear or read about the disgusting life style of the stars, many Hollywood's insiders knew a lot about what was going on. They talked about it, but fearing reprisals from the moguls and studios' bosses, did not discuss it in public, or report the scandals to the media. And almost in 90% of the cases, the media knew about all the scandals of Hollywood, but covered only a very insignificant amount of incidents and hard-to-hide scandals, for obvious reasons.

This book will take you behind the scene, and behind the desk of columnists, gossipists, and studios' bosses...and sometimes in the boudoir of drama queens, notorious nymphomaniacs, and...inside the mind of the mega stars who lived a double-life; the clean one on the silver screen, and the appalling one in their real and secret lives, that you have never read about.

Basically, the subject of this book is: "Hollywood's stars are the scum of the earth", and we are going to prove it!

Germaine Poitiers
Editor

Preface

Photo: Britney Spears says she knows her breasts are sexy, but she sometimes considers getting a reduction

Outrageous scandals...
Dirty gossip... Morbid accusations et al...
All are part of the fabric, soul, and daily existence of Hollywood.

Star-Dirt
Scandals caravan keeps on rolling...

All sorts of scandals have been historically linked with silver screen divas and goddesses since before there was even "talkies" in cinema.
They go back into the 1920s.
Before there were "talkies", there was talk of Hollywood's "It girl" Clara Bow taking on the entire USC football team. Arguably cinema's first-ever sex symbol, Bow quick became the subject of rampant sexual rumors after her disgruntled secretary leaked rumors to the press that the starlet had "relations" with the entire USC football team. All at once. On multiple occasions, said Devon Pollard.

Photo: Clara Bow.

According to Pollard, and Stuff Entertainment, politics was not the only arena that saw change in 2008, Hollywood also felt different as stars like Britney Spears and Robert Downey, Jr. overcame past personal troubles and let their work speak for Britney Spears: In 2007, the tabloids brimmed with celebrity scandals. Spears attacked a paparazzo with an umbrella and flashed her private parts in public.Then there was Britney Spears and her suspected romance with ex-Trojan volleyball player and Realtor-to-the-stars, Robert Edie. Now I'm not even going to list Britney's problems, because if you have a TV and a pulse, you know things have turned straight-jacket-crazy in the pop-icon's life.
But before she was suspected to be romantically involved with the Marshall business school grad, it was rumored she was playing tonsil hockey with Matt Leinart.
Celebrity heiress Paris Hilton spent three weeks in jail for violating probation in a case of driving under the influence, and actress Lindsay Lohan

28

saw her hard-partying life turn to DUI arrests and stints in rehab. She stood in stark contrast."
Things seem to be heating up in sunny Southern California, and we're not just talking about the weather. It seems every time the tabloids snap a picture of celluloids' most scandalous young starlets, there's a USC student or graduate standing beside them. Take the latest silver-screen scandal of the moment: Lindsay Lohan. Her rap-sheet is nearly as long as her IMDB profile. There's the multiple speeding tickets, the running red-lights, a hit-and-run, D.W.I, the drinking, the alleged cocaine possession, the rehab, and the revealing Marylin Monroe photos. And who was that scruffy guy with her in all the tabloid photos? That's USC graduate Spencer Guilburt. Lohan's has been caught with her (now-ex) hubby-of-the moment - 24 year old Guilbert, a graphic artist/clothing designer, kissing around town.
I would definitely say the golden age of the shock starlet seems to have ebbed," said Seth Abramovitch, editor of Defamer, a celebrity news website. "It peaked last year and they all sort of went into nesting mode." Spears, 27, began 2008 on a downturn as she was twice hospitalized for psychiatric evaluation. But her life soon quieted down as a Los Angeles family court granted her visits with her sons, and her father took over her affairs. Things got so slow for Spears that she told Rolling Stone magazine she felt old and boring. But quietude appears to have been a boon for the pop diva, because she released the chart-topping comeback album Circus. Since 2005, when he argued with TV interviewer Matt Lauer about psychiatry and jumped on Oprah Winfrey's couch proclaiming his love for Katie Holmes. Tom Cruise has battled his own image problems.
Finally, Cruise acknowledged his past issues, saying he acted "arrogant" and just could have "handled things better." He also won acclaim for his comedic role in the movie Tropic Thunder, parodying a nasty movie studio executive. "I think he's been very smart about the way he has been resuscitating his career and reshaping his image," said David Hauslaib, editorial director of celebrity website Jossip.
Celebrity watchers said Robert Downey Jr. returned to Hollywood's A-list and revived his drug- and arrest-plagued career by starring in hit comic book movie Iron Man, which earned US$582 million at worldwide box offices.
Downey also earned Golden Globe and Screen Actors Guild nominations for his role as an Australian actor playing a black American action hero in Tropic Thunder. "He is a success story in that he's also an inspiration for those younger people, like the Lindsays and the Britneys," said celebrity news blogger Perez Hilton. "He's been though rehab, he's been to jail and he's managed to come through it all," said Hilton, whose actual name is Mario Lavandeira. While many US stars stayed out of trouble in 2009, in Britain singer Amy Winehouse, 25, saw her battle with drug addiction overshadow her recording successes.
Along with Spears, Hilton and Lohan have also toned down their partying and settled into relationships. Hilton, 27, dated musician Benji Madden for months as Lohan, 22, became inseparable from gal pal Samantha Ronson, a celebrity DJ. "You have really your trio of tabloid cover girls, Lindsay Lohan, Paris Hilton and Britney Spears, and all three of them really have sort of cleaned up their act," Hauslaib said. Not to be left out is Nicole Richie, daughter of singer Lionel Richie and Hilton's co-star on TV show "The Simple Life." The one-time Hollywood party girl who spent time in jail in August 2007, had a baby with baby with rocker Joel Madden and stayed out of tabloid scandalous headlines.

Hollywood's Stars and Celebrities Scandals never stop

Photo: Marilyn Monroe

Stabbing Johnny Stompanato: In 1958, Lana Turner's daughter Cheryl, fearing that her mother's life was in danger, fatally stabbed her mother's former boyfriend Johnny Stompanato, who also happened to be a mobster. The death was called justifiable homicide.

Marilyn Monroe's death in 1962: It is still the object of much discussion, most of it centering on the Kennedys.

Roman Polanski's conviction of statutory rape: Director Roman Polanski's wife Sharon Tate was a victim of the madman Charlie Manson, and he was later convicted of statutory rape and fled the country to avoid jail.

Photo: Hedy Lamarr

Farrell Sues Sex Tape Scandal Model: The New World star Colin Farrell slapped model Candace Smith with a lawsuit for conspiring to sell an X-rated sex tape he made with her friend Nicole Narain. The 29-year-old alleged the model, who was a former Miss Ohio, conspired with Narain to distribute the tape. Farrell's lawyer Paul Berra confirmed that Smith was a main focal point of the case. Narain was also a defendant in the lawsuit according to Hollywood website TMZ.com. Smith appeared as a model on The Price Is Right in 2004 and also had a law degree from the University Law School in Chicago, Illinois.

Photo: Lindsay Lohan.

Hedy Lamar's shoplifting charges: Lamarr was famous for many scandals, most notably a 1966 arrest in which it was alleged that she stole an $85 pair of slippers. She was cleared of the charges, but that same year, her autobiography "Ecstasy and Me," which was actually penned by a ghostwriter, was published and further tarnished her image. The book gave unsavory details about her love life, even suggesting she was a nymphomaniac.

Actress Lindsay Lohan snoring cocaine: Lohan returned to her wild ways, after she was filmed allegedly snorting cocaine, less than two months after leaving rehab. The troubled star, who claimed to have sobered up after her recent stint at the Los Angeles Wonderland Center, was also reported to have bragged to friends about her sexual exploits with actors Jude Law and Spider-Man star James Franco as she partied at trendy Hollywood nightclub Teddy's. It was also published that time that the act of going to the rehabilitation center, was also a publicity stunt for Lindsay Lohan.

Singer R. Kelly's videotaping sex acts with a 14-year-old girl: In 2002, 35-year-old R&B singer R. Kelly, a married father of two, was charged of allegations that he videotaped sex acts with a 14-year-old girl. But this wasn't the first time Kelly's teenage love affairs made headlines. In August 1994, the singer married then 15-year-old Aaliyah just before her first album "Age Ain't Nothing But a Number", which Kelly produced. The marriage was annulled a few months later.
Sex with a 15 year old girl: Then in 1996, Tiffany Hawkins, one of Kelly's back-up singers, sued Kelly, claiming he made her have sex with him when she was 15 in order to keep her job. Kelly settled the Hawkins suit in 1998 for a reported $250,000. In 2001, Tracy Sampson, an intern at Epic Records, claimed in a civil suit that she lost her virginity to a coercive and deceitful Kelly when she was 17.
Juicy sex accusations: In 2005, a bitter former hotel security boss decided to breach her confidentiality agreement and revealed all about the celebrities' dirty secrets. Eloise Mohsin worked at the exclusive Phoenix Ritz-Carlton hotel in Arizona from 1999 to 2002, when she left amid a sexual harassment scandal. Mohsin told National Enquirer, that Paltrow once spent the night with pal Sheryl Crow at the hotel. Mohsin also alleged that supermodel Tyra Banks tried to romance Sean 'P Diddy' Combs when the pair were both guests at the hotel, by sending flowers and intimate notes to his room. But the most shocking revelation was a claim that a maid once found a used pregnancy kit in Justin Timberlake's room after Britney Spears spent a night with her then-boyfriend.

Photo: Kate Moss.

Wild sex-cocaine parties: In 2005, British newspaper the News of the World, claimed that Moss became wildly sexual during cocaine fuelled parties, and had orchestrated a number of lesbian romps with friends including Sadie Frost and British TV star Davinia Taylor.
Hollywood Celebrities Scandals reported that **Kate Moss** had also been accused of trying to seduce a personal assistant (PA) Rebecca White while under the influence of cocaine. Rebecca White, who claimed to have known Kate Moss since 1998, alleged that the British beauty lured her back to her hotel room and fondled her breasts.

And from Fatty Arbuckle to Michael Jackson...

Fatty Arbuckle, accused of killing Virginia Rappe
On Labor Day weekend in 1921, corpulent, baby-faced funny man Roscoe "Fatty" Arbuckle, beloved around the world by kids and adults for his silent-movie slapstick, celebrated his newly inked, record-setting $3 million contract with Paramount by throwing a wild party at the St. Francis Hotel in San Francisco. Witnesses claim that during the revelries, Arbuckle disappeared into a private suite with starlet Virginia Rappe. No one knows what happened next, but within days Rappe was dead, allegedly from acute peritonitis caused by "an extreme amount of external force." Arbuckle, suspected of sexual assault, was arrested and charged with manslaughter. After three headline-grabbing trials (the first two ended in hung juries), he was cleared. "Acquittal is not enough for Roscoe Arbuckle," the jury said in a statement. "A grave injustice has been done." But the comedian's career was ruined -- his contract canceled and his films banned. After spending a dozen years as a Tinseltown pariah, Arbuckle was finally on the comeback trail (he'd

just completed a series of shorts for Warner Bros.) when he died in his sleep of a heart attack at the age of 46.

Michael Jackson: 10 years of scandals, from molestation allegations to disfiguring plastic surgery. Every move Jackson has made in the past decade has been documented by an insatiable press for an obsessed public. The late Michael Jackson, who paid $15 million-plus to settle a 1993 child molestation lawsuit brought by a 13-year-old boy (Jackson was acquitted.) Smaller scandals have included Michael's marriages and subsequent divorces from Lisa Marie Presley and Debbie Rowe, with the latter producing two children (he says she bore them "as a present" to him) who don't look much like dad, though it's difficult to tell given their constantly veiled heads; his admission to British journalist Martin Bashir that he has "slept in a bed with many children ... It's very right. It's very loving "; and the infamous, November 2002 dangling of his then 11-month-old son (mother unknown) from a hotel balcony.

1942: Errol Flynn: Arrested for the statutory rape of two teenage girls. He's acquitted and the phrase "In like Flynn" is coined.
1949: Robert Mitchum: Busted for possession of marijuana. He serves 60 days in the pokey.
1959: Eddie Fisher leaves Debbie Reynolds for the recently widowed Elizabeth Taylor. Four years later, Taylor leaves Fisher for Richard Burton.

More scandals.
Here is a small list, from Hollywood's day one to the present:

- 1-The suicide of Olive Thomas in Paris, France (Hollywood's first recorded scandal).
- 2-Howard Hughes impregnation of Jean Harlow.
- 3-Humphrey Bogart's involvement in Jean Harlow's abortion.
- 4-Humphrey Bogart procuring male prostitutes to Howard Hughes.
- 5-Monaco Prince Rainier's list of his wife, Grace Kelly's lovers (Men and women)
- 6-Roscoe "Fatty" Arbuckle; accused of killing starlet Virginia Rapp.
- 7-The rape charge against Errol Flynn.
- 8-Silent film mega star Wallace Reid's tragic death from drug addiction.
- 9-The murder trial of Robert Blake, who has been accused of shooting and killing his wife.
- 10-Winona Ryder's infamous shoplifting charges, and trials.
- 11-Lana Turner's scandal: Daughter Cheryl stabbing to death hoodlum Johnny Stompanato, her mother's lover.
- 12-Robert Mitchum's arrest for drug possession.
- 13-The secret daughter of Clark Gable and Loretta Young.
- 14-Rock Hudson's AIDS.
- 15-Rudolph Valentino's homosexuality.
- 16-The shocking death of director William Desmond Taylor.
- 17-The Ingrid Bergman-Roberto Rossellini affair.
- 18-The murder of Nicole Brown Simpson.
- 19-The X-rated Rob Lowe sex video.
- 20-The Clara Bow's orgies, and gang-bang sex scandal.
  21-Sophia Loren-Carlo Ponti notorious affair and illegal marriage.
- 22-Bob Crane's baffling death.

- 23-Loretta Young and Clark Gable's secret love child.
- 24-Judy Garland's public disgrace.
- 25-Hedy Lamarr's arrest for shoplifting.
- 26-The Elizabeth Taylor-Debbie Reynolds-Eddie Fisher triangle.
  27-The affair between Elizabeth Taylor and Richard Burton.
- 28-Joan Crawford's affairs and dealings.
- 29-The killing of rapper Tupac Shakur.
- 30-The slaughter of Ramon Navarro.
- 31-Mary Astor's diary, 1935. The diary listed the names of her lovers, and described her extramarital affairs.
- 32-The baffling death of Thomas Ince aboard William Randolph Hearst's yacht "The Oneida". Did the magnate kill Ince, Hollywood style?

Does it stop? Oh no! It does not!

David Letterman admits sexual affairs; he claims he was extorted

October 2009: New York, Thursday October 1, 2009, Pop Eater/Wire Service-AOL News. The following was posted on AOL: In a stunningly candid admission during his show on Thursday night, David Letterman said that he has had sexual relationships with female employees of his show, and that someone tried to extort him by releasing information about the relationships. A CBS employee has since been arrested for the alleged extortion plot. During the taping of his CBS late-night show in New York, Letterman discussed receiving a threat to either pay $2 million or risk the relationships being made public. "In the back seat of my car, there's a package that I don't recognize. This is is a guy who is going to write a screenplay about me and he's going to take all the terrible stuff that he knows about my life and he's going to put it into a movie unless I give him some money," Letterman explained to the audience. "Now of course we get to what is it. What was all the creepy stuff that he was going to put into the screenplay and the movie, and the creepy stuff that I had ... sex with women who work for me on the show. Now, my response to that is yes, I have," he continued. The network said the person who was arrested works on the true-crime show "48 Hours" and has been suspended. A person with knowledge of the investigation said the suspect is Robert J. Halderman. The person spoke on condition of anonymity because authorities have not released the suspect's name. A "48 Hours" producer named Joe Halderman was part of a team nominated for an Emmy for outstanding continuing coverage of a news story in a news magazine in 2008.

Two numbers listed for Halderman were disconnected, and a message left at a third number was not immediately returned Thursday. RadarOnline.com was the first to report that Halderman was a suspect. As part of the case, Letterman said in a release that he testified before a grand jury and acknowledged sexual relationships with members of his staff. CBS spokesman Chris Ender says "Letterman's comments on the broadcast tonight speak for themselves."

Stars suicide scandals never stop!

May 2009: Spider-Man star, **Actress Lucy Gordon** has hanged herself in her apartment in Paris, France. The British actress, Lucy Gordon, was in movies such as Spider-Man 3, Serendipity, and Frost, was found dead Wednesday, days before her 29th birthday.

Photo: Actress Lucy Gordon

Lucy was devastated after the recent suicide of her close friend in the U.K. Gordon's body was discovered at her apartment at la Rue des Petites Ecuries after her boyfriend alerted a nearby shopkeeper.

It appears that the young woman took her own life." An officer told Sky News, "It was a horrific scene. The young woman had taken her own life in terrible circumstances. We are not seeking anyone else. It was a clear case of suicide."

Lucy Gordon had finished filming a movie about singer-songwriter Serge Gainsbourg in which she played British actress Jane Birkin.

Director Joann Sfar and producers Marc du Pontavice and Didier Lupfer said in a statement: "The film owes a lot to the generosity, gentleness and immense talent of Lucy Gordon."

Lucy Gordon's rep confirmed she had "ended her own days". That's so sad.

June 2008. Ruslana Korshunova, Russian actress and supermodel commits suicide: Ruslana Korshunova, a 20 year-old Russian actress/supermodel, plummets to her death in a suicide, from her ninth floor apartment in lower Manhattan.

The witnesses to the apparent suicide saw the barefoot woman, dressed in blue jeans and a purple tank top, and noticed her beauty immediately, although they did not realize at the time she was a world-famous model. Police stated there were no signs of struggle in her apartment. The window from which she fell had a balcony, which had construction netting around it that appeared to have been cut.

Ruslana Korshunova's death was ruled as a definite suicide.

Photo: Actor David Carradine: Murdered or suicide?

December 18, 2008. Soprano" actor John Costelloe commits suicide: John Costelloe, an actor best known to viewers of "The Sopranos" for his role as the gay lover of a mobster, has died Costelloe reportedly committed suicide by a self-inflicted gunshot. The Associated Press has reported that John Costelloe, 47, was found dead in his Brooklyn home on December 18, 2008. Costelloe, a

34

former New York City firefighter, was cast in "The Sopranos" in 2006 as a short-order cook, Jim Witowski, known as Johnny Cakes.

His character was the gay lover of Joseph Gannascoli, who played Vito Spatafore, a mob henchman seeking to keep his gay life on the down-low.

Photo: Star Mindy McCready

December 2008. Country star attempted suicide with pills, alcohol, and wrist slashed: Country singer, and superstar **Mindy McCready** was hospitalised after she cut her wrists and took several pills in an apparent suicide attempt, Nashville police said. A police report said McCready's brother discovered her at home on Wednesday. Timothy McCready told police his sister had been "very intoxicated" after a night out.

June, 2009. The legendary "Kung Fu" **actor, David Carradine,** was found dead in Bangkok at the age of 72. Many reports stated that Carradine was found hanged in his hotel room, but now new reports cited it was "accidental", possibly during a sex act such as autoerotic asphyxiation. Carradine's rep wants to put suicide rumors to rest and said the tragic death of the actor was accidental. An officer on the scene described finding Carradine's naked body hanging in his closet with rope around his neck as well as "other body parts". It sounds as if Carradine was engaging in a type of sex act and died accidentally. But the actor has spoken previously of suicide. In an interview in 2004, David Carradine stated: "I remember one time sitting in the window of the third or fourth floor of the Plaza Hotel for about an hour, thinking about just tipping off. And that was at a time when I was having more fun than you could imagine. "I just thought, 'Who the...cares, man? Why don't I just split?' Of course I didn't, so there you go." He also had said he considered committing suicide by shooting himself: "Look, there was a period in my life when I had a single action Colt 45, loaded, in my desk drawer. And every night I'd take it out and think about blowing my head off, and then decide not to and go on with my life. Put it back in the drawer and open up the laptop and continue writing my autobiography or whatever. But it was just to see." (Source: Stupid Celebrities) On June 5, 2009, the media had discovered that Carradine was murdered, because he was found with hands tied behind his back. Carradine's body was in a sitting position, with a yellow rope wrapped around the neck and attached to a closet bar, said police Col. Somprasong Yentuam, chief of the Lumpini area station. "We believe that Mr. David committed suicide but it is suspicious," said Yentuam. Even more information has come out which causes you to believe David Carradine's death was not a suicide. CNN is citing police sources who said police and rescue workers in Thailand told them "the actor's neck and genitals were found bound with rope."The CNN report says "a yellow nylon rope was tied around the actor's neck and a black rope was around his genitals."

Britney Spears: According to various reports, "After she shaved off her hair, Britney had a complete breakdown and tried to kill herself. Britney was crying and said she would kill herself if she lost the boys. Britney apparently tried walking directly into oncoming traffic, but a member of her staff grabbed her. During the night, she escaped and tried to walk into oncoming traffic. Britney said she wanted to kill herself. She later grabbed a bottle of Xanax and said she'd take the whole bottle – she didn't care what happened to her.

As you see, stars' scandals never stop, and this pattern is part of the daily life of the famous, the rich, and the "stars".

Tarnished Stars Find Ways to Get Their Shine Back
America loves a comeback story and getting there is big business in Hollywood

In a report from ABC news, "Hollywood is held to a very different standard," explains Eric Dezenhall, a Washington, D.C.-based damage control specialist and the author of Damage Control. "There is no pretense of morality." Of course, there are some scandals that aren't granted leniency, no matter how well-timed or sincere the apology. Paul Reubens, a comedian known for his kid-friendly role as Pee Wee Herman learned that lesson. After two arrests -- one for indecent exposure at an adult movie theater in 1991, and another for possession of child pornography a decade later -- his career is finished.

Eddie Murphy: After being caught red-handed with a transvestite prostitute in 1997, he managed to come back big with box office hits "Doctor Dolittle", "Norbit" and "Dreamgirls", among others. The latter not only earned $103.4 million at the domestic box office, but also an Oscar nomination for Murphy. Reubens is the exception.

Like most things in Tinseltown, there is a right -- and wrong -- way to stage a comeback. According to Shawn Sachs, a partner at New York's Sunshine, Sachs & Associates, a public relations firm that represents politicians and celebrities including Ben Affleck and Leonardo DiCaprio, the media and its audience are very forgiving. "They enjoy the pendulum shift," he explains. "They may love to tear you down, but then they love to build you back up."

On the "don'ts" list: lying, says Sachs. "It's PR 101: End the story," he says of coming clean. "If you're lying and misleading and trying to spin while there's still an open-ended story out there, you're going to get caught because there's just too much media." What it really comes down to is timing, says Dezenhall. His advice: "Go away for awhile and come back once the hurricane passes," he explains.

"It's very difficult to rebuild your house in the middle of a storm. You just have to wait." He applauds Lohan for doing just that. After two DUIs and a couple of stints in rehab, the struggling starlet has largely stayed away from the flashbulbs. But the "just shut up" strategy, as veteran celebrity publicity Howard Bragman has dubbed it, comes with its own set of challenges.

Namely: These people didn't get to be where they were by shutting up. That's why Bragman, who most recently mopped up the mess of "Grey's Anatomy" cast-off Isaiah Washington, tries very hard to convince his clients that just because they can get press, doesn't mean they should. Instead, he advises they wait until they're ready to come clean because it's always better to make one apology and do it well, than have to re-apologize and create another news cycle. In the meantime, crisis managers suggest disgraced celebrities focus on their art. Or, as Bragman puts it, "get back to what made you a star in the first place."

Disgraced Movie-Star Comebacks
Eddie Murphy (Left)

Scandal: Soliciting a transvestite prostitute in 1997.
Film: Doctor Doolittle (June, 1998). Box office gross: **$184.4 millions.**
Funnyman Eddie Murphy was caught red-handed in 1997 when police watched him pick up a transvestite prostitute in one of Hollywood's well-known sex-trade districts. Though image experts are quick to slam Murphy's handling of the event--rather than admitting fault, he resisted the charge--Murphy saw little fallout. Already on his way to PG-rated stardom--see *The Nutty Professor*--Murphy scored big with

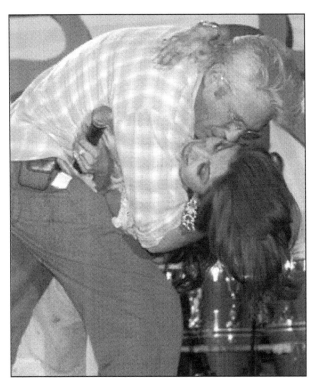

Doctor Doolittle. More recently, his work in the box office hit *Dreamgirls* earned him an Oscar nomination.

Photo: Scandal: Gere Kissing escapade in India in 2007.

Richard Gere: The superstar became the center of controversy in India when he swept Bollywood star Shilpa Shetty into his arms and kissed her several times during an AIDS awareness event in New Dehli.

In a locale where public displays of affection are still taboo, the action was enough to get Gere arrested (the order was soon overturned by the Supreme Court) and his figure burned in effigy throughout India. In spite of the much-publicized dust-up, Gere will head back to the theaters with 2008's *Nights in Rodanthe*, opposite Diane Lane.

Russell Crowe (Left)
Scandal: Assault charge for throwing a phone at a hotel concierge, in 2005.
Film: *Cinderella Man* (June 2005). **Box office gross: $65.8 millions.**
Since his 2005 phone-wielding altercation with a New York hotel concierge, Russell Crowe has worked hard at mending his embattled reputation with a Hugh Grant-style mea culpa tour. Though his tele-tantrum apology didn't translate at the box office for 2005's *Cinderella Man* or 2006's *A Good Year*, critics and fans alike are highly anticipating his return to action in this month's Ridley Scott crime epic *American Gangster*.

Roman Polanski (Left)
Scandal: Statutory rape in 1977.
Film: *Tess* (December 1980). **Box office gross: $53.8 millions.** Upon pleading guilty to a charge of unlawful intercourse with a 13-year-old in 1997, the renowned director of *Chinatown* and *Rosemary's Baby* fled the country to avoid sentencing. Though he remains in exile, the European-bound director continues to make noteworthy films. Among them: 2003 Oscar winner *The Pianist*.

Robert Downey, Jr.
Scandal: Drug possession. Date: Multiple arrests between 1996 and 2001.
Film: *The Singing Detective* (October 2003). **Box office gross:**

$382,138.

Despite his well-publicized battles with drugs--to say nothing of his various stints behind bars--Robert Downey, Jr. managed to keep his resume full, garnering high-profile roles during the drug-plagued period. It's clear the actor has his talent and general likeability to thank for his many Hollywood chances. While *The Singing Detective* failed to garner millions, his second post-scandal flick, *Gothika*, raked in $67.7 million in 2007 dollars. Newly remarried and reportedly clean, Downey, Jr. continues to snag films and fans alike.

Woody Allen (Left)
Scandal: Affair with his lover's college-aged daughter, in 1992.
Film: *Husbands and Wives* (September 1992). **Box office gross: $15.7 millions.**

Something of a tabloid target since his public affair (and later marriage) with lover Mia Farrow's adopted daughter, Woody Allen witnessed his cultural stock drop with his damaged reputation. In an ironic--if not bizarre--twist, Allen's first post-scandal film, *Husbands and Wives*, involved him playing a college professor who falls for a student.

While the film, much like many that followed, failed to pop at the box office, the actor/director has continued to garner film credits and headlines.

Hugh Grant (Left)
Scandal: Lewd conduct in the company of a prostitute, in 1995.
Film: *Nine Months* (July, 1995). **Box office gross: $95.3 millions.**

Still reeling from his 1994 hit, *Four Weddings and a Funeral*, Hugh Grant was caught with his pants down in 1995 in the company of a prostitute. Seeking clemency--not to mention an audience for his upcoming flick *Nine Months*--the boyish Brit staged what experts call a textbook mea culpa. Admitting fault on the talk show circuit proved successful: *Nine Months,* as well as future films *Bridget Jones's Diary, Love Actually* and *Music & Lyrics* all performed well at the box office.

Tom Cruise
Scandal: Couch jumping episode, media attacks, in 2005
Film: *Mission: Impossible III* (May 2006). **Box office gross: $138.6 millions.**

For most people, enthusiastically jumping up and down on a couch wouldn't be considered scandalous. But Tom Cruise is not most people. And those antics, combined with his calling Brooke Shields "irresponsible" for championing postpartum-depression drugs and dismissing

Today's Matt Lauer as "glib" while discussing Ritalin and kids, have alienated some of the once media-shy star's audience--at least according to Viacom chairman Sumner Redstone, who famously fired him last summer. In the months since, Cruise found a studio (United Artists) to run and will return to the silver screen this month in the shingle's Robert Redford-directed drama *Lions for Lambs*, co-starring Redford and Meryl Streep, as stated by Lacey Rose, Forbes, and ABC News.

Winona Ryder (Left)
Scandal: Shoplifting in 2001
Film: *Mr. Deeds* (June, 2002)
Box office gross*: $146.4 million
Ryder's film career had already taken a turn for the flop--see *Lost Souls* and *Autumn in New York*--when she was caught shoplifting at a Beverly Hills Saks Fifth Avenue in late 2001. Though the Oscar winner's first post-scandal film, *Mr. Deeds*, grossed $146.4 million at the U.S. box office when adjusted for inflation, it was her costar Adam Sandler who received much of the credit. Since then, she's continued to land roles but has had little to brag about at the box office.

Bottom line: The public and gossipists are equally hypocrite and responsible!

This book retraces all the colorful, juicy, and appaling episodes of stars and Hollywood's moguls' scandals caravans. The superstars' world is not a healthy environment.

PART ONE

Chapter 1
Airbrush her cleavage, maestro!

At the beginning, the names of early movie stars were not important.

Lillian Gish, once said: "We weren't important, only the picture was." Now, try to say this to Tom Cruise or Julia Roberts! They will tell you: We are the picture! The very first movies did not include the names of the actors and actresses in the credit titles. "Biograph" did not list the names of actors and actresses in the title credits before early 1914. Studios' executives thought that the film is the piece de resistance, not the name of the players (actors and actresses.) But, once it became certain to Hollywood's studios that moviegoers were mesmerized by the stars, then, and only then, studios' executives and producers understood that publicizing their stars would guarantee more revenues and dividends at the box office. Consequently, studios began to create and circulate fantastic and absolutely fictitious stories about their movie stars, and avalanches of stars' glamorous photos were sent to magazines and newspapers.

Ann Sothern once said: "Hollywood sold its stars on good looks and personality buildups. We weren't really actresses in the true sense. We were just big names--the products of a good publicity department. Today's crop of actresses and actors have real talent. Good looks are no longer an essential part of the business...Sometimes I'll watch an old movie on television and, once in a while, one of mine -- such as April Showers (1948) -- will come on and I'll watch it. And you know something? I'm always amazed at what a lousy actress I was. I guess in the old days we just got by on glamour."

The glamour syndrome:

Hollywood came up with two creations that catapulted and greased the wheel of movie stars' publicity campaigns and image making:

1-A special department solely created by the studios to print and distribute thousands of photographs of movie stars bearing their autographs in bold black ink. Later on, it was discovered that less than 1% of those autographed photos were in fact signed by the stars. The truth is, the studios assigned a fleet of clerks to imitate the signature of their leading men and women and mail photos in bulk to hungry and fanatic fans, who never knew the difference.

2-The glamour photography department. An entire mega sub-industry was invented. A huge undertaking placed under the direct creative control of "glamour photographers", such as Robert Richee and the legendary George Hurrell. These photographers had one thing on their mind: Creating new technology, lighting techniques, and developing innovative ideas and methods to make the stars look fantastic, mesmerizing and glamorous, in the most flattering and captivating way. The concept was simple: Idealizing the woman star, and elevating her to the rank of divine divas via suggestive romantic poses, positions, unusual artistic camera angles, special lighting techniques, against dark or sparkling backgrounds –depending on the theme- The photographs had to reflect romance, beauty of the silhouette, glamour and the "mystique" flair.

The combination of style, art and techniques of the camera created a new image and a new persona for the star. Thus, we have the "femme fatale", the "exotic star", the "divine", the "diva", the "all American", the "pin-up", you name it. The list of attributes is endless.

Airbrush her cleavage, maestro!

However, camera and lighting techniques alone were not good enough to convey the studio's preconceived message. The star had to be blessed with a natural beauty to start with. And that beauty had to be enrobed with high fashion and lavishly displayed with candidly revealing dresses. The display of the flesh was paramount, but the photographer had to be very careful when shooting an actress' cleavage. Meaning, the photographer had to be in compliance with the Production Code, thus, airbrushing the cleavage before releasing the photos to the media and the public was an utmost necessity.

Men's tastes and needs began to change.

Photo, below: Cyd Charisse's legs were considered a "national treasure" by Hollywood's standards.

By the end of the Second World War, men and particularly service men returning home lost interest in glamorous "shots."

For instance, Marlene Dietrich, Greta Garbo, Hedy Lamarr exotic and "divine" aura was replaced by more realistic and down to earth presentation and representation of the beautiful and idealistic woman. Beauty was replaced by healthy looking image, and romantic sensuality was dethroned by the figure of the simply beautiful next door girl. War and post war days changed men's tastes and preferences. Consequently, stars photos and pin-ups took a different look and a new format.

Now, men began to show a huge interest in women's legs and faces.

It is no longer the contour and silhouette of the body that attracted their attention, but simply a pair of legs. The era's living example and most convincing proof of this new phenomenon was the pin-up photo of Betty Grable in a swim-suit displaying the beauty of her legs, not her derriere as many suspicious minds thought so.

A new era of men's tastes and preferences has begun. Therefore, a beautifully shaped body reflecting physical health and a down to earth image became the soupe du jour. But this trend would not last long, and the pin-up photos appeal faded away with the publication of daring and very avant-garde magazines like "Playboy", generously showing photos of naked women.

No more talent is required...
The fascination of Hollywood with actresse' legs...

Photo: Elke Sommer

When Hollywood began a huge publicity campaign for Elke Sommer, most of her photos revealed a statuesque actress with fabulous legs.

The new discovery, Mae Britt was introduced to the American media and to the general public as a stunning European blonde with superb legs.

And now, England's new hottest commodity, Belinda Lee's legs were the center of attention of photographers of the era.

The studio "marketed" her as a diva with magnetizing legs.

Ann Miller's legs were insured by the studio for one million Dollars. Mitzi Gaynor's 20th Century Fox and her revealing pin-up photos displayed accentuated cleavage.

The time has changed, and so did Gaynor's photos. She is no longer a cleavage contender. Instead, her new image and glamorous photos focused on her shoulders and legs.

In France, ravishing Mistinguett's most valuable personal assets were her legs, and long before Miller and Lee, Marlene Dietrich's early striking stage and screen presence began with the display of her legendary legs.

The trend continued with Grable, Carole Landis and Cyd Charisse. During her contract years with MGM, Charisse 85% of her photos concentrated on her long legs. Only 15% rotated around her dancing. Glamour photographs of actresses cleavage and legs did not originate with European stars as many thought so.

This was Hollywood invention. And it took roots during the Second World War, starting with the legs of Betty Grable and the swim-suits of Esther Williams. It seems that men were always fascinated by women's legs.

Centuries before Dietrich, when ancient Greeks and Phoenicians began to set standards for the beauty of a woman, they started first with legs criteria such as the length of the legs, the shape of the knee and the elevation (height) of the arch of the foot.

Photo: Tina Louise

In France, several films titles were devoted to a woman's legs. The most famous one is Eric Rohmer's 1970 film "Le Genou de Claire" (Claire's Knee.)
Frank Capara, Vincent Minelli and George Cukors were the only directors in Hollywood who did not accord so many importance to an actress's legs. Instead, they focused on intelligent elegance, right makeup, refined hairdo and a special personal allure that could help an actress deliver a realistic and dignified performance. Those three directors gave respect and dignity to their actresses. No wonder why the critics called them "the directors of women." Insiders, gossipists, and columnists know very well that Hollywood's studios always paid extra for the actresses who had prosperous breasts and a fine pair of legs. Among the luckiest recipients were: Esther Williams, Tina Louise, Marlene Dietrich, Ann Miller, Cyd Charisse, Carole Landis, Betty Grable.

Marlene Dietrich's legs were insured for millions of Dollars!

43

Hollywood's silly press releases, publicity campaigns, and fictitious stories about actresses

---

Memorable press releases circulated by Hollywood's studios in 1962 stated that Jill St. John (The actress who starred in the 1971 James Bond's Diamonds for Ever) is an easy going, fun-loving, down to earth actress, but had 80 pairs of shoes, she smoked 50 dollar pipes and kept in her home, a huge elephant as a pet.

Always in search of a fresh publicity angle, Florenz Ziegfeld (famous creator of the Ziegfeld Folies) got an idea from the milky bath mixture Ann Held used to condition her skin. He informed the press that Miss Anna Held bathed in several gallons of fresh milk every day, and reinforced the story by saying he had returned one shipment from a local dairy because it had gone sour.

The dairy owner sued Ziegfeld for libel and the hoax was eventually exposed. But Held's name made headlines every step of the way.

At its time, the milk bath incident made titillating headlines for weeks and started a fad; an auspicious beginning for Ziegfeld's aggressive publicity blitz for Anna Held. "The name of the young woman became as well known in this country as the name of the President," wrote the New York World.

One silly and steamy press release told how Debra Paget (The actress who starred in "The Ten Commandments") had a special bed made for her in India perfumed with rare flowers and plants that had magical healing powers, the release also referred to the diamonds and precious stones that were encrusted in the dashboard of her Cadillac.

This press release infuriated an entertainment columnist who later wrote: "Debra Paget is one of the silliest girls in Hollywood...she had too many publicity angles for her own good."

Stars are not necessarily the good or bad characters they play on the screen or the cliché/stereotype given to them by the media.

"Hollywood is a synonym for wealth and glamour; it has also become a synonym for sin. As a symbol of sin, it should be noted, Hollywood is a scapegoat for traditional hostilities, the embodiment of Bohemia to all the Philistines on the face of the globe." - Leo Rosten, 1941.

Russell Aiuto wrote:
Hooray for Hollywood
That phony, super Coney, Hollywood
Where any movie goddess
Can be an addict
Or be ecstatic
With just a pusher or two,
And any starlet
Can be in the market
To keep her honey from being blue.

*** *** ***

Scandals, and cover-ups

Adrienne L. McLean and David Cook brilliantly stated that Hollywood has had a long association with scandal-with covering it up, with managing its effects, in some cases with creating and directing it. However, another recurring feature of our conversations about scandal was their tendency to devolve into gossip sessions, in that our attempts to establish the limits of scandalous behavior by recounting anecdotes ourselves about Hollywood and its stars would inevitably be met at some point with an astonished "I didn't know that!" We are also interested, therefore, in how we learn about scandalous deeds, where our information comes from and when, and who controls the terms of our knowledge.

Even the most canonical Hollywood scandals, if one may call them that...

- Roscoe "Fatty" Arbuckle's arrest for his involvement in the death of starlet Virginia Rappe in 1921;
- The unsolved murder of director William Desmond Taylor in 1922;
- Matinee idol Wallace Reid's death from the effects of morphine addiction in 1923;
- the publication of sexually explicit excerpts from Mary Astor's diary in 1935;
- Errol Flynn's trial for the statutory rape of two teenaged girls in 1942;
- Robert Mitchum's arrest and incarceration in 1948 for possession of marijuana;
- The extramarital affairs of Rita Hayworth and Ingrid Bergman in 1949, and the birth of Bergman's "love child" in 1950;
- The death of Lana Turner's mob boyfriend Johnny Stompanato, apparently stabbed in the stomach by Turner's daughter Cheryl in 1958.

Hollywood's hypocrisy

Instead of being a morality tale about debauchery, licentiousness, and the arrogance of unearned wealth, Arbuckle's story is now more often employed in film scholarship, for instance, as exemplary of Hollywood's hypocrisy.
Hollywood has it all.
"It has a famous director of silent films shot in the back.
It has, among the suspects, a dope-possessed movie star, several sex-crazed female movie stars, a young up-and-coming screen goddess with an insatiable lust for the director, the starlet's monster of a stage mother, hit men, drug pushers, and the victim's brother. If this were not enough, there's an embezzling chauffeur, a gay housekeeper, charges of gay and bisexual escapades, hysterical and dishonest movie executives, and a district attorney who seemed to want to produce a cover-up."- Turner Entertainment Digital Network.

Publishers Weekly in reviewing Charles Higham's book "Merchants of Dream" stated that movie mogul Louis B. Mayer (1885-1957) is often depicted as a lecherous ogre, but film biographer Higham (Errol Flynn) humanizes the M.G.M. titan in this revelatory, wonderfully vivid biography based on archival files and interviews with the Mayer family and surviving M.G.M. executives. The multifaceted Mayer is portrayed as a hypochondriac haunted by his mother's painful death, an absentee husband whose extramarital romances pushed his mentally disturbed wife to multiple suicide attempts, and a stern yet loving despot who protected his homosexual stars and covered up alleged acts of manslaughter by John Huston and by Clark Gable.

Higham reveals how director Victor Saville, a British intelligence agent in WW II, swayed Mayer to make anti-Hitler movies. He offers new details about Mayer's close ties with Herbert Hoover, his betrayals of and by Irving Thalberg and his detestation of Greta Garbo, for whom he provided a cover when she worked as a British agent fighting Hitler.

Photo: Cinematographer **Hendrik Sartov**, director **King Vidor**, Thalberg, and **Lillian Gish** on the *La Boheme* (1926) set.

Nicknamed the "Boy Wonder," Irving G. Thalberg was a notorious sex maniac. In a 2004 interview with author Scott Feinberg, Anita Page said, that her refusal to meet demands for sexual favors by MGM head of production, Irving Thalberg, who was married to Norma Shearer, supported by Studio chief Louis B. Mayer, is what truly ended her career.

In 2005, The Guardian published a fascinating article about Hollywood's confidentiality, image making, "selling a star" secret past and lifestyles of contemporary stars. Here is an excerpt: "When actors were hired at MGM, they would meet with movie mogul Louis B Mayer, and be sent immediately to Strickling's office, where he would ask, after hearing their life story, 'Are you holding anything back? Is there anything embarrassing in your past that we should know about? If you tell me now, I can make sure anything like that stays out of the press.'

Contractually speaking, the studios owned the stars, so their lives were stage-managed, and when that wasn't possible, they were rewritten with happier endings. Strickling, in the words of his biographer EJ Fleming, 'was as likely to arrange a wedding as cover up a death... Fourth of April 1958: another Hollywood blonde, another dead body. When Johnny Stompanato was murdered at Lana Turner's house in Beverly Hills, Turner called her mother.

Did her mother call the police? Did she call an ambulance?

No, she - or someone - called Jerry Giesler, the Hollywood lawyer dubbed 'defender of the damned'. The studio system had more or less fallen apart by then, and stars were left suddenly unprotected. Louis B Mayer had died a year earlier, Turner was no longer under contract to MGM, and Strickling, who had covered up abortions and a suicide attempt for her in the past, was unavailable. It wasn't just the emergencies that needed handling: what about everyday life?

Photo: Joan Crawford...a nymphomaniac with an insatiable sex appetite...

Some were always destined to be OK: Crawford knew the difference between herself and 'Joan Crawford'; Hepburn's East Coast confidence was unshakable. As for others, Lana Turner among them - their images had been so carefully controlled for so long that they didn't know who they were any more... Pat Kingsley is in many respects the most powerful woman in Hollywood. She is feared by the press and revered by her clients. Stories of her techniques are legion and legendary - believing overexposure to be one of the prime risks of celebrity, she will drastically curb the number of interviews her clients give, she'll demand that her stars appear on the covers of magazines or not at all, that they have the right of veto over writers and photographers, that they get copy approval, and often she herself will be present throughout the interview.

In short, she will ensure that nothing escapes her control. She is rumoured to have said to one editor: 'Why do you get to decide who goes on your cover?' If she doesn't like what a writer or magazine has done with one of her clients, she is reputed to forbid them access to all of her other clients for ever more - and she represents everyone (or did until recently).

Photo: Leslee Dart

In the past 18 months she has been fired by Tom Cruise in favour of his fellow Scientologist sister (resulting in outlandish behaviour that vindicates, to most eyes, Kingsley's keep-shtoom methods), and she herself has fired the former president of her company, Leslee Dart, who took with her some of their more luminary clients.

Still, no one who relies on celebrity interviews to keep their circulation up dares to cross her. If you've ever read an interview with, say, Al Pacino, Jodie Foster, Courtney Love, or, in the past, Nicole Kidman, Julia Roberts or Tom Cruise, and found it somewhat unrevealing, you have Kingsley to thank. 'I don't like interesting stories,' she has said. 'Boring is good. Good reporting and good writing don't help my client.

New information is usually controversial. I don't need that.'

This may sound at first like a mere media story, to do with the problems of journalists and not the interests of readers or viewers or movie goers. And that may be partly true (who cares what journalists have to go through in order to do their jobs?). But it would be hard to overstate the reach of Kingsley's invisible touch. For instance, many of her clients have come to rely on her opinion so extensively that they ask for her advice on scripts they are sent. Another example: the work of Kingsley's company, PMK/HBH, is 30 per cent corporate - they represent American Express, AOL, Reebok, Cadillac, among others, and their aim is to fuse their entertainment contacts with their corporate clients.

So Cadillacs are used to chauffeur stars to the Oscars; for Tom Cruise's film Minority Report, Kingsley arranged for it to be worked into the script that Cruise would walk into a shopping mall and see ads for Guinness then buy clothes at the Gap. Her influence may be subliminal, but that's why it works - on all of us. Now she's about to open an office in London.

When I told one of my Los Angeles friends I was coming to meet Pat Kingsley, she gasped and said: 'Here, that's like saying you're coming to meet the Queen.' How much of her job is firefighting, I wonder? 'Well,' she says, 'there's always some of that. Sometimes you are called upon to be a suppress agent. It's not always just to get somebody publicity.'

The Hollywood's 'dream factory'

Photo: Hollywood's big mouth, gossip columnist, Hedda Hopper.

From 1946 to 1947, an anthropologist with the unlikely name of Hortense Powdermaker studied the Hollywood 'dream factory' using some of the techniques she'd perfected while observing cannibal chiefs in the South Pacific. Actors, she found, were 'looked down upon as a kind of subhuman species' within the industry; she was struck by the intensity of people's reactions. 'So rarely does anyone have a good word to say for them!' she exclaimed in a rare moment of unscientific surprise. And nowhere was there stronger mutual hostility than between actors and their publicists. '"All actors stink" is the practically universal attitude of Hollywood publicity men,' wrote Powdermaker.

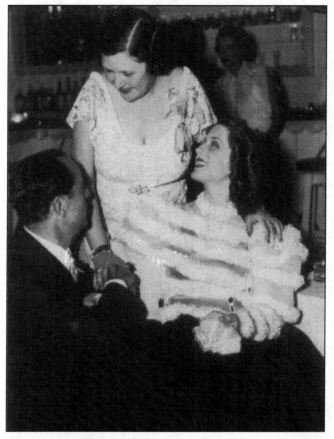

Photo: Hedda Hopper with Louella Parsons

Since then, publicists have gradually become more powerful than journalists.
Far more. There is no one now, Kingsley says with confidence, 'who could make or break a career' like Winchell could, or like Hedda Hopper or Louella Parsons, all of whom Kingsley overlapped with for a time... When Russell Crowe punches a paparazzo, when Tom Cruise gets up and jumps on a talk show sofa, or openly criticises his fellow actors - can you blame them? Any time you wonder, 'Who do they think they are?' or, 'What do they think they're doing?' consider it proof that the system works. After all, maybe they just believe their own publicity."

While she was still in her teens, Debra Paget's personal publicity emphasised her innocence and insisted that she was a sweet family girl. Magazines informed their readers that Debra still lived with her family and shared a bedroom with her sister.

Debra confided that she was a "Mama's girl" and had never been kissed by a man in real life. In the so-called "Swinging Sixties" people became more cynical and less sentimental, more confident and less deferential; and with the passage of time a new generation became the cinema-going public. These new film-goers were still impressed by flamboyant glamour and by an obviously exciting lifestyle, and this in part explains the huge public interest in Elizabeth Taylor and Ursula Andress throughout the 1960s.

Elizabeth Taylor was conspicuously unlike the general public because she lived on a grand scale, and earned and spent fortunes ostentatiously. Ursula Andress was also different from normal people. She was always being photographed at airports, in expensive restaurants or exclusive holiday resorts, and this gave the impression that she too lived in another world.

By contrast, throughout the 1960s Sophia tried to win public sympathy by constantly talking in interviews about her childhood poverty, her wish to have children, and her anguish at her failure to do so. She did this so often and so repeatedly that eventually there was no need to read a magazine article about her or an interview with her, because the contents could be predicted. This damaged Sophia's status with the film going public in two ways.

Photo, from L to R; Stars' maker and breaker, Walter Winchell with Major Harry Martin, whose wife was, the gossip Hollywood maven, Louella Parsons.

First, by eternally lamenting her failure to have children, Sophia reminded film-goers - who were predominately very young people - that she was not some remote Goddess, not even some-one remarkable and unusual, but was in fact no different from normal people.

Second, in a climate of jaunty opportunism and jovial cynicism, there was contempt, not sympathy for some-one who so obviously felt sorry for herself despite having a far better life than most people. (Martha Hyer, the wife of Hal Wallis is almost the only raconteur who has anything good to say about working with Humphrey Bogart or anything bad to say about Rock Hudson. While she was still in her teens, Elizabeth began to receive publicity about her private life. By now she had discovered the opposite sex and was actively indulging her curiosity.

Photo: Movie star Kate Hudson is obsessed with splashing water over herself to protect herself from "negative" Hollywood peers.

For a time, MGM tried to protect her innocence. (Towards the end of his life, Peter Lawford told in an interview how he was warned by MGM. W.E.N.N., reported that movie star Kate Hudson is obsessed with splashing water over herself to protect her from her "negative" Hollywood peers. The almost famous actress, who is married to The Black Crowes frontman Chris Robinson, is terrified of attracting bad karma, and wears sacred crystals to protect herself. The 26-year-old says, "When I'm around people who have bad energy, I usually carry some water and I just kind of, like, put it on myself. It's not like a holy water, just something to cleanse myself if someone's really negative. And I carry around crystals too. I feel it's important to protect yourself."

*** *** ***

52

Chapter 2: Editorial cartoon of the era...

How bad Hollywood's stars were they? They were awfully bad!

Immorality did not concern them!

The message:
The public is fed up with stars who play virtuous roles on the big screen, while in real life, they are scandalous, greedy, without shame, and far from being virtuous.

The message:
Mrs. Grundy and Death at Hollywood's box office.

The message:
The rotten foundation of Hollywwod.

NEW YORK DAILY NEWS   Feb. 9, 1922

The message:
The shocking inside world of Hollywood.

The message:
The movie industry submerged by scandals, vices, murder, dope parties...

The message:
Uncle Sam is watching Hollywood's scandals.

WHAT THE "ANGEL" MOTHER SHOULD DO TO HER "ANGELIC" CHILD!

DENVER POST   Feb. 10, 1922

The message:
Los Angeles should put an end to Hollywood's immorality.

The message:
Did Will Hays succeed in cleaning up Hollywood and getting rid of movies' scandals?

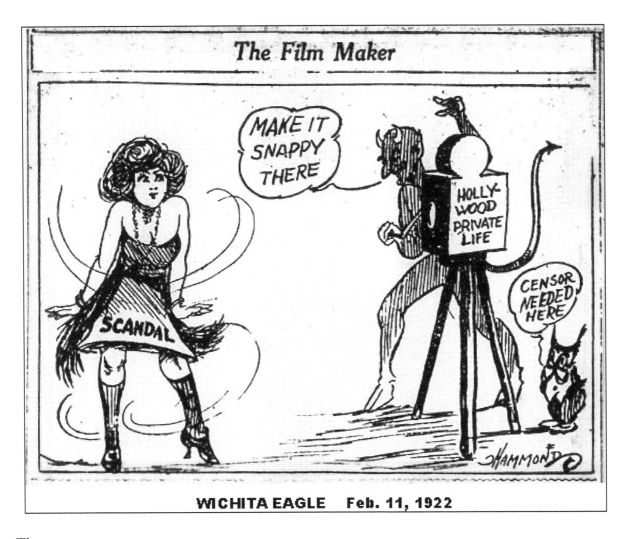

The message:
Hollywood's stars private lives are directed by the devil.

SAN FRANCISCO CALL-POST   Feb. 11, 1922

The message:
In Hollywood's world, high salaries, immaturity, loose living, drugs, scandals, and alcohol are exploding.

ROCHESTER TIMES-UNION   Feb. 13, 1922

The message:
Hollywood needs help, because its motion picture industry is being carried away by Satan; the devil of immorality and scandals.

They'll Have to Cut This Part Out

SAN ANTONIO EXPRESS   Feb. 19, 1922

The message:
Scandals, violence, wild parties, murder, rapes and orgies scenes, must be totally cut from all movies.

66

"SHAME!"
By ALBERT T. REID

RUTLAND HERALD   Feb. 20, 1922

67

The message:
Hollywood's way of life: Crime, insanity, booze, and new scandals en route.

The message:
A fan of a Hollywood's star is saddened because she has been named in a murder scandal.

THE DOUBLE EXPOSURE.

LOS ANGELES TIMES   Feb. 26, 1922

The message:
Double exposure is a vital part of Hollywood and the media hypocrisy.

Chapter 3: A juicy synopsis
From Hollywood's grapevine, and what it seems to be true!

Photo from L to R: James Dean. A well-known homosexual in the close circle of Hollywood. 2-Marilyn Monroe; they said "Bob and John Kennedy killed her."

"The morals of yesterday are no more. They are as dead as the day they were lived."-*Norma Shearer*

WHY THIS LIST?
Because it tells you a lot about Hollywood's moguls, and stars' character, persona, personality, demeanors, behaviors, morality, ethics, way of life, and the world they live in!!

*** *** ***

Hollywood is not a healthy place, and its people are the scum of the earth!

- Jean Harlow's husband of two months, Paul Bern, blew his brains out after discovering he was impotent and couldn't satisfy the "Platinum Blonde."

Left: Forgotten film star, the stunning Florence Lawrence.
Right: Marion Davies. In fact, Davies was a terrific woman, a loving person, and generous to a fault!
When William Randolph Hearst faced bankruptcy, she was the only one who came to rescue him, and to pay his debts.
This woman was so unjustly under-rated by critics. In my book, Marion Davies was a hell of an actress.

- "There's one thing I want to make clear right off: my baby was a virgin the day she met Errol Flynn." — First line of *The Big Love*, written by Florence Aadland, about her 15-year-old daughter Beverly's relationship with the *Robin Hood* star

- Louis B. Mayer's last words: "Nothing matters. Nothing matters."

- "Every man I've known has fallen in love with Gilda and wakened with me."-Rita Hayworth.

- In January 1959, Carl "Alfalfa" Switzer was shot to death by a hunting buddy during a drunken brawl over a $50 debt. Police ruled the slaying a "justifiable homicide." Alfalfa was just 33 years old.

- "Who do I fuck to get off this picture?"-Anonymous Hollywood actress, ca. 1930.

- Gore Vidal on Grace Kelly: "Grace almost always laid the leading man. She was famous for that in this town."

- John Garfield died of a heart attack in 1952, shortly after being placed on the Hollywood blacklist.

- "My fun days are over."-James Dean, shortly before his fatal car crash, 1955.

- In 1932, Peg Entwistle became the first aspiring starlet to leap to her death off the "Hollywood" sign. In her suicide note, Entwistle wrote: "I'm afraid I'm a coward. I'm sorry for everything."

- "Cocaine isn't habit-forming. Hey! I should know, I've been using it for years."-Tallulah Bankhead
- Frank Sinatra had *Suddenly* pulled from theaters when he discovered that Lee Harvey Oswald had viewed the film a couple of days before he was arrested for assassinating JFK.
- Marilyn Monroe died of a drug overdose on August 5, 1962, at the age of 36. According to the coroner, Monroe swallowed 47 tablets of Nembutal. The rumor mill has actively churned over the years, implicating just about everyone except the Maytag Repairman, including the CIA, JFK, RFK and the mob.
- Rock Hudson rarely brushed his teeth. They said, he had the worst breath in Hollywood. Larry King did mention this on his show!
- Silent film stars Lillian and Dorothy Gish were more than sisters. They were lovers!
- Washed-up actor Sal Mineo (*Rebel without a Cause*) was knifed to death by a robber outside his West Hollywood apartment in 1974. He was 37 years old.

Cary Grant and Randolph Scott; two lovers in a "cachette".

- Cary Grant and Randolph Scott were more than just roommates when they shared a house together in the 1940s.
- Randolph Scott had several discreet male lovers. The list included Robert Taylor and Cary Grant.
- **Nazimova and the Garden of Alla (Allah):**

The Garden Of Alla started as one large mansion bought in 1918 by Alla Nazimova. Nazimova, a silent screen actor, added 25 bungalows to the property, which stood near Crescent Heights and Sunset. She bought the mansion in 1919 for $65,000, according to TheOldDyke.UK site.

Orgies and voyeurism

She then spent another small fortune landscaping it and putting in a pool that supposedly was shaped like the Black Sea and had underwater lights, supposedly. Whether all that's true or not, the new Garden of Alla was the Chateau Marmont of its day--the place to stay in Hollywood for the rich and famous. The hotel that Nazimova eventually made of her mansion was home to the most brilliant, scandalous, and witty Hollywood personalities.

Many (like George S. Kaufman, Alexander Wollcott, Dorothy Parker and Robert Benchly) were transitioning from New York to Hollywood, in the early days of talking movies. Chaplin, Theda Bara, Gloria Swanson, Fatty Arbuckle, John Barrymore, Clara Bow, Talullah Bankhead, Lillian and Dorothy Gish--they all participated in steamy sexual orgies, voyeurism, and masturbation acts at the Garden of Alla.

Barrymore, in fact, kept a bicycle handy so he could get to parties and bars quickly. A spicy online version of the Garden of Alla story, written by Walter Lockley, includes a story from Harpo Marx's biography *Harpo Speaks*, about a "royal battle of the bands" between him and a noisy neighbor-- who turned out to be Serge Rachmaninoff, famed composer. Harpo grew annoyed by his neighbor's all-day practising. So he fought back and drove Rachmaninoff away by playing the first four bars of Rachmaninoff's Prelude in C # Minor, over and over again.

During Prohibition, when no liquor could be legally bought in Los Angeles, the inhabitants of the Garden of Alla made a valiant attempt to fill the swimming pool with their empty liquor bottles. They failed, but they tried really, really hard. The impoverished Nazimov lost ownership of the place, either during the Depression, or even earlier, as her film career fizzled. The new owners added an "h" was added to the name: Garden of Allah. For a decade or so, it continued as a trendy abode for transplanted New Yorkers and celebrities-hiding-out.

F. Scott Fitzgerald, Lawrence Olivier, Talullah Bankhead, Orson Welles, Charles Laughton and Elsa Lanchester were some of the denizens who favored it then. Nazimova herself moved back in 1939, taking bit parts in movies until she died in 1945. The Garden of Allah slowly decayed into a sleazy dive, and in 1959 fell victim to the bulldozers, wrote Vickey K.

The "Party House" in Time magazine:

Time magazine published an article on the Garden of Alla. Here are some excerpts:

Title: Show Business: End of the House Party.

The text:

I'll be damned if I'll believe anyone lives in a place called "The Garden of Allah."-Thomas Wolfe, in a letter to F. Scott Fitzgerald, July 26, 1937. Even Tom Wolfe, the country boy from North Carolina, should have known better. Everyone lived at the Garden of Allah Hotel—everyone, that is, who was part of the Hollywood elite in the old days when the town still managed to be wacky in the grand manner.

Through the late, intoxicated '20s and '30s, the Garden was more house party than hotel. Robert Benchley was resident clown; John Barrymore kept a bicycle there so as not to waste drinking time walking between the separate celebrations in the sprawling, movie-Spanish villas.

Woollcott, Hemingway, Brice, Olivier, Welles, Bogart, Dietrich all lived at the Garden during its green years.

Last week architects were busy drawing plans for an office building to replace the Garden—long since gone to seed—while bartenders and chambermaids were out hunting new jobs. Come fall, bulldozers will grunt across the grounds, toppling the tall cypresses and pepperwoods. Tons of earth will be dumped into the swimming pool in which wobbly guests once cooled their hangovers. Soon, sightseeing buses will drive along the curve of Sunset Boulevard between Schwab's Drugstore and the gabled Marmont Chateau, with rubberneck guides remembering nasally: "Alla Nazimova lived here once. Paramount built her a mansion. The swimming pool was in the shape of the Black Sea to remind her of Yalta, where she was born."

Men in White. Like Tom Wolfe before them, tourists will find it hard to believe that there was once a Garden of Allah. But it blossomed in lush profusion from the day in 1927 when Nazimova turned her once private domain into a super hostelry; 23 guest villas were added to the great stucco manor house—and an h was added to the mistress' first name, recalling the movie Garden of Allah. Alla objected to the spelling, but her modest protests were drowned in the gin-laced hubbub.

"Nothing," says Columnist Lucius Beebe, who became a steady visitor, "interrupted the continual tumult that was life at the Garden of Allah. Now and then the men in white came with a van and took somebody away, or bankruptcy or divorce or even jail claimed a participant in its strictly unstately sarabands. Nobody paid any mind."

Nobody paid any mind the morning a throaty Broadway actress gulped down some repairs for the damage of the night before and strode about her villa in the buff with a pet monkey perched on her shoulder. Only an outsider—a Western Union boy—was shocked. When he delivered a telegram, the boy took one look at the apparition bowing low before him, shoved the message into the monkey's paw and fled.

Splash in the Night.

Everyone was delighted when Humorist Benchley moved in, accompanied by Columnist John McClain, who trundled Bob from party to party in a wheelbarrow when walking was out of the question. At the Garden Benchley created some of his most memorable epigrams.

There, when a friend said that drink was a slow poison, Bob, nose down in a beaker of martinis, answered: "Somehow, the party went on and on. Holdup men knocked over the front office from time to time (and once murdered a clerk), a waitress was arrested for peddling narcotics; the switchboard was taken over by a telephone operator who claimed to read character from voices, and who refused to put through calls from types he disliked. Still the guests came, and still they dropped into the pool. "I used to wait for them to come home and fall in," remembers Playwright Arthur Kober. "It was like waiting for a shoe to drop. I'd hear the splashes and then I'd go to sleep."

That's all right. I'm in no hurry."

But in 1941, when Alla herself returned from Broadway to live in one of her own villas as a paying guest, an era was ending. The old faces were fading fast; the place was soon overrun by roaches and call girls. The last big spender was a happy drunk from Kansas City who made his fortune turning out horror pictures for the kiddies. For months last year, all drinks served in the Garden bar were put on his tab, and eventually he broke the record rung up by Benchley and his pals.

The achievement does not seem impressive mainly because it is far from enough to keep the Garden going. "It's all rundown now," mourned one of the maids last week, "but it's still got a lot of what you'd call dignity. The same people keep coming back. Oh, they go away complaining, but they come back because there's nowhere else like this. Now where will they go?" as reported in Time, July 27, 1959.

- Clara Blandick ("Auntie Em") took a one-way trip to the Land of Oz in 1962 by slipping a plastic bag over her head.
- Alan Ladd's career was in a nosedive at the time of his death at the age of 50. At first he was nearly killed by an "accidental" self-inflicted gunshot wound and then he succeeded in his mission with an overdose of sedatives.
- "Put my ashes in a box and tell the messenger to bring them to Louis B. Mayer's office with a farewell message from me. Then when the messenger gets to Louis' desk, I want him to open the box and blow the ashes in the bastard's face." - B.P. Schulberg
- In 1958, Lana Turner's 14-year-old daughter, Cheryl, stabbed to death Lana's boyfriend, underworld mobster Johnny Stompanato. The slaying was declared a "justifiable homicide."
- Once billed as the "next Garbo," actress Frances Farmer soon slipped into a nightmare world of drunkenness, drug abuse and years in a "sleazy mental institution."
- In 1920, silent film actress Olive Thomas committed suicide in Paris after being unable to find a supply of cocaine. She was 20 years old.
- "Far from being the world's favorite uncle, Disney was a vicious anti-Semite and hater of communists, who for twenty-five years was a Hollywood spy for J. Edgar Hoover's FBI." — "The Mouse That Bores," A User's Guide to the Millennium, J.G. Ballard, 1996.
- Alan Ladd's career was in a nosedive at the time of his death at the age of 50. At first he was nearly killed by an "accidental" self-inflicted gunshot wound and then he succeeded in his mission with an overdose of sedatives.
- The actor who played Andy Hardy's father, Lewis Stone, died of a heart attack while chasing a gang of youths who were throwing rocks at his house.
- During the promotion tour of the film Tattoo, Bruce Dern swore that he and costar Maude Adams actually had sex during the film's final sex scenes, a claim vehemently denied by Adams.
- In 1935, 30-year-old actress Thelma Todd was found "slumped over the steering wheel of her Lincoln Phaeton Touring car." Her demise was declared an "accidental death from carbon monoxide poisoning," although everyone from her ex-husband to a jealous lover to Lucky Luciano's hit men has been implicated in the murder of the "Ice-Cream Blonde."
- Jack Lemmon once revealed that he was suffering from alcoholism when he played an alcoholic in Days of Wine and Roses.
- Jayne Mansfield, who "dabbled in devil worship," was killed in a car accident with a slow-moving tractor-trailer in 1967.
- Slogan for The Outlaw: "What are the two biggest reasons for Jane Russell's success?"
- When Anthony Perkins married Berinthia Berenson on Cape Cod in 1973, his pet collie, Murray, served as best man.
- After Montgomery Clift's automobile accident in 1957, there were rumors of heavy drinking, drug abuse and strange behavior on and off the set. Clift died of a "heart attack" at the age of 45.
- The Eskimo who was showcased in Robert Flaherty's classic documentary, Nanook of the North (1922), died of starvation two years after Flaherty completed filming.

- Silent film director Thomas Ince died of a "heart attack" aboard William Randolph Hearst's yacht. However, rumor has it that Hearst suspected another yacht guest, silent film legend Charlie Chaplin, of having an affair with his mistress, Marion Davies. Hearst aimed his gun at Chaplin, and Ince was accidentally shot while trying to shield Chaplin and Davies. Chaplin denied being on the yacht.
- Aspiring film actress Elizabeth Short, the notorious "Black Dahlia," was found in a vacant lot in Los Angeles in 1947, her body "savagely mutilated" and "hacked in half at the waist." No one has ever been arrested in connection with the murder.
- Was 32-year-old martial arts legend Bruce Lee poisoned by jealous "Chinese martial arts lords" for revealing trade secrets in his popular films such as *Enter the Dragon*? Tragically, Lee's son, Brandon, was accidentally shot and killed by a gun that was supposed to be filled with blanks during the filming of *The Crow* in 1993.
- After a boozy all-night revel in 1921, silent film comedian Roscoe "Fatty" Arbuckle was accused of raping and murdering a young model named Virginia Rappe. Rumor has it that an impotent Arbuckle ravaged Rappe with a Coke bottle and she died of internal injuries. Although he was acquitted after three trials, the rotund actor kissed his career goodbye, started drinking heavily and died in 1933 at the age of 46. (Source: Alternative Reels)
- "I've got America's best writer for $300 a week."-Jack L. Warner, on signing William Faulkner
- Although Disney had a strict rule against drinking on studio property, Walt himself was known to imbibe regularly in his office during the afternoon.
- In 1988, Disney was fined $150,000 by the Florida Department of Environmental Regulation for hazardous waste leaks.
- In the months before his death, Walt Disney allegedly made a series of films of his ideas for the theme park that were played at monthly staff meetings so he could keep control of the enterprise from beyond the grave.
- "A woman's ass is for her husband, not theatergoers."-Louis B. Mayer
- William Randolph Hearst served as the inspiration for Charles Foster Kane in Orson Welles' masterpiece *Citizen Kane*. Hearst's mistress Marion Davies' clitoris served as the inspiration for the mysterious "Rosebud," the dying words on Kane's lips.
- Natalie Wood's body was found floating facedown off Catalina Island in 1981, completing the *Rebel Without a Cause* curse that also claimed costars James Dean, Sal Mineo and Nick Adams. Was her death an "accidental drowning," suicide or murder?
- Errol Flynn's drinking buddies placed six bottles of whiskey in his casket.
- One of England's most-promising directors, Michael Reeves, overdosed on sleeping pills in 1969. He was 25 years old.
- Disney secretly purchased 27,433 acres of swampland (formerly known as "Mosquito County") in Central Florida in the mid-'60s for about $180 an acre. Today, Disney World encompasses 30,500 acres (43 square miles), approximately the size of San Francisco and twice as large as Manhattan.
- Walt Disney required all of his staff members to punch in and out on time clocks even if they were just going to get a drink at the water cooler or take a trip to the "shitter."
- Walt Disney relied mostly on the music of dead composers to score *Fantasia* so he wouldn't have to shell out any royalties.
- Walt Disney became a domestic spy for the Federal Bureau of Investigation starting in the early 1940s and helped usher in the infamous Hollywood Blacklist.

- In 1996, the National Labor Committee filed a report that detailed worker abuses in Haitian factories manufacturing Disney apparel. It was reported that Haitian workers took home about 28 cents an hour while Disney CEO Michael Eisner garnered $189 million in salary and bonuses that year.
- EuroDisney has strict rules for its Parisian employees—no facial hair, no long hair for men, no jewelry and no fingernails past the ends of fingers.
- The late, great jazz singer Peggy Lee had to go to court in order to force Disney to fork over residuals for her voice-overs in the video release of *Lady and the Tramp*.
- Peter Lawford told in an interview how he was warned by MGM. W.E.N.N., reported that movie star Kate Hudson is obsessed with splashing water over herself to protect her from her "negative" Hollywood peers.
- Dick Haymes (born on September 13, 1916 in Buenos Aires, Argentina, died from lung cancer on March 28, 1980 in Los Angeles, California) renounced his United States citizenship in 1944 and registered himself as resident alien. Not very patriotic!
- Bing Crosby: In 1925 Crosby and his friend Al Riker (who was the younger brother of the singer Mildred Bailey, already successful in her own career) started a duo, which they named "Two Boys and a Piano." They were hired by the Paul Whitman's orchestra, and remained with him until 1930. They were not very successful with the audiences, and Whitman decided to dismiss them.

However, one of the violinists on the show, Matty Malneck, helped them to team up with Harry Barris as a third vocalist. The trio called themselves "The Rhythm Boys." Their luck changed due to a song Barris wrote, "Mississippi Mud," and with Malneck's help they turned the song into a hit. And so The Rhythm Boys were invited back into the Paul Whiteman's Orchestra. The trio's only movie together was called *The King of Jazz* and Bing Crosby was supposed to sing a solo of "The Song of the Dawn." Unfortunately, this was not the first time Crosby got in trouble for drinking. He was so drunk that he could not perform, and John Boles took his place. This generated bad publicity, since this was prohibition time, and sadly, it was not the last time Crosby would get in trouble for alcoholism.

- **Billie Dove** (1902-1997) and **Flo Ziegfeld**:
Photo: Billie Dove

Ziegfeld saw the statuesque model on the cover of a magazine, and became interested in her. When he contacted her, he found out that she was only fourteen. He waited until she was 16 and hired in his 1919 Follies. In 1920, she appeared in the "Midnight Frolic". Soon after, Ziegfeld began an affair with Billie Dove. His other Billie in real life, his wife, Billie Burke, knew about the affair, and behind his back, shipped Dove to Hollywood. In 1923, Dove reached stardom on the silent screen.

- **Billie Burke** (1885-1970), and **Flo Ziegfeld**:
Burke, the child of an heiress and a singing clown was the second wife of Florenz Ziegfeld. She was beautiful, wealthy and highly educated. Burke was known for her tempestuous character, fine manners and graceful acting on stage.

Photo: Billie Burke

She began her career as a teenager singer in 1903, and became a sensation overnight. On New Year's Eve 1913, she met Florenz Ziegfeld at a ball and fell in love with him, to the chagrin of everybody. Friends advised her to forget about Ziegfeld, for he was known for his daring affairs and notorious infidelity, but she would not listen.

Ziegfeld and Burke got married in 1914. In 1916, Ziegfeld encouraged her entry into movies. In 1922, Billie Burke was voted the public's favorite actress. When Ziegfeld went bankrupt, she bailed him out financially on many occasions.

Even after his death, she struggled for years to clear his debts, and was forced out to sell the magnificent "Ziegfeld Follies" to her husband's long time rivals and enemies, the Schuberts. Billie Burke is remembered for her role as the good witch Glinda in "The Wizard of Oz."

- **Joan Diener**

She was famous, and she took the media by storm. Today, she is totally forgotten. Even Life magazine honored her by having her photo on the cover.

She died in May 2006, with $43 and six cents in her bank account. Joan Diener captured the *Life* cover on September 20, 1948, after her Broadway début in "Small Wonder."

It was heard from the grapevine that "Diener was famously thrown into a pool by Fernando Lamas during a 1953 dinner at the Beverly Hills Hotel, after throwing her arms around him, crying, "You look divine!"– in the middle of a huge feud between Lamas and his then-lover Lana Turner!" Showbiz is unmerciful! And many wonderful actresses ended their career almost homeless or least alone, destitute and penniless... When they were on the top of the world, the world was their oyster...and when their fame faded away, they became yesterday's news.

- **Rudolph Valentino**:

Photo: Rudolph Valentino

He landed in New York where he worked for a while as a dancer and obtained a certain local fame. It has been said that during this period he also was a gigolo and that he had judicial troubles for prostitution-related matters. He next joined an operetta company that soon disbanded in Utah; from there he reached San Francisco, California, where he met the actor Norman Kerry, who

79

Jean Harlow, a bona fide sex maniac.

Photo: Humphrey Bogart procured male escorts for the bisexual Howard Hughes.

convinced him to try a career in cinema, still in the silent era. After a dozen films, that made him quite famous, in 1919 he was married for a few hours to Jean Acker (1893-1978), a part-Cherokee film starlet who was a lesbian; the marriage was reportedly never consummated and they were divorced in 1923. He then achieved full success in films in 1921 with "The Four Horsemen of the Apocalypse". On May 13, 1922, in Mexicali, Mexico, Valentino married actress Natacha Rambova. This resulted in him being jailed for bigamy, since his divorce from Acker was not yet final. They remarried a year later. (Read more on page 395.)

- **Humphrey Bogart, Howard Hughes and Jean Harlow's abortion.**
A book detailing the alleged secret life of legendary Hollywood actor Humphrey Bogart caused a huge controversy in Hollywood. The tome *The Secret Life Of* Humphrey Bogart, penned by scribe Darwin Porter is based on a manuscript full of incredible gossip written by the Casablanca star's friend - actor Kenneth Mackenna. In the book, Porter alleges that Bogart took on an undercover role for tycoon Howard Hughes, after being frightened that the mogul knew too much about his philandering.

80

Jean Harlow...Howard Hughes got her pregnant, and Humphrey Bogart took her to an abortion clinic.

Bogey was afraid Hughes would tell all to his then-wife Mary Philips. According to Porter, Bogart procured male escorts for the reportedly bisexual businessman, took Jean Harlow to the abortion clinic after Hughes got her pregnant and slept with gossip queen Louella Parsons in order to get good press. In 1932, Harlow was paid $250 a week. It was during the making of Red Dust that Harlow's second husband, MGM producer Paul Bern died in an incident that remains mysterious to this day: He was found nude, in his wife's bedroom, shot in the head, and drenched in his wife's perfume. Years later, it was suggested by screenwriter Ben Hecht that Bern was murdered by an unbalanced former lover, Dorothy Millette, who did actually commit suicide the next day.

Photos: Jean Harlow

Photo: Jean Harlow at age 17. Got paid $ 45 to pose naked.

(Years later, the Bern-Harlow house became the home of Jay Sebring and his lover, Sharon Tate, who were both murdered by Charles Manson and his followers.)

Because of Harlow's indiscreet affair with boxer Max Baer, his wife threatened divorce proceedings naming Harlow as a co-defendant for "alienation of affection," then the common term for adultery.

MGM arranged a sudden marriage between Jean Harlow and Harold Rosson, a cinematographer.

Following the end of her third marriage, Harlow met superstar, William Powell.

They reportedly were engaged for two years, but differences kept them from marrying swiftly (she wanted children, he did not). Harlow also said that studio head Louis B. Mayer would never allow them to wed.

Jean Harlow

While filming Saratoga (1937) with Clark Gable, she was hospitalized with uremic poisoning. She died shortly afterward at the age of 26, and is buried at the Forest Lawn Memorial Park, in Glendale, California. William Powell paid for her tomb, which bears the simple inscription "Our Baby."

- Clark Gable had an illegitimate daughter (Judy Lewis, born on November 6, 1935) from his affair with actress Loretta Young. His well-known girlfriend was Olivia de Havilland.
- James Cagney had a tough adolescence. At Stuyvesant Highschool in New York, his schoolmates called him "The Irish redhead." He used to pick up fights all the time, never lost one, and quite often, ended his fist fight by giving his embarrassed beaten one chew gum and candies.
- **Secret wedding of Jan Peters and Howard Hughes.**

Jan Peters made front page news when she married Howard Hughes, who had zillions of affairs and sexual relationships with many stars, including: Gene Tierney, Bette Davis, Billie Dove,

Katharine Hepburn, Carole Lombard, Ava Gardner, Marian Marsh, Ida Lupino, Lillian Bond, Jean Harlow, Mary Rogers, Nancy Belle Bayly, and Olivia de Havilland.

Don't try to look for their wedding ceremony pictures, you will not find any, because the marriage was kept secret. Hughes also maintained Terry Moore in Beverly Hills hotel, and secretly wed her. According to Guy Rocha, Nevada State Archivist, a myth has seemingly developed around multi-millionaire and eccentric Howard Hughes's secretive second marriage to Hollywood actress Jean Peters in Tonopah.

We know from marriage records and other later biographical accounts that early in the morning on January 12, 1957, Hughes, Peters, and a few select Hughes' associates, flew from the LA area to the former Tonopah Army Air Base in a new 120-passenger TWA Constellation (Hughes owned TWA at the time). The commonly-accepted story goes the troupe was shuttled to the Mizpah Hotel, where several rooms had been reserved.

Under the assumed names of G. A. Johnson of Las Vegas (Hughes) and Marian Evans of Los Angeles (Peters), the couple was married. Their first honeymoon night was not spent in Tonopah, but rather in LA following a quick return flight. According to the account in *Empire*, a Hughes biography published in 1979, "the entire operation took about three hours." Hughes' veil of secrecy lasted for quite some time.

Rumor abounded in Hollywood and elsewhere of the marriage, but no press accounts appeared until March 1957, and they were full of distortions as to when and where the couple were wedded. Tonopah was not mentioned in any of the stories. In fact, the Nye County marriage certificate with the fictitious names was not filed in the county recorder's office until May 27 by District Attorney William P. Beko (later long-time district judge).

Eventually, the facts came out that Hughes and Peters were actually married in Tonopah. Yet according to LeRoy David, a Nye County Democratic Assemblyman at the time, Mr. and Mrs. Hughes, a.k.a. the Johnsons, were married in his apartment at the L&L Motel (razed in 2005) and not at the Mizpah Hotel (the biography *Empire* referred to a second-floor room in "a nondescript motel"). David, late in life, had mistakenly credited Justice of the Peace Tom McCulloch with marrying the couple--McCulloch was not elected JP until November 1958. Actually the marriage certificate shows long-time JP Walter Bowler conducted the brief wedding ceremony.

In an interview in 2002 with Associated Press reporter Martin Griffith, a former Hughes attorney, D. Martin Cook, said, "the only people in the motel room other than the happy couple and himself were Hughes aide James Arditto and Justice of the Peace Walter Bowler, who performed the five-minute ceremony."

Jean Peters filed and obtained a divorce from Howard Hughes in Tonopah on June 18, 1971. Hughes and Peters had not lived together for several years. Records show that Peters asked a lifetime alimony of $70,000 per year. In return, Peters agreed to waive all claims to Howard Hughes' estate. Hughes' lawyer claimed that his client offered Peters a settlement of over a million dollars, but Peters refused, because she wanted more.

A secret agreement was signed between the two. Hughes never spoke a bad word about Peters. And Peters never discussed her life with Hughes, and refused many lucrative offers to publish a memoir in which she would talk about Hughes. The only comment she made about Hughes is that she had not seen him for many years (during and after the marriage) because of his health condition and psychological problems that forced him to stay alone in a separate room. However, the couple did talk to each other by phone. Once heard through the grapevine that Peters married Howard Hughes, everybody in Hollywood and Las Vegas wanted to be close to Jan Peters. After the divorce, and for a very short time, only publishers and gossip columnists showed interest in Peters. She became yesterday news and her so-called friends and confidents vanished from her entourage.

- **Veronica Lake; she died alone, penniless and destitute.**

Her life was not a happy one; she struggled with broken marriages, alcoholism, poverty and

mental illness. Veronica Lake was charged with disorderly conduct, and was arrested for being drunk in public. She filed bankruptcy in 1951.

Peers, who worked with her in Hollywood, claimed that she was a very difficult woman, bossy and hysterical. Actor Eddie Bracken, who co-starred with her in the film "Star Spangled Rhythm" once said: "She is known as 'The Bitch' and she deserved the title." Alan Ladd who co-starred with Lake in the 1946 film "Blue Dahlia" called her "Moronica Lake".

Paramount had enough of Lake, and terminated her contract in 1948.

It was reported in the media on October 4, 2004, that Veronica Lake's ashes have been discovered in a New York antique store, 30 years after her death. Her ashes were thought to have been scattered off the Florida coastline, but it has emerged some of them have remained on dry land. Laura Levine, who owns Homer and Langley's Mystery Spot in the Catskills, upstate New York, was amazed with the find.

Levine said "It's a strange little footnote to a fascinating legacy." Betty Davis, once said about Veronica Lake: "the most beautiful person who ever came to Hollywood." Paramount producer Arthur Hornblow Jr., changed her name (née Constance Frances Marie Ockelman) to Veronica Lake.) He said: I chose Veronica because when I think about Veronica, I think about classic, and, Veronica Lake's beauty is a classical beauty...and Lake after her blue eyes."

At Paramount, in 1943, Veronica Blake was making $4,500 a week.

- **Ann Savage** was born on February 19, 1921 in Columbia, South Carolina. She was Hollywood's femme fatale of the 40's. Even though, she lasted only one decade, Ann Savage remains to this day, a cult favorite. She made her eternal mark in the 1945 film "Detour" shot in six days at the cost of $35.000. Detour is unquestionably one of the greatest surreal film noirs of the era.

She retired from Hollywood in 1953. After her husband's death in 1969, Ann Savage became flat broke. Penniless and forgotten, she began to look for a job, and found one as a secretary in a small law firm. Same thing happened to Gene Tierney who spent the last years of her life working as a small clerk in a department store, and barely surviving on the small wages she got.

Barbara Payton or one of Hollywood's worst human tragedies!

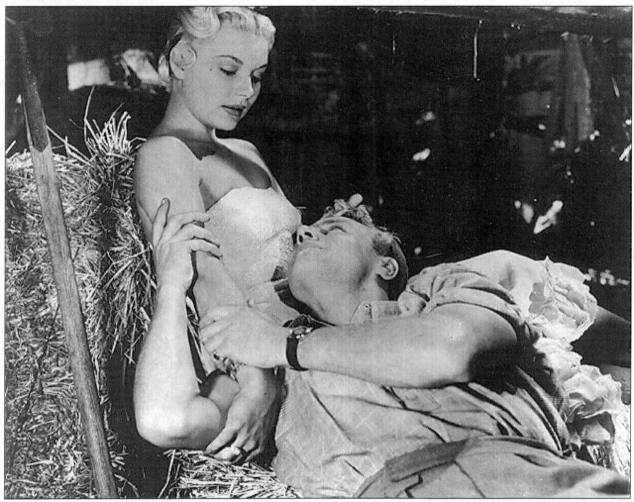

The stunning Barbara Payton and Tony Wright in a scene from "Bad Blonde."

Barbara Payton, one of the most beautiful actresses in Hollywood ended her career as a street prostitute...just to survive! Promising careers that don't pan out, I always want to find out what caused it," John O'Dowd told the *Star Ledger*. "Superstars, of today in particular, are written about all the time. I find that their (those whose careers were cut short due to tragedy or hardships) stories are more fascinating." O'Dowd is the author of *Kiss Tomorrow Goodbye: The Barbara Payton Story* (softcover, 480 pages, US$29.95), which has been recently published by BearManor Media.

Now, Barbara Payton? According to O'Dowd, Barbara Payton was a star in the making in the early 1950s. While under contract with Warner Bros., Payton was earning $10,000 a week. She was James Cagney's leading lady in Gordon Douglas' crime drama *Kiss Tomorrow Goodbye* (1950), had the second female lead in Douglas' *Dallas* (1950), playing opposite Gary Cooper and Ruth Roman, and was Gregory Peck's love interest in the Western *Only the Valiant* (1951).

Barbara Payton and Lloyd Bridges, in a scene from the 1949 thriller "Trapped."

Payton's highly unstable personal life, which later involved drug and alcohol abuse, ended up destroying both her film career and her rollercoaster marriage to respected actor Franchot Tone. She ended her days performing menial chores and, at one point, working as a street prostitute in Los Angeles. In May 1967, Payton — her luscious beauty long gone — died of heart and liver failure at her parents' home in San Diego. She was 39. O'Dowd says he decided to write Payton's life story because he could relate to some of her darker moments, as he himself had been involved with drugs in his youth. His interviews and articles have appeared in a number of publications, including *Filmfax*, *Discoveries*, and Glamour Girls: Then and Now.

He has kindly consented to answer a few questions about Barbara Payton for the Alternative Film Guide. Here is the interview (As is, unedited):

Q. Who was Barbara Payton? And what made you interested in writing a book on her?

A. Barbara Payton was a beautiful young actress who worked in Hollywood films from the late 1940s to the mid-1950s. She was a sexy and charismatic blonde with a nice shape and gorgeous blue eyes, and she possessed a sizable amount of raw acting ability. Barbara had a lot of potential, but for several reasons she wasn't able to parlay all these strengths into a successful career. It was

Barbara's unfulfilled promise as a performer that initially intrigued me and motivated my interest in wanting to research and write her life story.

She was absolutely riveting on-screen and she possessed all the ingredients necessary in those years to really succeed in films.

Photo: Barbara Payton and Stephen Murray in "Four-Sided Triangle."

The things I later discovered about her life shocked and haunted me (and still do).

Even now, after working on this project for nearly eight years, it is still almost inconceivable to me that there was actually a well-known actress who went from starring roles in "A" pictures at Warner Bros. —namely, *Kiss Tomorrow Goodbye, Dallas*, and *Only the Valiant* — to living as a penniless and alcoholic prostitute on Los Angeles' Skid Row.

When I really stop to think about it, it seems impossible. How could something like that have happened? How could the people in her life allow it to happen? Barbara's life is, by far, one of the most harrowing, "real-life horror stories" I have ever come across. At the risk of sounding grandiose, I believe her saga and its almost epic misery reads like a Greek tragedy or like something out of the Grand Guignol shows of the late 19th century. I mean, all the elements are there: a reckless and relentlessly debauched lifestyle that included all night bacchanals filled with lots of drugs and alcohol, a stabbing, beatings, mobsters, blackmail attempts, gang murders, several well-publicized arrests, losing custody of her son, a slow and horrendous physical deterioration, sexual degradation of the worst kind, severe mental illness ... My God, it is almost unreal. Everything that could go wrong in a person's life seems to have happened to Barbara and it is almost overwhelming when one stops to really consider all that she endured. Paris Hilton, Lindsay Lohan, Britney Spears, and all those other troubled young girls in today's Hollywood have nothing on Barbara! She was doing all they're doing now — and more! — over 50 years ago. But I don't want to see any of those girls (or guys, for that matter) trying to outdo Barbara or even following the same path she took, because just look how she ended up. She lost everything. It's a real sin, I think, to throw away one's good fortune and the blessings in one's life. It's not fair to the people themselves or to those who love and care about them. I wish Barbara had cared enough about herself and about the people she loved to get help.

Q. According to the IMDb, Barbara Payton appeared in only 14 films between 1949 and 1955. Why such a brief career?

A. Barbara's personal life, tangled and screwed up as it was, always took precedence over her acting career. If she had been more focused and goal-oriented and had reined herself in more, she could have had a longer and much more meaningful career. Barbara's freewheeling, no-holds-barred lifestyle literally blackballed her in Hollywood. She became a pariah that people whispered about and delighted in raking over the coals. The town used her (as she used it) and then it threw her to the curb. She treated herself like a worthless piece of trash and the industry responded in kind.

Photo: the classy and stunning Barbara Payton with Franchot Tone at a film premiere.

Barbara was under contract to both Universal and WB and if she had lived a different kind of lifestyle she could have acted in many more films. (In a perfect world, instead of making only 14 films she could have made 40 or 50, you know?)

But for some reason Barbara unwisely allowed her many personal excesses to get in the way of whatever career goals she may have had.

I believe that Barbara did take her acting career seriously — at least in the beginning, when she first started out. Some of her former co-workers insist that she really studied and worked hard at improving her craft. It's a shame she never sought help to try to conquer her demons but as one person who knew her said in my book *Kiss Tomorrow Goodbye*, "Barbara was having so much fun in the '50s her attitude always was: 'Why stop'?" With that kind of flippant and careless attitude I don't believe she ever had a chance at having a decent life or career. On the surface, Barbara didn't exude the endearing vulnerability that Marilyn Monroe had and she was usually pretty ballsy and brash. Still, I feel sorry for her. Many people don't, but knowing the damage that was done to her psyche as a child ...I do.

Q. What was Barbara Payton like as an actress?

Any memorable film performances or was she just a screen presence?

A. Barbara Payton had a kind of casual and intuitive acting style that was nonetheless very effective, and in my opinion she could have developed into a really strong performer. That said, her performances in the 14 films she made are, alas, rather a mixed lot.

Photo: Barbara at her best, circa 1950s.

She was totally believable in the James Cagney film *Kiss Tomorrow Goodbye* (her character, a naïve blonde named Holiday Carleton, that Cagney shacks up with, was both wild and innocent, which many people who knew Barbara insist was her real persona) and in the Lloyd Bridges film noir *Trapped*.

But she seemed completely adrift in her two British films, *Bad Blonde* and *Four-Sided Triangle* among others. She delivered an irritatingly abrasive and one-note performance in the former and just seemed disconnected in the latter. I don't know if she would have fared any better with different and mores skillful directors, but I tend to think that the quality of her performances was always contingent on what was going on in her personal life. For instance, she and her boyfriend Tom Neal (the star of the classic B film noir *Detour*) were allegedly drinking and fighting a lot when she was filming in England and I believe these distractions negatively impacted her ability to concentrate on the job at hand.

Q. Barbara Payton was briefly married to Franchot Tone in the early 1950s [1951-1952]. What was their marriage like? And how was Payton's relationship with B-movie actor Tom Neal?

A. Barbara and Franchot Tone were totally ill-suited for one another and I believe their marriage was doomed from the start. While they initially had a respect and a genuine affection for each other, this quickly disappeared after Franchot realized that Barbara couldn't remain faithful. Later, their relationship was filled with duplicitous and vengeful acts fueled by obsessive jealousy and game-playing, and an almost sadomasochistic feeding off of each other's weaknesses and most fragile emotions. Simply put, their relationship was a mistake from the get-go and highly dysfunctional (with a capital "D"). Barbara's relationship with Tom Neal was another exercise in masochism, I believe. They were both externally rough and irreverent, and they seemingly had over-the-top sex drives that they indulged often with not a thought (or care) to the possible consequences. Neal was also said to have an explosive temper — easy to anger and to react in an often physically aggressive manner — and for some inexplicable reason Barbara seemed to enjoy needling him and invoking his anger.

Barbara had serious self-worth issues as well as some heavy psychological baggage and severe emotional problems. I have no doubt that she was mentally ill.

I don't think Barbara ever stood a chance at succeeding in relationships with either Franchot Tone or Tom Neal, or with anyone else, for that matter. She needed intense, long-term psychotherapy, something that she, sadly, never received.

Q. What did Barbara Payton do once her film career came to a halt?

A. Barbara lived a kind of aimless and almost nomadic existence after her film career ended. She wandered about — from California and Nevada to Arizona and Mexico and God knows where else — trying to find herself, I guess. She worked a series of menial jobs in the 1960s, and earlier had tried her hand at running a few businesses, including a combination restaurant and nightclub in

California. When things were really bad, she took whatever job she could find. Cleaning motel rooms on Skid Row, working as a shampoo girl in a beauty parlor and waiting on drunks in a strip club, scrubbing toilets...Barbara always did whatever she had to do to survive. She showed tremendous fortitude. Unfortunately, every job she ever held was ruined by her personal problems and the often tumultuous events in her life.

Q. Barbara Payton died in 1967, at the age of 39. Why so young?

A. Barbara suffered from a longstanding battle with alcohol and drug abuse, and both diseases played a part in her early demise. Near the end of her life she also experienced several prolonged bouts of homelessness where she often went days without eating, and I believe her spirit and her desire to live declined hand-in-hand with the steady decline of her physical health. By the time that Barbara died at 39 she was extremely worn out — physically, psychologically, and spiritually. Although she officially died of heart and liver failure, I personally believe she had also lost the will to live years earlier and sort of just "faded away."

Q. Anything you'd like to say about her 1963 autobiography "I Am Not Ashamed"?

A. The book's content has been criticized a lot over the years, and while it's clear that Barbara didn't "write" it herself I feel that she likely shared a lot of anecdotes from her life with the book's real author, Leo Guild, who wound up putting his own spin on them. I think you have to kind of weed through it to separate the wheat from the chafe, but there are definitely little nuggets of

information in there that help explain who Barbara was. I tried like hell to find out if the reel-to-reel audio tapes of Barbara's and Guild's interview still exist — I even hired a private detective to search for them — but unfortunately I came up empty handed. I'm sure they would have revealed a lot about her state of mind at the time and the extent of Leo Guild's influence on the finished product.

Q. During your research, did you uncover much new information on Barbara Payton? Could you provide us with an example?

A. Yes, thanks to her family and friends I learned a lot of things about Barbara that had never been documented before. For instance, she was an excellent cook going back to her adolescence, and in fact she was described by several people who knew her as actually being "a gourmet cook." She was also adept at interior decorating and design, and she had the true temperament of an artist. Barbara was also a very warm and nurturing person — which is something of a revelation as it flies in direct contrast to the widely held notion that she was a selfish and cold-hearted bitch. I'm not saying she couldn't be tough — believe me, she could — but her normal, every-day demeanor (especially when she wasn't feeling threatened or frightened or attacked by the press, etc.) was very kind and affectionate. She was compassionate, loathed any kind of mistreatment or injustice, and had a deep affinity for the underdog — things that totally won me over. Barbara loved affection: giving it and getting it. She craved love, affection, and attention, and she was probably as needy as any one person can be. She was a most fascinating creature and I hope the book will help reveal some of her very special inner qualities.

As someone said about her, "She was a worthwhile human being and I only wish she had believed that." I couldn't agree more. Interview by Alternative Film Guide. Note: Kiss Tomorrow Goodbye: The Barbara Payton Story can be purchased on line. It is the best book ever written on Payton.

- **Barbara LaMarr, Hedy Lamarr, and Louis B. Mayer.**
Photo: Barbara Lamarr

Barbara LaMarr was a notorious heroin addict. When she died suddenly at the age of 29 in 1926, the studio blamed it on "too rigorous dieting." An illegitimate son she claimed to have adopted was inherited by Zasu Pitts. He underwent a name change, went on to date Elizabeth Taylor, and now lives in Puerto Vallarta, Mexico. When Viennese beauty Hedwig Keisler arrived in Hollywood, MGM mogul Louis B. Mayer named her Hedy Lamarr because of her resemblance to the silent star. (Source: Claroscureau) Louis B. Mayer, the master of propaganda par excellence, introduced his new "find", Barbara LaMarr (Name at birth: Reatha Watson, 1896-1926, known to fans and the public as "The Girl Who Was Too Beautiful") to the media as a talented actress with "high moral virtues." In fact, LaMarr was everything but an ethical woman. She collected lovers by the dozens, had six husbands, bankrupted two of them, and died from an overdose of heroin at the age of twenty six.

Later on, Mayer claimed that she died from anorexia! At MGM, cover-ups and conspiracies were the plat du jour. They never stop! And it appeared that Mayer was fascinated, perhaps obsessed with Barbara LaMarr, for he changed the name of his second "great find" Austrian actress Hedwig Kiesler to Hedy Lamarr. Hedy Lamarr stated, that her name change occurred aboard a ship that brought her to America. Now you know, how and why we got Hedy Lamarr! And this one was not a saint either, for she was the first European actress to appear totally nude in the 1933 Czech film "Ecstasy". In Europe, the film was banned for reason of obscenity.

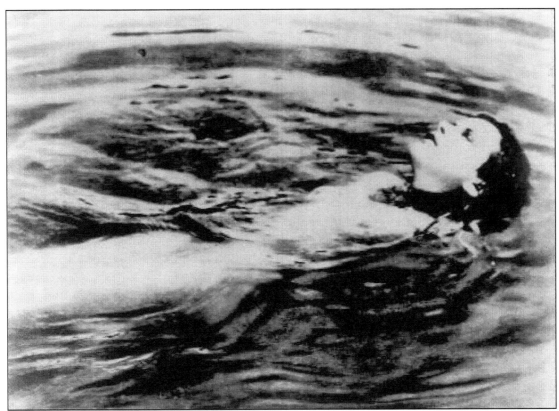

Photo: Lamarr swimming naked in a scene from the film.

Photo: Lamarr running naked in the forest; a scene from the 1933 film "Ecstasy". Considered by cinema historians to be the first nude scene on film.

Lamarr's first husband, Fritz Mandl, tried very hard to buy all the available copies of the 1933 infamous film "Ecstasy" in which Lamarr appeared naked. He made a comment to the film producer about one particular scene in the film, later to be known as "Lamarr's Orgasm" scene. He asked him if indeed his wife had an orgasm during that scene, and the produced said absolutely not. Then, during the conversation, something unexpected popped up; the producer told Mandl, that before filming Lamarr totally nude in the "forest scene", she asked the cinematographer if he is going to take closeup frames, and he replied "some shots", then surprisingly, Hedy Lamarr asked for a comb to comb her pubic hair!!

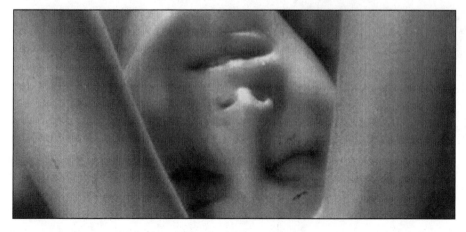

"Hedy Lamarr's Orgasm" scene in the 1933 film "Ecstasy," directed by Gustav Machaty.

94

Barbara LaMarr is the first silent movies star to do a bath tub scene.

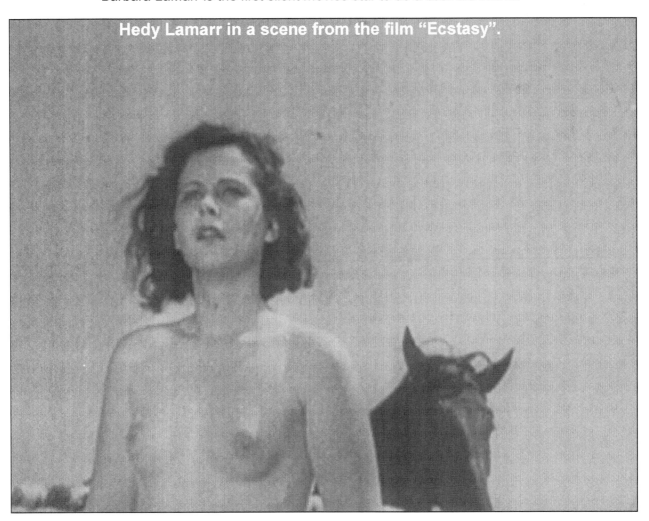

Hedy Lamarr in a scene from the film "Ecstasy".

95

Spout reported that this notorious Czechoslovakian production wasn't the first non-pornographic film to depict sexual intercourse, but it is considered the first theatrically released movie to feature an actress (Hedy Lamarr, in her star-making role) simulating an orgasm on-screen. Censorship, bans and denouncements of the film from the U.S. Department of the Treasury, Adolph Hitler and Pope Pius XII were partly due to Lamarr's infamous non-sexual nude scene, but the close-ups on the actress' face as she expresses sexual pleasure were certainly as objectionable, if not more so, for the time.

Marina Vlady in the 1961 film "La Ragazza in Vetrina" (The Woman in the Window) by Luciano Emmer. A major discovery at the Torino International Film Festival 2004. The film was censored on release.

Fritz Mandl felt that his reputation was tarnished because of his wife's nudity scenes; he retired from society for a long time, and imposed on his wife a kind of a house arrest. He locked her up inside the home for six long months. But Lamarr disguised as a servant, managed to escape.
Films like "Ecstasy" were always well received in international film festivals. Nudity scenes were viewed by liberal film critics as a direct response, and/or a form of rebellion against governments' rules and authority.

To the critics and some hypocrite producers, sex and nudity scenes expressed a new art platform. Marina Vlady's 1961 film "La Ragazza in Vetrina" (The Woman in the Window), directed by Luciano Emmer, was a major discovery at the 2004 Torino International Film Festival, because the film was censored on release, and the prostitute's display scenes were not seen by the general public. Worth mentioning here, that Vlady became an international sensation, after the release of "The Woman in the Window."

Marina Vlady was the winner of the best actress award at the 1963 Cannes Film Festival, for her most unusual and explosive performance in the film "The Conjugal Bed". Lamarr's "Ecstasy" was an immense success at the 1934 International Film Exposition in Venice. It made Lamarr an international star; not because of her artistic talent, but rather because of her nudity and orgasm scenes. The Catholic Church was appalled, and Pope Pius XI condemned the film, and put it on "The Index"; a term to mean banned or condemned.

In the United States, cinemagoers could not see the nudity scenes, because Henry Morgenthau Jr., then Secretary of the Treasury, managed to convince the American government, the Catholic Church, and heads of the cinema industry to ban the film as immoral and indecent. Consequently, a new and edited version of the film was released in the United States in February 1937.

- **Hedy Lamarr arrested for shoplifting:** In 1965, Hedy Lamarr, a once glamorous movie star was picked up by the police, at Los Angeles' Mays & Co department store for trying to lift an $86 pair of slippers. (Not deterred from such felonies, Lamarr repeated her crime of shoplifting again in 1977.) But she was later cleared of all charges.

For most superstars, scandal like this might destroy their image, but for Hedy Lamarr, this was just another notch in her tumultuous life, full of scandals, and shocking adventures. However, Lamarr lost a chance to play in "Picture Mommy Dead", because of that shoplifting incident. This gave Zsa Zsa Gabor the opportunity to replace her.

Photo: Florence Lawrence

Again, in 1991 in Florida, Lamarr was charged with shoplifting. It was really unfortunate, because the charge this time was for stealing eye drops and laxatives worth $21.48. Lamarr's attorney stated that the shoplifting was actually a case of absentmindedness. Lamarr, 77, had been shopping with two other friends, and had in fact paid for the other items she had bought at the store. She could have contested the charges, but preferred to plead "no contest" so she would not have to appear in court and face a barrage of tabloid reporters. Through her attorney, the quite wealthy former actress promised she would refrain from breaking any laws for a year, and the charges were dropped. Rumors that Hedy Lamarr was a kleptomaniac seem to have absolutely no basis in reality.

Worth mentioning here, that Lamarr filed a $21 million lawsuit against ghostwriters Leo Guild and Sy Rice, alleging that they had turned her purportedly autobiography, the highly readable *Ecstasy and Me: My Life As a Woman* (1966), into a book that was "fictional, false, vulgar, scandalous, libelous, and obscene." Wrote Andreas Soarez.

- Forgotten film star **Florence Lawrence**, once known as "The Imp Girl," committed suicide by swallowing ant paste in 1938 at the age of 52.

- **Wallace Reid**

Hollywood's legend and the biggest star in the early 1920s, Wallace Reid was Hollywood's first victim of drugs, morphine, heroin, and cocaine.

Photo: Superstar Wallace Reid…he was just a façade.

The cinemagoers took him for a role model; little they did know about his drug addiction and nasty character. On the silver screen, he shined as a hero, "An All American clean-cut type", and the charming, perfect gentleman. In real life, he was a mess, and a mental case. And the studios covered up all his macabre side, addictions, mental illness, and scandalous affairs.

Reid became so weak, disillusioned and out of control, to a point where he could no longer walk. He collapsed twice during the shooting of the 1919 "The Valley of the Giants." And in the 1922 film "The World's Champs", Reid was totally unable to stand straight on his feet. And during all these years, the studios kept on portraying Reid as a hero and a perfect American role model. But finally, they went public, because they could no longer hide the truth. Reid passed away on January 18, 1923. He relinquished his last breath in the arms of his wife, actress Florence Reid.

- **Mae West arrested on obscenity charges…and she not a good mother!**

While struggling in Vaudeville, Mae West had a son when she was in her young teens. Some say he was a relative. Others, that he was fathered by Frank Wallace who she briefly, secretly married but split with shortly after. In those days there was a process called family adoption, and one of Mae's cousins took the boy and raised him along with her other children. Mae went on to do her thing on the stage, even getting arrested on obscenity charges. When Hollywood called, she went. After stealing the show as a bit player in a George Raft movie, Paramount put her in a series of sex comedies that saved the studio from bankruptcy in the lean early 1930's. She came up with her own stories, but was illiterate. She told the writers what to write, then took credit for their work. After hitting it big, Mae's father and siblings moved to Los Angeles, and she set them up with jobs and houses of their own. Mae's son, who only knew her as a distant cousin he saw in the movies, showed up on her doorstep in Hollywood one day asking her to help him get a job. She knew right away who the handsome young man was, but said nothing. Neither did the handful of others who knew the secret. Since she was between bodybuilders at the time, she kept him on, and eventually Mae's flirting led to a sexual encounter between them. Then another. And another. That continued for about six months, several times a week. Eventually (one would hope her conscience finally got the better of her), Mae set the young man up with an extra from one of her films and the two hit it off and moved back to New York. Shortly after their return, someone, either the young man or his fiancée, told a family member what he'd been up to with Cousin Mae. The relative confronted Mae and she admitted it, but begged them to keep it quiet, and it was.

In her later years, the aging sexpot retreated to her tacky gold-and-white apartment, holding court with nude statue of herself under crystal chandeliers. She often entertained the waning crowd of admirers with tales of the men she'd had, and once or twice let slip about the time her son came up to see her, stated Claroscureaux.

- ### Norma Talmadge: Her husband never trusted her. And he was right, unfortunately!

Photo: Norma Talmadge

1916 was also the year Norma met Joseph M. Schenck, a wealthy exhibitor itching to produce his own films.

Norma was 23; Schenck, a homely Russian gnome of 38. He proposed marriage and her own film studio, and with Peg's blessing, the two were married in October. She called Joe "Daddy." Daddy vowed to make his hot young wife the greatest star of all, an actress for the ages, and spared nothing to prove it.

In 1917, they formed the Norma Talmadge Film Corporation and it was a cash cow. It was rumored that Schenck was so worried about losing his young wife, he only hired gay actors as her leading men. Eugene O'Brien played opposite Norma ten times; Harrison Ford, four (as well as ten of Constance's comedies). He had reason to worry. When Norma finally got a straight leading man -- Mexican stud Gilbert Roland -- in a modern version of *Camille* (1926), she fell in love with him and the two began a passionate affair. Norma asked for a divorce and Schenck refused; as a producer he was loath to break up a moneymaking team, and he cast Roland opposite his wife in three more films. *Camille* was the last film Norma released through First National and her last big hit. Whether true or not, that's just what she did.

Norma was one of the wealthiest women in the country. In 1932, she ended her affair with Gilbert Roland. He was twelve years younger, and she knew one day he would leave her for a younger woman. She instead took up with Joe Schenck's poker buddy, comedian George Jessel. In 1934, after seven years of separation, Schenck gave Norma her divorce. She married Jessel and made a few appearances on his radio show but that didn't last, and neither did the marriage, ending in 1939. She seemed happy out of the spotlight.

Coming out of a restaurant, the glamorous former star was stopped by autograph seekers. "Go away, dears," she reportedly told them. "I don't need you anymore." Norma died of a stroke on Christmas Eve, 1957, wrote Claroscureaux.

Photo: Eroll Flynn aboard his yacht, the "Sirroco." Flynn wanted to call his autobiography "In Like Me", which would have been brilliant, unfortunately the publisher insisted on "My Wicked Wicked Ways."

Errol Flynn (1909-1959)
According to Hollywood Scandals, and Mental Floss blogs, Eroll Flynn set the gold standard for celebrity debauchery. A fan of drinking, fighting and fooling around, he was thrice tried on statutory rape charges, and of course acquitted by an all-women jury.

He was accused of being a Nazi spy (according to biographer Charles Higham, although subsequent biographies have denounced this particular claim). One of Flynn's most infamous scandals involved his close friend John Barrymore. Flynn's posse stole Barrymore's body from the morgue and propped it up inside Flynn's home so Flynn could be "greeted" by his old friend. The police didn't find the charade so funny, and neither did the newspapers or public. Flynn's mischief did not end with his death – he is said to be buried with six bottles of whiskey as a parting gift from friends.For a short time, Flynn was the neighbor of volatile and Mexican hurricane Velez Lupez, known for constantly punching the face of her husband, Tarzan Johnny Weissmuller, and picking up fights on the set and in the streets. She was a wild hot pepper. Flynn didn't mind. He loved wild women; in fact, he loved everything that had a jupon on. So, he took the liberty to invite himself into Lupez Zappata volcano bedroom. He walked in, and boom, headed directly to her boudoir. He took his clothes off, and threw himself over her enormous bed full with Maharaja's pillows of all imaginable colors, shapes and designs. And he waited. Flynn is ready for action. But Volcano Lupe was kneeling before an enormous black crucifix decorated with Mexican circus motifs...she was asking Santa Maria and Jesus forgiveness, for she was about to commit an act of sin. Then she asked the Lord for his understanding, and boom dived into Flynn who was already masturbating. The handsome pirate and Mexican "bomba" kept digging into each others for hours.
Worth mentioning here that Flynn had his socks on all the time...while playing pirate trapeze on the huge net of Lupe. In court, during his rape trial, Betty Hansen, one of the girls who accused him of raping her, said "Flynn had undressed, but had kept his socks on throughout."
Is it a Flynn's trademark?
Flynn was booked that day, but released on bail. In another rape case, Peggy Satterlee accused Flyn of raping her on his yacht, in 1941, and penetrating her in front of "every porthole." Flynn had a yacht christened Sirocco, and he nicknamed his crew "FFF", which stands for "Flynn Flying Fuckers." And he used to acknowledge their hard work by awarding them a medal shaped like a penis. Badges were also distributed to the crew; they bear the figure of a large penis with dangling testicles on both sides of the badge. What a guy! He was a certified insatiable sick sex-maniac.
According to authors Robin Cross and John Marriot, "By the early 1950s, he was a puffy shadow of his former self, but still grimly fulfilling his sexual quota...he contacted hepatitis from a dirty needle. In hospital, he kept his pecker up with the aid of twice-daily visits from a couple of streetwalkers who administered oral sex."

Flynn with his 16-year old mistress, Beverly Aadland, at the Lido Club, on Swallow Street, a little lane that runs between Piccadilly and Regent Street. Errol Flynn was purportedly to have once said: 'I like my whisky old, and my women young'. The above photo, whilst not saying anything about his choice of whisky, although there is an impressive array of glasses in front of him, certainly says something about his taste in women, or should I say girls. This photo was taken on the 5th of May,1959, a month or so before his fiftieth birthday. According to Beverley's mother, who wrote about Flynn and Aadland's romance in a book called 'The Big Love', by the the time of this meal they had already been together for a year, as reported by Nickel in the Machine.

Photo: Is she saying: "For the last time, he is not my father."

101

In secret, Flynn used to travel to Mexico City, searching for teenage girls and boys. On more than one occasion, he was caught in the act with two Mexican men, and once with Tyrone Power engaging into anal sex.

In Hollywood, his homosexuality exploded in close circles, mainly at his friend residence, director Edmund Goulding. Randolph Scott was a regular participant. Flynn was both an exhibitionist and a voyeur. He had the habit of exposing himself totally naked to macho men, and playing with himself.

Confirmed: Flynn had slept with baby-faced 18 year old Truman Capote, said Marilyn Monroe.

According to Cross, his guests, "might have found the performance less amusing, had they known that one of the Flynn's lovers had been the baby-faced 18 year old Truman Capote, with whom, Flynn had slept in New York in 1943. Years later, Marilyn Monroe asked Capote if he had enjoyed the experience. Capote replied, "If it hadn't been Flynn, I wouldn't have remembered it."

According to the book "Errol Flynn: The Untold Story", evidence was cited to support claims that: 1) Errol Flynn had bisexual tendencies and bedded little boys, as well as many of Hollywood's closet homosexuals, and 2) Errol Flynn spied on behalf of the Nazi Party before and during WWII. According to Higham and his sources, Flynn was an anti-Semitic bastard, who got off watching himself having sex with men from a mirror on the ceiling of his bedroom at Mulholland House.

Photo: Flynn with his 16-year old mistress, Beverly Aadland. He was in a very bad shape. Photo taken a few weeks before he died in Vancouver, in 1959 from a heart attack.

- **Jack Pickford "Mr. Syphillis"**

Photo: Jack Pickford andwife, Olive Thomas, sailing to scandal.

Mary Pickford's little brother Jack got his first taste of sex at 13, when Biograph studio hands took him to a whorehouse. Promoted as "the boy next door" in films, Jack Pickford's performances still hold up today. Subdued by the standards of the day, he was also a likeable character and could have been a major player, but as an actor he only coasted, preferring to expand his energy on alcohol, drugs, and womanizing. All three of his wives were Ziegfeld girls-turned-film actresses. The first was sprightly Olive Thomas, in 1916. She was just as wild as her young husband and the union was a rocky one punctuated by bitter fights and passionate reunions. Saintly sister Mary and formidable mother Charlotte disapproved of common little Ollie. After the US entered World War I, Jack enlisted in the US Navy in early 1918 and began using his famous name in a scheme where wealthy young men paid bribes to avoid military service, as well as pimping young girls to officers. Pickford came close to being dishonorably discharged, but mysteriously wasn't. It's believed that Mary Pickford, with more clout than the Pope then, arranged for him to give evidence to authorities in exchange for a medical discharge. In 1920, Jack and Olive went on a second honeymoon to Paris hoping to patch up their marriage, and inaugurated the first of the great Hollywood scandals.

Photo: Jack Pickford's 1920 passport photo.

After a night scouring the dives of Montparnasse looking for drugs, the couple returned to their suite at the Hotel Crillon about 3 A.M. Jack either fell asleep, or went out looking for more dope. Olive is believed to have done some cocaine that night. Unable to sleep, she went into the bathroom presumably for a sedative, felt around in the medicine cabinet without turning on the light and accidentally drank the mercury bichloride prescribed for Jack's chronic syphilis.

She lingered three days in excruciating agony as the mercury ate her insides. Jack was reportedly devastated and attempted to jump overboard while crossing the Atlantic with Olive's body. An abusive second marriage to Broadway star Marilyn Miller in 1922 ended with a Paris divorce five years later.

His last came in 1930. In-between came more scandals, more trips to Pickfair for money and to raid sister Mary's hidden stashes of hooch. In her autobiography, Mary remembered the last time she saw her brother in 1933. By then, Mary herself had turned to the bottle. Jack was emaciated, his clothes hanging off his narrow frame reminding her of a coat hanger.

As she was walking him to the port corchere, he said to her, "Don't come down, Mary dear, I can go alone." That's the last time you'll see Jack." As reported by Claroscureaux.

- **Horny, vulgarissimo Spencer Tracy**

Born: April 5, 1900 in Milwaukee, Wisconsin. Died: June 10, 1967 in Hollywood, California from a heart failure. Remained married to Louise Treadwell until his death, despite his passionate relationship with actress Katharine Hepburn. Tracy had numerous extra-marital affairs. Although, Hepburn was the love of his life, Tracy was a notorious womanizer, and his "approaches and advances" were not always civilized.

Irene Dunne was the first actress who told us about Tracy's vulgar behavior and horny demeanor. According to Dunne, while they were shooting the 1943 film "A Guy Named Joe", Tracy whispered in her ear "I want to put it deep in you." After the filming of a scene, Tracy went back to Irene Dunne, and told her in a very graphic manner, what he wanted to do with her. Apparently the sex maniac Tracy was referring to anal sex.

Dunne was appalled and reported the incident to Louis B. Mayer, who rushed on the set to "fix things", and whisper in the ear of horny Tracy "something made Tracy furious, yet he was laughing..." said Dunne.

- **No hygiene whatsoever for Lee Marvin, Clark Gable, and Rock Hudson.**

Photos from L to R: Lee Marvin, Vivien Leigh with Clark Gable in "Gone with Wind".

Vivien Leigh almost quit starring with Clark Gable for a reason totally unknown to the general public. Leigh said, that Clark Gable had the worst and most intoxicating mouth breath apparently caused by 2 bridges and third rate dentures.

She added that she could not breathe every time she had to kiss the "king". This was neither the first, nor the last nightmarish experience Leigh had experienced. According to Leigh, Lee Marvin was as bad as Gable. She almost refused to kiss the rugged Marvin while filming "Ship of Fools". His breath was so awful, she could not come close to him...and his body's odor was equally "suffocating." And as it was reported by Larry King on his show, Rock Hudson would spend weeks before brushing his teeth! Yuck!

- **Gary Cooper's threesome session with Marlene Dietrich, Tallulah Bankhead, and Grace Kelly.**

Born: May 7, 1901 in Helena, Montana. Died: May 14, 1961 in Beverly Hills, California from a lung cancer. He had numerous affairs with Hollywood's leading ladies. Among his mistresses were: Tallulah Bankhead, Grace Kelly, Patricia Neal, and Ingrid Bergman. His well-known girlfriends were: Carol Lombard, Marlene Dietrich (who though he was dumb), Tallulah Bankhead, and volatile Lupe Velez, known for seriously scratching the face of her husband Johnny Weissmuller.

Cooper liked underage girls, but fortunately for him, he was never caught.

Gary Cooper with his mother.

Mother seems amiable enough, "except when crossed" (to quote Dr. Pretorious). The photo was taken for a compulsory Mother's Day just-plain-folks sitting at Paramount in 1936. By then, the wandering boy had been subdued and brought into the corral by Sandra Shaw, former social lioness, and now Mrs. Gary Cooper.

Shaw was not a very happy wife, because she caught Cooper in the act, and on one occasion, she found him in a threesome session with Marlene Dietrich, Tallulah Bankhead, and Grace Kelly.

Gary Cooper with his wife Sandra Shaw. People used to say she was a tough cookie. But obviously, she had her reasons.

Photo: Sophia Loren in 1960, in Rome, Italy.

- **Sophia Loren**

The exotic Sophia Loren always felt uncomfortable when studios' executives and films producers focused their attention on her breast rather than on her talent.

Loren had already encountered a déjà vu experience when Director Stanley Kramer on the set of "The Pride & the Passion", (starring Frank Sinatra as the rebel leader, Cary Grant as an ordnance officer from England and Sophia Loren in her first English language role as a peasant girl in love with two men) said: "Might I add I was not unimpressed with the heaving bosom of Ms. Loren, which was not so securely encased in a low-cut blouse that I doubt any peasant could have afforded in 1810." To Frank Sinatra, another sex maniac, Stanley Kramer said: "I love to suck on those tits (Loren's tits, that is.)

1810.

Photo: Frank Sinatra, Sophia Loren and director Stanley Kramer on location during the filming of "The Pride & the Passion."
This was Sophia Loren's first English-language role. During the shooting of the film, Stanley Kramer made numerous remarks about Sophia Loren's breast. In that troubled film, Loren wore a bra no Spanish peasant girl wore in

So why did she pose naked? She told Clark Gable "We were so poor; we ate meat, once a year."

107

Photo: Husband Carlo Ponti with Sophia Loren who overcame church and legal obstacles to their marriage, including spending years exiled in France.

This was her explanation! She got paid the equivalent of $15 per photo. Responding to a question by a reporter from La Corriere Della Sera about her success in movies, Loren sharply replied: "You are absolutely right, at the beginning, my looks helped me get noticed, but once the opportunity to act was given to me after so many struggles, my talent took over. I was born an actress, and my poverty taught it a lot...I just needed a break and a little fine-tuning. Few actresses in the world made it because they had talent. You pay your dues, and to start with, you compromise, you go along, you give up lots of your dignity and freedom, but once you show world what you can do, you set up your own rules and you stay firm without forgetting where you came from. Let me tell you, showbiz is the most difficult and unpredictable business in the world."

Carlo Ponti, the Oscar-winning film producer who discovered Sophia Loren and then defied bigamy charges and excommunication to marry her, died at the age of 94 on Thursday, 11th January 2007. Ponti was 40 when he met Sophia Loren in 1950. She was a 15-year-old contestant in a beauty pageant. The Scotsman reported that Ponti, who insisted his first marriage to Giuliana, with whom he had two children, was already over, sought an annulment from the Roman Catholic Church, as divorce was illegal in Italy. When this failed, he instructed his lawyers to seek a divorce in Mexico, and once this was obtained, they arranged for the couple to be married by proxy. This, however, did not prevent a scandal over the divorce. Ponti was charged with bigamy and Loren was charged with being a concubine. Loren said later: "I was being threatened with excommunication, with the everlasting fire, and for what reason? I had fallen in love with a man whose own marriage had ended long before." The scandal forced the couple to live in exile in France, and only after the Mexican marriage was annulled and the charge of bigamy dropped did they return in secret to Italy. During this period, Ponti produced the film La Ciociara, known in English as Two Women, for which Loren won an Oscar in 1962. Ponti and Loren finally beat Italian law by becoming French citizens, and they married for a second time in

Paris in 1966. In an interview in 2002, he said: "I have done everything for love of Sophia. I have always believed in her."

Cary Grant fell in love with her and proposed. She turned him down three times. Her sister, Anna Maria Scicolone's former husband, Romano Mussolini, was the third son of Italy's fascist dictator Benito Mussolini. In 2006, Sophia Loren and Jessica Lange teamed up to raise global awareness of children who are HIV-positive in Russia. A reporter from Il Tempo once asked her: "Any regrets for posing nude?" Loren answered: "I was hungry...I had to eat. When you are hungry, and nobody is there to give you a helping hand, you will do anything to survive. No sir, no regrets at all!" Marilyn Monroe said the same thing, when she appeared nude in Playboy magazine.

Jayne Mansfield: "My boobs... is all what I have."

Sophia Loren and Jayne Mansfield at Romanoff's (Beverly Hills, 1957). Obviously Loren has noticed something unusual!! It is self-explanatory.

Howard Hughes, Jane Russell's bra, and his obsession with large breasts.

Photo: What passed for risqué in the early 1950s?: Jane Russell.

Born-again Christian, and sex maniac, Howard Hughes was fascinated by women's long necks and prosperous breasts. So he instructed his studio wizards to design a seamless underwire brassiere for Jane Russell to showcase her breasts. It was the era state of the art bra, especially engineered to lift up and separate Jane Russell's 38-D breasts, leaving no trace of support lines. Russell in one of her candid interviews said that she did not wear "that thing" during the shooting of the film. Instead she wore her own bras, but she added two extra layers of tissue paper over the cups. And Hughes never knew the difference. Jane Russell ushered in the concept of large breasts, and created in the general public an enthusiasm for opulent figures. This is how Russell entered the world of cinema and became a huge star. Despite the fact, that Howard Hughes slept with the most beautiful stars in Hollywood, and had orgies upon orgies for years, he loved to masturbate while looking at Jean Harlow and Jane Russell naked photos.

Breasts! So ironically then, and as a nice kick in the arse for the PCA, the publicity agent Russel Birdwell built interest in the film, and emphasised on Jane Russell and her breasts.
His plan worked out so well that people wanted to see her, magazines wanted to publish her photos, and everyone knew who she was before her debut film had even been released.

In 1940, Hughes was producing "The Outlaw", a Western to be directed by Howard Hawks. The two stars had already been chosen, but Hughes was aware that David O. Selznick had secured publicity for "Gone With The Wind" by searching for an actress to play Scarlett O'Hara. Hughes decided to test several other young hopefuls, and when he saw Jane's photograph, he added her to the list. Jane's screen test was directed by Howard Hawks himself, with Lucien Ballard as cinematographer.

110

Photo: Is this the real Howard Hughes?

Ballard was still in the early stages of his career, but developed to become arguably the most versatile and accomplished American cinematographer of his generation. Years later, Ballard recalled testing Jane. "Well, I worked with Howard Hawks shooting tests for "The Outlaw" for Howard Hughes. We filmed these tests on 16mm in Hughes' basement. They were testing a hundred boys and a hundred girls for the leads, as a publicity stunt of course. Hughes had already picked the two he wanted, but we went ahead anyway. So after a while I told Howard I wanted to do some tests on my own, and I took Jane Russell, because she'd been hanging around me for a while, always asking why I did that and why I did this - she was just a kid at the time. So Howard said OK, and asked me to use Jack Buetel, who he liked quite a bit for the role. Anyway, I made these tests in the haystack, used cross-lights so her tits show big, and Hughes went wild for it. I didn't know it then, but he had a thing for tits. He had the scene made into a loop, and he'd run it over and over again. So anyway, he cancelled the two people he'd signed for the leads, and decided to use Jane Russell and Jack Buetel."

Jane was the first star whose glamour pictures unashamedly emphasised her bust. In 1940, most Hollywood glamour stars had economical figures - some had almost no figure at all - and the few stars of bounteous femininity had always been very discreet in their publicity photographs. Jane's pictures were not discreet. They showed her lounging in low-cut blouses with a surly expression on her face. Frequently the blouse was far too large and was slipping. A picture of Jane in a haystack became one of the three photographs most requested by American servicemen during World War Two. "Mean, moody and magnificent" was the descriptive slogan. "The Outlaw" itself ran into problems, and after a few weeks, Howard Hawks and Lucien Ballard were fired. Howard Hughes began directing the movie. Hughes was also engaged in a running battle with the Breen Office which was responsible for enforcing the Production Code. The Breen Office had warned Hughes as to what was permissible, and when they saw "The Outlaw" in 1941, they refused a certificate until and unless major changes were made. After further skirmishing, "The Outlaw" was given a Seal Of Approval in 1943, but Howard Hughes was now fully occupied supplying equipment for the Second World War. Hughes decided that he would not release "The Outlaw" until the war was over! He refused to allow Jane to make any other movies, but instructed his publicity chief, Russell Birdwell, to continue promoting her. Birdwell did this very successfully, and throughout the war Jane Russell was a movie star without a movie, a pioneering glamour queen who could be seen in magazines, but not on the silver screen.

In 1946, with The Second World War over, Hughes and Birdwell began a sales campaign of unbridled vulgarity. Enormous pictures of Jane Russell with plunging necklines were spread across advertising hoardings, accompanied by slogans like "What Are the Two Great Reasons For Jane Russell's Rise to Stardom?" The general public flocked to "The Outlaw", and Jane was now an authentic star. She became an influential star. Other well-endowed actresses began to flaunt their mammary assets in an attempt to achieve star status, and one ambitious starlet, Marie McDonald, labeled herself "The Body". Breasts in general became bigger, not only in movies, but in advertisements and calendars and in the new medium, television.

*** *** ***

111

- **Juanita Hansen**
Photo: Juanita Hansen

To Hollywood milieu, she was known as "The original Mack Sennett Girl"; a bathing beauty! Big deal! As one of the leading stars of the early days of Hollywood, Hansen made lots of money, and her huge earnings allowed her to pay $80 for one once of cocaine. Hansen was on the Black List of California law enforcement. The Black List was officially called the "Doom Book." Very a propos.

Most certainly, all those who have used cocaine and heroine ended up in the gutters, including the biggest names in the business. However, some big stars managed to stay in their mansion, and in the public eye, such as the rude Jack Nicholson, and the very talented Nick Nolte. But almost all the heavy users lost their shirt. And I have no sympathy for them. But Hansen had a strong will, and she fought her addiction. In fact, she did more than that; she established the "Juanita Hansen Foundation", as a tool to wage a war on pushers and narcotics. However, because of her arrest, her career came to an end. And soon, the bubbly and very wealthy actress was completely forgotten. On more than one occasion, she was not allowed to enter a church.

- **Tallulah Bankhead and her boobs' enhancement display**
Photo: Tallulah Bankhead

One night at the Stork Club, Tallulah Bankhead brushed shoulders with Marlene Dietrich and her escort, Otto Preminger. Bankhead greeted them with her famous "Daaaaahling...Daaaaahling" stuff, and did not waste a second to tell them, that she had a job done on her boobs. Tallulah continued, "Look look here, I've just had them done..." directing Marlene Dietrich and Preminger attention to her boobs, "Aren't they marvelous? Do you like my new breasts?" she added, and Boom Kaboum, Tallulah flashes out her enhanced boobs in front of all the diners. Now here we are talking about a woman (Tallulah) who often spoke of herself as "clean as a whistle", and trashed the reputation of almost every star in Hollywood, except those who appeared free of charge on her radio show. Smiling, and perhaps confused, Preminger asked Tallulah "They are fine...what are you going to do with them?", and Talullah answered "Daaaaahling...Daaaaahling...that's the new Me. I wish my fans could see them on the air!" When asked why she was moving to Hollywood, Tallulah replied, sucking on her index, "To fuck the diviiiiiiiine Gary Cooper, Daaaaaaaahling!" Upon her short return to Broadway, another nymphomaniac asked her about Coop, and Talllu replied: "Mission accomplished. It was fabulous, Coop lived up to his reputation."

Mabel Normand:
Photo: Mabel Normand with Mack Sennett, in 1918.

On the unusually cold evening of February 1, 1922, Mabel visited William Desmond Taylor for about an hour at his bungalow court apartment. They drank gin cocktails, discussed Nietzsche, Freud and film, Mabel played some comic riffs on the piano, then left. She was the last person to see him alive. Minutes after walking her to her chauffeured car at 7:45, he was shot to death. Next morning, Mabel's friend and Taylor's neighbor, Chaplin co-star Edna Purviance, phoned Mabel to let her know all hell had broke loose. When police arrived, they found studio brass from Famous Players-Lasky (Taylor's employers) burning papers and poking around with Taylor's stiff body nearby. On Taylor's watch chain was a locket with Mabel's photo.

Mabel was investigated by police and was never considered a serious suspect. She insisted their relationship was platonic, even after love letters she'd written were found in his apartment. The investigation also uncovered her $2,000 a week cocaine habit. It was expected that Hollywood would close ranks on Mabel and make a pariah of her out of fear for their own careers, but her good friend Norma Talmadge braved it to visit her in broad daylight and in full view of the reporters camped outside her house.

Photo: Mack Sennett organized the Mabel Normand Feature Film Company and gave her a studio of her own in late 1916.

Taylor's murder remains unsolved and there are a number of theories about who did it. One of the most popular that's been around from Day 1 is that he was rubbed out by Mabel's dope dealers because he was trying to get her free of both drugs and almost certainly extortion fees.

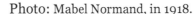

Photo: Mabel Normand, in 1918.

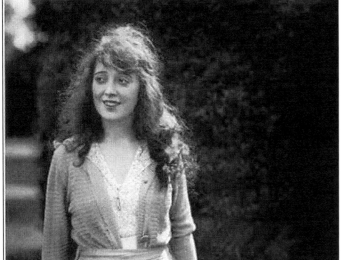

Mabel sailed to Europe to escape the glare of publicity, and Sennett delayed the release of *Suzanna* for nearly a year. Both *Suzanna* and her next feature, *The Extra Girl*, were hits.

Her career had taken a big ding, but was still intact. On New Year's Day, 1924, Mabel was partying with Edna Purviance at the apartment of Purviance's boyfriend, tycoon Courtland Dines. Mabel's chauffeur Joe Kelly (aka Horace Greer, an ex-con) got into an argument with Dines and left, returning later and shooting him twice with a pistol belonging to Mabel. Dines

113

recovered and didn't press charges against Kelly, who claimed the shooting was in self-defense, but it was disastrous for both Mabel and Edna.

Photo: Sam Goldwyn, Mabel and Charlie Chaplin.

The Ohio Board of Film Censorship banned Mabel's films, and the state of Kansas and the cities of Boston and Detroit were considering the same. Mabel attempted to clear her name with a nationwide publicity tour promoting *The Extra Girl*. She was somewhat successful; it didn't help that she mocked the wife of a midwest mayor behind her back. Mack dropped her. *The Extra Girl* was the last film she did for him.

Photo: Photo of Mabel Normand with a note to William Desmond "To my dearest", found by the police, on Desmond's desk, allegedly linking her to his murder.

1924 was a busy year anyway. She was also named in the divorce proceedings of a wealthy couple named Church. Mr. Church told his wife he'd had an affair with Mabel in 1923 while they were patients in the same hospital. An attempt at a new career back east on the stage fizzled out almost before it began, and by 1926 she was back in Hollywood grinding out sad little comedies for Hal Roach while Mary Pickford waxed poetic in the fan mags welcoming her back.

She even took a stab at matrimony with *Mickey* co-star Lew Cody, but Mabel was played out, her days numbered. Her last three years were plagued with bouts of pneumonia, but it was tuberculosis that finally got her in February, 1930. She was 38. In 1950, Billy Wilder used the names of both Mabel and William Desmond Taylor to create the character of Norma Desmond. (Source: Claroscureaux)

- **Alma Rubens** (February 19, 1897- January 22, 1931)

Photo: Alma Rubens

Alma Rubens was a heavy user of narcotics and a mental case. She died of drug-induced pneumonia. She was 33 years old.

But it is necessary to mention, that Rubens was a terrific actress, and a performer through and through, gracing the screen with an uncanny charisma and flair for the dramatic gesture before her untimely death. Her first role was in 1913 in a film called *Banzai*, and she followed that with several films in 1914 and 1915 – including an uncredited role in one of the first cinema classics of all time, D.W. Griffith's *The Birth of a Nation*, but of course, her first big breakthrough came in 1916, when she made a film called *Reggie Mixes In*.

Rubens starred in several successful films, such as the 1924 "The Firefly of Tough Luck", "The Half-Breed", "Judith of the Cumberlands", and "Intolerance (another great classic.) "The Half-Breed" was probably the film that catapulted her into the galaxy of stardom, wrote Tammy Stone. But drugs destroyed her life and career.

Her life was a tragedy, and the worst act of it, is what happened in January 1929; people in the streets watched her running like a totally crazy woman, all the way to the end of Hollywood Boulevard, followed by two unidentified men. Rubens began to scream "I have been kidnapped, help, help!" When the two men cornered her near a gas station, Rubens attacked them with a concealed knife.

But in reality, the two men were not kidnappers, but her physician and an assistant registered nurse, who have tried earlier to commit her to a nursing home. A few months later, Rubens was transferred to a psychiatric ward in the Los Angeles General Hospital. But this is not the end of the story. In January 1931, Alma Rubens was arrested again in San Diego's Grant Hotel, hiding in one of her gowns, 44 cubes of morphine. And that incident sealed her fate. It is really a tragedy, because that woman was a hell of an actress, and a wonderful human being.

But drugs are stronger than any virtue or talent!

- **Frances Farmer's multiple arrests** (1913-1970)

Photo: The glamorous Frances Farmer with Tyrone Power in *Son of Fury*, released in 1942.

In 1943, the Seattle Times wrote, the once-promising career of Seattle-born actress Frances Farmer had declined by the early 1940s. A talented but troubled woman, she was relegated to minor roles in low-budget films and then dropped by the major studios altogether. In 1944, after a period of increasingly erratic behavior, she was declared legally insane and institutionalized. She attempted a comeback in the 1950s but never regained the momentum of her early years in Hollywood and on Broadway. Since her death in 1970, however, she has become something of a cult figure, better known for her harrowing personal life than for her relatively brief career.

In her purported autobiography, written with the help of a friend and published two years after her death, she said she spent most of that time alone. Isolated and bitter, she felt herself "beginning to slip away." She began to work on her memoirs, hoping that she might be able to "purge" herself through self-examination (Farmer, 234).

She was also drinking heavily and becoming increasingly dependent on amphetamines. A woman who worried constantly about her weight, Farmer began using amphetamines (marketed as Benzedrine) soon after she arrived in Hollywood. At the time, the drug was widely available and often recommended by doctors as an appetite suppressant. Not until the 1970s was it discovered that amphetamines are highly addictive, have unpredictable side effects, and -- taken in sufficient quantities -- can produce symptoms similar to those of schizophrenia. Whether she was mentally ill or simply suffering the effects of alcohol and drug abuse may never be known. In any case, her downward spiral accelerated on October 19, 1942, when a policeman in Santa Monica stopped her for driving with her bright headlights on in a wartime "dim-out" zone. She got into an altercation with the officer (reportedly telling him "You bore me"), and was arrested on charges of drunken driving, driving without a license, and failure to obey dim-out restrictions. She was fined $250 and sentenced to 180 days in jail, suspended. After paying half the fine (promising to pay the rest later), she went to Mexico to work on a film for an independent production company. She quit after two weeks and returned home, to find that her relatives had moved her out of her rented bungalow and into a hotel in Hollywood, apparently because she was running out of money.

In January 1943, Farmer was hired for a role in a low-budget melodrama called *No Escape*. On the first day of filming, she slapped a studio hairdresser, causing her to fall and dislocate her jaw. The hairdresser went to the police, who found there was already a warrant out for Farmer's arrest because she had not paid the remaining half of her drunk driving fine. She was arrested at her hotel later that night and booked into jail on charges of assault and violation of probation.

The wire services reported that "It was no movie glamour girl who faced the bench" the next morning. Her eyes were bloodshot, her blonde hair matted, and her blue suit wrinkled. She was defiant and sarcastic.

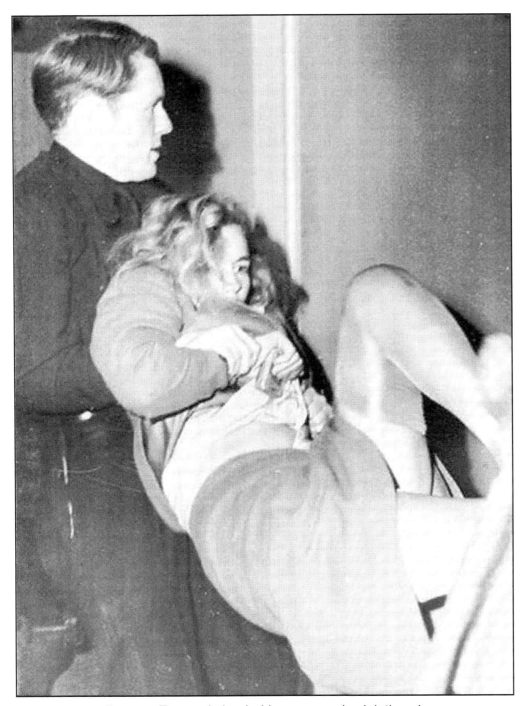

Frances Farmer is hauled in on a parole violation charge.

When the judge asked her if she'd had anything to drink since last appearing in court in October, she said, "Yes, I drank everything I could get, including Benzedrine." When he asked if she had been in a fight in a Hollywood nightclub the previous evening, she said, "Yes, I was fighting for my country and myself." The judge sentenced her to serve her original 180-day sentence. Denied permission to call a lawyer, she caused a melee, knocking one policeman to the floor and bruising another officer and a matron before she was carried out of the courtroom, screaming, "Have you ever had a broken heart?"

Pictures of the once-haughty star being hauled off by police after her sentencing appeared on the front pages of newspapers all around the country. Back in Seattle, her mother said the arrest might have been only a publicity stunt, designed to give Farmer some real-life experience as a jail inmate in preparation for an upcoming role. Later, her mother would say Farmer was suffering from "nervous exhaustion" caused by "consistently being cast as a professional harlot in motion pictures" (*P-I*, 1943). Eventually, she would blame her daughter's breakdown on international Communism.

Farmer spent one more night in jail and then, after the intercession of a psychiatrist who had been contacted by her family, she was transferred to the psychiatric ward of the Los Angeles General Hospital. The psychiatrist told reporters that she was suffering from "manic depressive psychosis," which he considered "probably the forerunner of a definite dementia praecox." To the headline writers, this meant "Her Sanity Held in Doubt." A few days later, she was committed to the screen actors' sanitarium at La Crescenta in the San Fernando Valley. Meanwhile, producer Frank King announced that she was being replaced in the film *No Escape*. Farmer would spend most of the next seven years in mental institutions, beginning with seven and a half months at La Crescenta, for treatment of what was variously diagnosed as "manic depressive psychosis," a "split personality," "schizophrenia with paranoid illusions [sic]," or simple depression. Her treatment included insulin shock, a therapy that had been developed by the eminent psychiatrist Manfred Sakel in Vienna in 1927. Patients were injected with overdoses of insulin to induce convulsions and coma, in the belief that such trauma could jolt a disordered brain back into normal functioning. Later this treatment was found to be both dangerous and ineffective, but in 1943 it was accepted psychiatric procedure. Farmer described insulin shock as "a brutal physical attack which not only stunned the brain cells, but shocked the body as well and left the patient racked with nausea and pain" (Farmer, 246). She complained so bitterly about its effects that her mother finally arranged for her release.

She returned to Seattle with her mother in September 1943. However, relations between the two women soon became strained. "Since the time of my release," Farmer wrote, "Mamma and I had fought, argued, threatened, and screamed until it had finally come down to a climax of two exhausted women sitting across from each other in a small, cluttered kitchen. We were enemies who had grown tired of pretending" (Farmer, 13). Less than six months later, Lillian Farmer filed a complaint in King County Superior Court asking that her daughter (identified by her married name, Mrs. F. E. Anderson) be designated "an insane person" and committed to King County Hospital at Harborview for observation and treatment. During a hearing held before the King County Sanity Commission on March 23, 1944, two psychiatrists testified that Farmer was legally insane, as shown by signs of agitation, delusions, and paranoia. They thought "marital difficulty" might have been a "a pre-disposing cause of the insanity" (*Seattle Times*, 1944). Farmer's court-appointed *guardian ad litem* waived her right to a jury trial. The presiding judge then ordered her committed to the Western (Washington) State Hospital for the Insane at Steilacoom, about 35 miles south of Seattle.

At Western State Hospital, the treatment of choice was electroconvulsive shock therapy, which was considered safer than insulin shock. The treatment (still in use, although less common) involves passing a low voltage electric current through the brain for one to two seconds. As with other forms of shock therapy, the side effects include disorientation and memory loss. Farmer apparently underwent a standard course of electric shock therapy soon after she was admitted to Western, undergoing shocks two or three times a week for three months. The results convinced her doctors that their famous patient had made a "complete recovery" and she was remanded to her mother's custody. In Seattle, Dr. Donald A. Nicholson -- one of the two psychiatrists who had certified Farmer as insane -- told an audience: "I think this case demonstrates just how successfully antisocial behavior can be modified. Three months ago this woman was totally unresponsive and today she is being returned to her family completely cured. This marks a significant victory for the mental hygiene movement in Washington state" (Arnold, 187).

Interviewed at her mother's home a day after her release, Farmer said "It's all been like a terrible dream," and that she hoped to get back to work soon, after a month or two of rest at an aunt's ranch near Reno, Nevada (*The Seattle Times*, 1944). In fact, it would be nearly 15 years before she worked as an actress again. Less than a month after her discharge, Farmer was arrested on a charge of vagrancy in Antioch, California. She was penniless and apparently seeking work as a fruit picker. A photograph taken at the time of her arrest showed her wearing a work shirt and dungarees, scowling and holding a cigarette.

Farmer ignored offers of help that came from San Francisco, Hollywood, and New York. After spending the night in jail, she pled guilty, was fined $10, suspended, and released to the custody of her parents. But it was an uneasy interlude. By May 1945, she was back at Steilacoom, recommitted -- at her mother's request -- on the grounds that it was not safe for her to be at large. She did not set foot outside that institution again for five years.

The allegation that Farmer was lobotomized was advanced by Seattle writer William Arnold in his 1978 book *Shadowland*, amplified by the 1982 film *Frances*, and has since been widely accepted as fact. However, Farmer's family, friends, and others insist she did not undergo a lobotomy, by Freeman or anyone else.

Farmer herself addressed the issue in a 1968 tape-recorded interview with Lois Kibbee, a New York writer and actress who was collaborating with her on her autobiography. She said she had heard women on her ward "pleading" for lobotomies, because "They had been told the operation would sever the little nerve that controls one's sense of grief" (*Indianapolis Star*). But she reportedly told Kibbee and other friends that she did not have the operation.

In a memoir published in 1978, Farmer's sister, Edith Farmer Elliot, said hospital authorities had sought her parents' permission to perform the operation but they refused. She said her father had been "horrified" by the request and had threatened to sue "if they tried any of their guinea pig operations on her" (Elliot, 153). Interviewed after the release of the movie *Frances*, three nurses who had worked at the hospital during the 1940s also denied that Farmer had had a lobotomy. "I worked on all the patients who had lobotomies, and Frances Farmer never came to that ward," said Beverly Tibbetts (*P-I*, 1983).

Her full civil rights were not restored until 1953, when she petitioned the Superior Court in "The Matter of the Insanity of Mrs. Frances Anderson" to void her mother's guardianship. On the day her petition was approved, she went to the Olympic Hotel -- the same place where she had once been honored as the hometown girl who had made good -- and got a job sorting laundry. In April 1954, she married again. In a newspaper interview, she cautiously predicted that she and her new husband, a heavy equipment operator named Alfred H. Lobley, would be "contentedly happy" (*Seattle Times*). Six months later, she abruptly left her husband and her parents and bought a one-way ticket bus ticket to Eureka, California, choosing that destination because it was as far from Seattle as her money would take her. She spent the next three years living quietly and anonymously, working as a secretary under the name of Frances Anderson. She had no further contact with her parents. Her mother died in 1955, followed by her father the next year. She was named her mother's sole heir, gaining title to the family home in West Seattle. She sold the house, for $5,500, and stayed on in Eureka.

The Final Years

Farmer seemed to settle easily into life in Indianapolis. Her TV show, *Frances Farmer Presents*, was a local hit, giving her both a steady income and a comfortable niche in the community. She introduced the movies shown on the program and often interviewed visiting celebrities on the air.

She was also in great demand as a public speaker. In addition, she served as actress-in-residence at Purdue University, mentoring drama students and appearing in university productions such as *The Sea Gull* in 1962. Then she seemed to deteriorate. She became more erratic, demonstrating outbursts of temper and sometimes showing up for work drunk. "All of a sudden, on certain days, and for whatever reasons, Frances was talking like a truck driver," one of her co-workers said. "This lovely, charming, elegant, sensitive lady would chew out the program director or someone, then go storming out the back door, pop in her Edsel and go flying out of the parking lot" (*Indianapolis Star*).

Finally, in April 1964, the station's general manager fired her. He hired her back two months later, but fired her again at the end of the summer. Despite these problems, Farmer went back on stage that summer, appearing as the self-centered mother in a Purdue Summer Theatre production of *Look Homeward, Angel*. Midway through the two-week run, she was arrested for drunk driving. She finished the play anyway, but it was the end of her acting career. After she lost her job in television, Farmer went into two business ventures with a friend, but both failed. She was arrested once more for drunk driving, and had her license suspended for a year.

In 1968, she resumed work on her autobiography. The book was not yet completed when she died, of esophageal cancer, on August 1, 1970, six weeks before her 57th birthday, leaving unanswered many questions about the sad trajectory of her life. She was buried in Indianapolis. Six women friends served as pallbearers, said Cassandra Tate.

Ingrid Bergman is condemned by the Senate (Read more in section: Hollywwod's sex scandals, pages 222, 223.)

Photo: Isabella Rossellini, mother of Elettra Wiedemann and daughter of Ingrid Bergman, and director Roberto Rossellini.

Ingrid Bergman's impeccable image as an Oscar-winning actress for "Gaslight" and devoted wife and mother (she and surgeon Petter Lindstrom had a 10-year-old daughter, Pia) was destroyed in 1949 when she began an affair with married Italian director Roberto Rossellini on the set of "Stromboli", and became pregnant with his child.

Public condemnation -- fueled by sensationalistic stories from Hollywood gossip columnists -- was swift, with religious groups calling for Bergman's films to be banned and Senator Edwin C. Johnson denouncing the Swedish-born actress on the Senate floor as "a powerful influence for evil" and suggesting she be barred from the country for "moral turpitude" (The Senate officially apologized to Bergman in 1972).

The couple wed soon after Bergman gave birth to Rossellini's son (she lost custody of Pia in the divorce) and they produced five more films and twin daughters -- Isabella and Ingrid -- before separating in 1956. The following year, Hollywood welcomed Bergman back from exile with a Best Actress Oscar win for "Anastasia". (Source: Kat Giantis)

Photo: Ingrid Bergman, Roberto Rossellini, and Bergman-Rossellini baby.

- **Clara Bow**

Born in a grimy Brooklyn tenement during a killing heat wave, her mother Sarah, a part-time prostitute and full-time schizophrenic, hoped she and her baby would die in the heat and didn't bother calling a doctor or getting a birth certificate.

Clara grew up criminally neglected, filthy, always hungry and in ratty clothes, the constant victim of taunts from other girls. So she became a tomboy, running with a pack of neighborhood boys. A boy named Johnny was severely burned and supposedly died in her arms when she was 9; years later, she would make herself cry at will on movie sets by asking the band to play "Rock-a-bye Baby" because it reminded her of him.

Ignored at home, with no friends, she spent a lot of time in movie houses and dreamed of being a star. In 1921, the sixteen year-old entered Motion Picture Magazine's "Fame and Fortune" contest. Her alcoholic father Robert took her to a cheap Coney Island photographer and took two photos she later described as "terrible." She delivered them at the magazine offices herself, and the secretary taking them noted on her application, "Called in person. Very pretty." Clara won the grand prize, a role in a feature film, then was humiliated when it was released and all footage of her had been removed. Years later the film was re-issued to capitalize on her success, with the missing scenes restored.

Clara's crazy mother equated actresses with prostitutes. One night, she awoke to find Sarah holding a butcher knife at her throat, saying she would make it all better before collapsing in a seizure. The incident marked the start of Clara's lifelong losing battle with insomnia. Another attack followed a few weeks later with Sarah chasing Clara out of the house, again with a knife. Traumatized, Clara wandered Coney Island for two days before her father found her. Robert Bow had Sarah committed to an asylum and she died shortly afterwards. For the rest of her life, Clara blamed herself for her mother's death, believing her choice of career was responsible. The freak show wasn't yet over. With Sarah out of the way, Robert allegedly raped his teenage daughter.

According to actress Louise Brooks, "coming from the Brooklyn slums to work in Hollywood, Ben Schulberg automatically labeled Clara a cheap little whore, a category she never escaped."

Clara stole almost every scene in every bit part he threw her into, and audiences were taking notice. Rather than create projects for her, Schulberg made money loaning her out. In 1924, Clara was selected as a WAMPAS Baby Star. At this point in her career she was adored by the people she worked with.

121

Clara Bow

78

122

She brought her drunken father to Hollywood, then bankrolled several businesses to keep him out of her hair, but all failed. He began hanging around her sets trying to pick up young girls by telling them he was Clara Bow's father.

In 1925, Schulberg brought Clara to Paramount, sorely in need of a new star. She fit the dress. After Schulberg cast her in *The Plastic Age,* Clara became the studio's most popular actress. Co-star Gilbert Roland became the first of many fiancés. While filming her next feature, *Mantrap,* she fell in love with director Victor Fleming, twice her age, and divided her time up between both. They were just the first of a parade of lovers that would eventually include Gary "The stud" Cooper, John Wayne, and creepy Bela Lugosi.

As Clara's star rose -- and rise it did, to spectacular heights when she made It ("it" being sex appeal) in 1927, she was shunned by the rest of Hollywood, a phenomenon observed by Louise Brooks when she tried to get husband Eddie Sutherland to invite her to one of their famous parties. Despite labeling Clara a "half-witted little girl," Brooks liked her, and liked her a lot.

"Eddie recoiled in horror -- 'Oh, heavens, no, we can't have her, she--we don't know what she'd do, she's from Brooklyn.' Her accent and dreadful manners would reproach the producers of their common origins... Everyone at Paramount said of course she's the greatest actress... but she wasn't acceptable, and she knew that and it made her feel bad." She wasn't even invited to the premieres of her own films. Larger than life, Clara tore through Hollywood in a flame-red Kissel convertible with chows dyed to match her flaming red hair, the epitome of the liberated flapper flaunting her affairs, and thousands of women wanted to be her. Henna sales hit an all-time high.

Under Schulberg, she was working in as many as three films at a time, thirteen in 1925 alone. The roles didn't call for much, and she didn't have the confidence to ask for better scripts. Schulberg and the rest of Paramount's suits considered her stupid and gullible and treated her as such. Most of the tripe still managed to break box office records, and between 1927 and 1930, she was one of Hollywood's top five box office attractions.

Schulberg dropped her after selling her contract to Paramount for $150,000 when he became infatuated with Sylvia Sidney. And then came the talkies. Louise Brooks recalled meeting Clara for the first time at Pomeroy's sound studio, when she was Hollywood's top female star and receiving 30,000 fan letters a month, and remembered her as "stunned and helpless," convinced her voice would never make it. Brooks said: "Schulberg told her, her Brooklyn accent was awful, but it really wasn't at all...When talkies came in in '28, I was told to go over to the sound studio... But I wasn't told Clara was going to make the test with me. I'd never met her, and I walked into the studio and there was a big couch and she was sitting in a corner of it, all curled up wearing her usual sweater and skirt, and I sat down and we began to talk and I have no recollection of them lighting the scene, or taking it or stopping it. She just began to talk, she knew all about me, I was supposed to be very sophisticated in Hollywood, that was purely on the strength of my Paris-New York wardrobe and of course being very sniffy... I really was just a hick from Kansas. I felt Clara wanted something from me as we sat talking. She was telling me how dreadfully Schulberg was treating her and I said, 'Well, what's he doing?' This is after she moved to this very expensive house in Beverly Hills and her life was being run by her hairdresser... She says, "Schulberg sent Ruth Chatterton (a stage actress turned a vocal coach) up to my house on Thursday and I beat it out the back door because they make me feel so terrible that I can't talk." I looked at her, and I have never seen anyone so beautiful in her features. She had skin just like a baby, she had this soft fluffy baby hair...It's funny, in 1928 she already knew that she was finished." Like her mother before her, Clara's own mental illness began to set in and she developed a pathological fear of the mike. MGM gave Garbo two years to prepare for her first sound film. Paramount gave Clara Bow two weeks. After a shaky start in her first talkie, *The Wild Party*, her performances in sound films improved quickly, her box office appeal undiminished.

Photo: Gloria Grahame. Grahame's big break came in 1946 while on loan to RKO Pictures, playing party girl Violet in Frank Capra's *It's A Wonderful Life*. She worked constantly through the late 40s and into the early 50s, despite personal problems, crippling self-doubt, and a stormy reputation that dogged her career.

A marriage to *Rebel Without A Cause* director Nicholas Ray (the second of four) began in trouble and ended in lurid scandal, though he directed her in *In A Lonely Place* (1950), probably her best performance, stated Blue Movies Review.

Overworked and taken advantage of by Paramount, she had several breakdowns and the studio went all out to humiliate her by canceling her films, docking her pay, charging her for unreturned costumes and insisting she pay for her publicity photographs.

The last straw was the sensational trial of former assistant Daisy DeVoe, when Clara's scandalous private life was picked over for public consumption.

Her nerves shattered, she retreated to a sanatorium in 1931 and Paramount released her from her contract a short time late.

She returned to Hollywood for a two-picture deal with Fox Film Corporation and made the early talkie classic *Call Her Savage* (1932), The film was a hit, but Clara decided to go in for marriage with cowboy actor Rex Bell and motherhood. *Hoop-La,* released the following year, marked the end of her career.

Clara died of a heart attack in September, 1965, while watching a Gary Cooper movie on TV, Claroscureaux reported.

- **Gloria Grahame:** "I married Nicholas Ray, the director. People yawned. Later on I married his son, and from the press's reaction - you'd have thought I was committing incest or robbing the cradle!" -Gloria Grahame. Nicholas Ray (director, *Rebel Without a Cause*, *Johnny Guitar*, etc.) divorced Grahame after he found her in bed with his teenaged son, Tony.

- **The death of Lou Costello's toddler son is a well-known Hollywood tragedy.**
Less familiar, even to some of his fans, is a similar incident which was visited upon W.C. Fields on March 15, 1941, when the two and a half year old son of actors Anthony Quinn and Katherine

DeMille (Quinn states in his memoirs that the child was actually three at the time) wandered across the street from his grandfather's home, fell into Field's backyard fish pond, and drowned. According to Anthony Quinn's recollection, he and the family were visiting Cecil B. DeMille that Sunday afternoon, and somehow the boy had gotten separated from his nanny. Fields kept a little sailboat in the pond, and that's presumably what attracted him. Emergency personnel worked over the child for several hours, but it was hopeless. In the aftermath of the incident, Fields "went into retreat for three or four days", and wouldn't talk to anybody.

Of course, the parents never got over it, as Anthony Quinn recounted, and this would further erode the already weak underpinnings of their marriage. Fields never wanted to go near the pond again.

- "I really blew everything after *Footloose*. I spent a fortune on drink and drugs. I had two houses and just gambled away most of my money." -**Chris Penn**
- "I'm going to die young. I just can't stop destroying myself."-**John Belushi**, shortly before his fatal overdose of cocaine and heroin.
- In 1920, silent film actress Olive Thomas committed suicide in Paris after being unable to find a supply of cocaine. She was 20 years old.

- **Buster Keaton's wife and his in-laws**

Photo: Nathalie Talmadge, who took Buster Keaton's fortune and refused any contact with his sons.

After a lifetime on Vaudeville stages with his knockabout family act, Buster Keaton finally left the show because of his father Joe's drinking. In New York City on a February afternoon in 1917, he went to the Talmadge Studios looking for work, despite his reservations about the medium of film (back then a film actor was even more disreputable than a stage performer), and met Roscoe "Fatty" Arbuckle, under contract to producer Joseph M. Schenck. According to Keaton, the first thing he had to do was find out how the camera worked, so he borrowed one and took it back to his hotel room, dismantling and reassembling it to understand its mechanics.

He returned to the studio the next day and was hired at first as Roscoe Arbuckle's co-star and gag man, then Arbuckle's second director and his entire gag department. The two became great friends. Schenck soon gave Buster his own production unit and he made a series of successful two-reel comedies.

He met Schenck's sister-in-law Natalie Talmadge at the studio where she worked as script girl and sometime-bit player. Her older sister Norma (Schenck's wife) and younger sister Constance were stars; "Nate," the ugly duckling of the trio, wasn't. Their courtship was unusual. At one point they dated, but it was never serious. They hadn't seen one another for two years, or even exchanged any love letters, but in January 1921, Natalie wrote to Buster in Hollywood proposing marriage.

Photo: Nathalie's new digs, 1926.

According to Claroscureaux, and as stated in his wonderful research, Buster took a train east and married Natalie at Norma and Joe's Long Island estate in May.

The reason for the marriage has never been explained from either side. According to Keaton's third wife Eleanor, Natalie's sisters and formidable mother Peg looked down on Buster, who they considered a lowly comic and not good enough for their sister. They began to undermine the match even before the vows were exchanged. It's believed that Joe Schenck, who produced both Keaton's and Norma's films and, like 99.9% of film producers a crooked bastard at his core, engineered the union to keep the business in the family.

The couple had two sons during the first three years of their marriage. Natalie, not to be outdone by Norma or Constance, spent a fortune on clothes and several more moving her family from one mansion to another, culminating in the construction of a 10,000-square-foot Italian villa in Beverly Hills. It was after the birth of their second son Robert, Buster remembered in his autobiography, that the relationship hit the rocks. Natalie, under pressure from her sisters and mother not to have any more children, refused to sleep with him. He never understood why. Only 28 at the time, he made it clear to Natalie and Peg that he wasn't going to do without sex, and would get it elsewhere. He took up with a couple of actresses including Dorothy Sebastian; their every move noted by the private detective Natalie had hired. Attempted reconciliations failed, and the marriage ended in a bitter divorce in 1932.

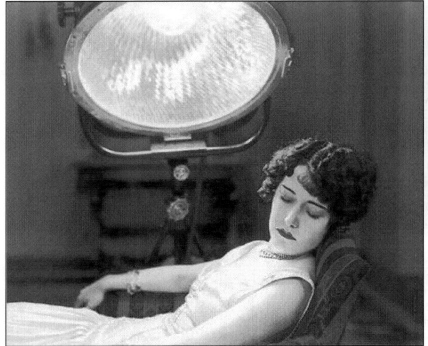

Photo, left: Dorothy Sebastian
Photo, right: Keaton with his wife, Eleanor Norris.

Natalie took Buster's fortune and refused any contact with his sons, whose surnames were legally changed to Talmadge, and who he wouldn't see for a decade.

The failure of his marriage and the loss of his independence as a filmmaker (brother-in-law Joseph Schenck sold him out, screwed him royally, in fact) drop-kicked Keaton into one long lost weekend of alcoholism that lasted until 1940, when he married Eleanor Norris, a 23 years younger than Keaton, who is credited with saving his life. The two were happily married until Keaton's death in 1966.

According to Classic Movies:

- Back in 1920, when actress **Olive Thomas** died of poisoning in Paris, all kinds of rumors surfaced regarding the last few hours of her life, and questions are raised regarding her relationship with Jack Pickford and life insurance policies taken out on her the year before. Some claimed her death (or suicide) was planned by her wicked husband. (Sources:
- **Charlie Chaplin** was hounded by red-baiters and tax-collectors to the point where he left the United States and lived in Switzerland. He was also well-known for his sexual activities; one biographer claimed that Nabokov's "Lolita" was inspired by Chaplin's relationship with Lita Grey.
- **Jean Harlow**'s life was filled with scandals, in particular the suicide of her second husband, Paul Bern, not to mention her relationships with gangsters, nude photos taken at the age of 17, and a reported abortion of a child fathered by William Powell. Winona Ryder is a saint compared to Harlow, or at least her public persona!
- Silent film actress **Margaret Campbell,** was murdered in 1939 by her son with her former husband, German-born actor Josef Swickard. She was sexually assaulted and bludgeoned to death with a hammer. The son was also charged with 2 other murders, a Russian dancer, who was bludgeoned to death, and actress Delia Bogard, who survived the attack. Swickard died a year later from natural causes. He was falsely rumored to have jumped from the Hollywood sign.
- "**Joan Crawford** slept with every star at MGM of both sexes," said Bette Davis. There was some truth in this. Most of Crawford's leading men had succumbed to her sexual magnetism and she counted several female stars, including Greta Garbo, Marlene Dietrich, Barbara Stanwyck and later Marilyn Monroe, among her lovers.
- **Durango Jones,** a scandalous exhibitionist of a golden age, a lost boy-man, a male nymphomaniac, thrilled millions. He was a smiling, golden-haired, blue-eyed hunk turned sexual predator during the early days of Hollywood. Who slept with Mary Pickford's three husbands, her two brothers-in-law, and her brother? Durango Jones, that's who! as stated by Hollywood Closet.
- **Cary Grant: LSD and orgies.** The suave and refined Grant had a double-personality. On the screen, he was the gentleman type par excellence. In his private life, he was a different story. Of course, he kept his refined manners in society, and retained his sophisticated aura, but in the privacy of his home, Mr. Grant participated in multiple orgies, and the guest stars were Joan Crawford and Grace Kelly. Little known to the general public is the fact that Grant enjoyed drugs, and particularly LSD. In many of these orgies, Grace Kelly would ask Grant to undress her piece by piece, while the elite audience puffed and snored all sorts of drugs. Special packages of drugs were shipped to Grant's huge house from Mexico, and FBI's Hoover knew about it, but closed his eyes, for Grant was a United States spy, and an informer working for both the CIA and the FBI. Grant also had a strong connection with the underground and organized crime. His chauffeur was a convicted felon and a hoodlum, and served as a liaison between Grant and shady characters.
- **Jack Nicholson:** "In 1978, Jack Nicholson, a heavy cocaine user, directed and starred in "Goin' South", a rambling comedy western. Much cocaine was snored during filming.

When the film was released, Time magazine's film reviewer referred to Nicholson's "somewhat stoned eyes." The Los Angeles Tribune's Charles Champlin observed: "Somewhat confusingly, Jack Nicholson plays the whole role like the before half of a Dristan commercial, with nasal passages blocked. Why? I don't know, and don't care to ask." Message received and understood. As reported in Hollywood Scandals by Robin Cross and John Marriot, Time magazine; and The Los Angeles Tribune.

- **George Raft: A hoodlum who became a superstar.**

Photo: George Raft

From humble beginnings as a barely literate street kid in Manhattan, and talented hoofer, George Raft, born in 1895 (died 1980) to a German father and Italian mother, rose to prominence as a Hollywood actor. But he could not divorce himself from his roots; Raft's tough-guy persona on the silver screen was not an act—gangsters were his heroes (and sometime mentors). Because of Raft's alleged ties to infamous mobsters he became a marked man, resulting in the compilation (between 1944 and 1967) of a 127-page FBI George Raft dossier (of which there are 111discernable pages). What follows is a page from that file."

Raft was interviewed by agents of the Bureau in 1938 in connection with the investigation looking to the location of Louis 'Lepke' Buchalter. At that time Raft admitted association with Benjamin 'Bugs' Siegel, who was a member of the 'Big Six,' a group of leaders of gangs in New York City during the late Prohibition era.

He also admitted knowing of [name redacted], a close associate of Buchalter and Jacob Shapiro. Raft at this time stated that when he arrived in California in 1927, he was picked up by the authorities due to his past connections in the café business in New York, but that after a short time they discontinued bothering him. [Redacted], Paramount Pictures, Inc., stated that, according to his understanding, before Raft became a movie star he was a collector of beer money in New York when Prohibition was in effect.

Gary Cooper, the movie actor, was interviewed at this time also, and he advised Raft was an individual who was somewhat unable to keep pace with the salary he was receiving, and that Raft had a distorted sense of loyalty to his old New York associates, who were not always of the best type. In 1939, Harry 'Champ' Segal, a former New York City racketeer, advised he had associated with George Raft in Hollywood. At the time of the Buchalter investigation, information was also received that Raft had induced one [name redacted] to come to Hollywood from New York City."

Benny Siegel often spoke of George Raft as a great star, an actor whose gangster characterizations were so authentic they defied imitation and comparison. Raft replied, in turn, that Siegel "tried to imitate me and tried to copy my style."

Raft did not dissemble when asked about his acquaintances: "I met Meyer Lansky, but I never associated with him. In my time I knew them all. Al Capone, Joe Adonis, Frank Castello, Vito Genovese, Dutch Schultz, 'Machine Gun' Jack McGurn, Lucky Luciano, Vinnie Coll. I'll tell you the truth, I admired them." (Quoted in Lewis Yablonsky, George Raft, 1974.)

George Raft was born on September 26, 1895, in a ten-family tenement on New York's 41st Street between Ninth and Tenth Avenues, in a densely-packed immigrant neighborhood called Hell's

Kitchen. Those were the streets that produced such luminaries as Vincent 'Mad Dog' Coll, heavyweight champ Gene Tunney and Owney Madden, an immigrant from Liverpool, England, who would become a powerful mob boss.

George's father, Conrad Ranft, was of German descent. Conrad met and married into an Italian family from Little Italy. Eva Ranft was a striking, dark, swarthy woman. Her parents had a small produce business, selling vegetables from a horse-drawn wagon. Disowned by his parents because he had married an Italian, Conrad decided to strike out on his own.

He worked as a delivery man and was eventually promoted to route supervisor in the Wanamaker Department Store's warehouse. George lived the life of a layabout, scrounging for sustenance where he could. (On occasion, Madden would slip George a few dollars to tide him over the rough spots.) He rode the rails to seek work in the upstate orchids and had a few hassles with the "bulls." When his dream of playing professional baseball did not materialize ("You can field, but you can't hit."), he turned to boxing. His last fight sent him to the hospital with a broken nose and a ripped ear that required twenty-two stitches. The pool room was a better fit. He won often enough to pay for his keep.

Raft was initiated into the gangster life in the early years of Prohibition. He trained as a driver to ride shotgun ahead or behind beer trucks from Madden's illegal brewery in Lower Manhattan. In the dead of night the convoy would go hell bent to 110th Street (to prevent hijacking by other gangs) where Dutch Schultz would then take command for the remaining run to customers north of the city.

In 1927, Raft left New York for the West Coast where the possibility of a film career awaited. Given his exotic looks he was judged as a potential replacement for the recently deceased Rudolfo Valentino. In his first film (*Queen of the Nightclub*, 1929), he displayed his dancing talents. During the next few years, he watched his resources deplete as opportunities become fewer and far between.

George's breakout film (*Scarface*, 1932) was his first gangster role and triggered a complete career turn and the end of his Latin Lover stereotype. George favored the high life, the night life, good clothes, and fine wines. He was a big spender. Money for him was not be flipped but to slip effortlessly through his fingers. In his late years when asked what happened to the millions he had earned from his seventy-six films, with his quick wit he responded, "Part of the ten million I spent on gambling, part on booze, part on women. The rest I spent foolishly." As stated by Mike La Sorte.

His career was marked by numerous tough-guy roles, often a gangster or convict.

The believability with which he played these, together with his lifelong associations with such real-life gangsters as Owney Madden and Bugsy Siegel, added to persistent rumors that he also was a gangster.

The shady reputation may have helped his popularity early on, but it made him somewhat undesirable to movie executives later in his career.

Raft had several mistresses and lovers, to name a few: Carole Landis, Betty Grable, Cleatus Caldwell, Joi Lansing, Mae West, and Mari Blanchard.

*** *** ***

129

• Gene Tierney

Stacy Conradt stated that Tierney became incredibly successful on Broadway by the age of 20. She soon found herself in roles opposite Rory Calhoun, Rex Harrison, Tyrone Power, Clark Gable and Humphrey Bogart.

It was Bogart who discovered how deep Gene's mental problems ran while they were filming *The Left Hand of God* in 1953.

He encouraged her to seek help, so when the movie wrapped, she was admitted to Harkness Pavilion in New York and then the Institute of Living in Hartford, Connecticut, where she received 27 shock treatments. It was too much for her and she tried to escape the asylum, but she was caught and reinstitutionalized. She tried to commit suicide in 1957 by jumping off of a ledge but was stopped just in time. It was thought that her bipolar disorder was triggered when she gave birth to her first daughter, who was born deaf, partially blind and had some mental handicaps.

Tierney's close friend Howard Hughes saw to it that her daughter receive the best care possible. Although she never admitted to an affair with Howard Hughes, she did have affairs with John F. Kennedy and Tyrone Power while separated from her husband, Oleg Cassini, one of Jacqueline Kennedy's favorite designers.

- **Alan Ladd's** career was in a nose dive at the time of his death at the age of 50. At first he was nearly killed by an "accidental" self-inflicted gunshot wound and then he succeeded in his mission with an overdose of sedatives.

- During the promotion tour of the film *Tattoo*, **Bruce Dern** swore that he and costar **Maude Adams** actually had sex during the film's final sex scenes, a claim vehemently denied by Adams.

- In 1935, 30-year-old actress **Thelma Todd** was found slumped over the steering wheel of her Lincoln Phaeton Touring car. Her demise was declared an "accidental death from carbon monoxide poisoning," although everyone from her ex-husband to a jealous lover to Lucky Luciano's hit men has been implicated in the murder of the "Ice-Cream Blonde."

- "Everyone's just laughing at me. I hate it. Big breasts, big ass, big deal. Can't I be anything else?"-**Marilyn Monroe**.

- **Tom Neal's scandals**

Photo: Tragic accident; Tom Neal accidentally strangled Ann Savage in the classic low-budget thriller *Detour*.

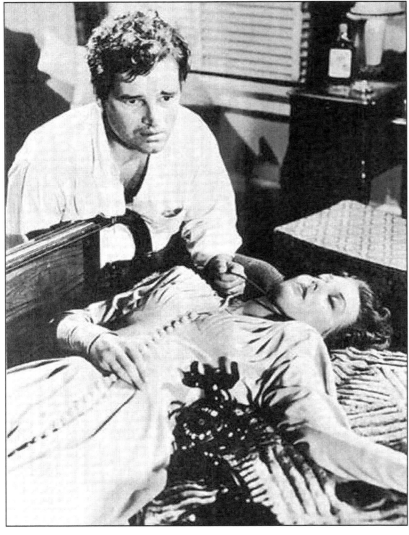

Handsome Tom Neal was born into a wealthy family in Evanston, Illinois, on January 28, 1914.

Neal attended Northwestern University, where he excelled on the boxing team, and graduated from Harvard Law School at the age of 24. Neal never intended to practice law, preferring instead to be an actor. After doing some work in summer stock, he made his Broadway debut in the mid 1930s, right before starting law school.

In the late 1930s, Neal went to Hollywood where he was put under contract to MGM. But the studio didn't give him a big build-up, loaning him out instead to smaller studios.

After his contract ended in 1942, Neal freelanced with great success, appearing in films frequently with beautiful B movie queen Ann Savage. The war years proved to be the best of Tom Neal's film career. Neal's career began to sag a bit after the end of World War II, yet he kept getting roles. His film career ended with a scandal surrounding his involvement with actress **Barbara Payton.** Payton was engaged to actor Franchot Tone but had a roving eye. She began seeing Neal on the sly, about which Tone quickly learned. During a confrontation in September 1951, Tone and Neal brawled over her affections. Tone caught the worst end of the fight and was hospitalized for several days and required plastic surgery. Payton and Tone married a couple of weeks after the altercation, but their marriage ended just a few months later. Afterward, Neal and Payton married, but this union ended quickly. The Franchot Tone-Barbara Payton-Tom Neal triangle made headlines in 1951 and effectively killed the film careers of all three principals. The Franchot Tone-Barbara Payton scandal was not the last or the worst for Tom Neal. In 1961, he married **Gale Bennett,** his fourth wife. Four years later, Neal shot his wife in the head, killing her instantly. Although Neal maintained that the killing was an accident, he was convicted of involuntary manslaughter and sentenced to 15 years. After serving six years of his sentence with good behavior, he was paroled in late 1971 and returned to the Los Angeles area, where he and his teenaged son shared an apartment. Sadly, Tom Neal died suddenly of a heart attack at age 58 in August 1972. His son, Tom Neal Jr., has also dabbled in acting, as reported by Brian Drive-in Theater.

- Aspiring film actress **Elizabeth Short**, the notorious "Black Dahlia," was found in a vacant lot in Los Angeles in 1947, her body savagely mutilated and hacked in half at the waist. No one has ever been arrested in connection with the murder.

- **Were the silent film stars Lillian and Dorothy Gish more than sisters?**
Photo: Lillian and Dorothy Gish. Lillian Diana de Guiche (October 14, 1893-February 27, 1993), was an American actress known as Lillian Gish. Born in Springfield, Ohio, she was the elder sister of actress Dorothy Gish. John Gilbert was infatuated with Lillian Gish, and would mess up his "love scenes" with her in the filming of Boheme, La (1926) on purpose, so he could keep kissing her. Lillian Gish never married or had children. She ended her relationship with George Jean Nathan when she discovered he was Jewish by birth, although his mother was a convent-educated convert to Roman Catholicism and he himself shared Gish's conservative views.

In 1912, Mary Pickford introduced the sisters to D.W. Griffith, and she got them contracts with Biograph Studios. Their first role was in Griffith's short film *An Unseen Enemy.* Lillian went on to star in many of Griffith's most acclaimed films, among these: *The Birth of a Nation, Intolerance, Broken Blossoms, Way Down East,* and *Orphans of the Storm.* Although Lillian never married, the Gish-Griffith association was so close that it was suspected that Lillian was Griffith's lover, though the evidence is circumstantial at best. Alleged relationships were affairs with Charles Duell, a producer, to whom Lillian was reportedly engaged, and the drama critic and editor George Jean Nathan, although Gish was posthumously outed as a lesbian in several books, including one by Boze Hadleigh called Hollywood Lesbians (1996), and another by Axel Madsen titled The Hollywood Sewing Circle (2002). Many insiders insisted that in fact, they were passionate lovers, wrote Spiritus Temporis.

Lillian Gish

Photo: Lillian and Dorothy Gish.

Gossip about the sisters' romantic and sexual affair appeared in newspapers' columns and were widely circulated in Hollywood.

Lillian Gish once said: "Marriage is a business. A woman cannot combine a career and marriage. I should not wish to unite the two. I believe that marriage is a career in itself. I have preferred a stage career to a marriage career." (1919)

Another quote by Lillian Gish: "Lionel Barrymore first played my grandfather, later my father, and finally, he played my husband. If he'd lived, I'm sure I'd have played his mother. That's the way it is in Hollywood. The men get younger and the women get older."

According to Who Dated Who, Lillian and Dorothy Gish both started working for D.W. Griffith in the early days of 'American Mutoscope & Biograph. While it's been claimed that Griffith was immediately infatuated with Lillian, in their first film for him, Biograph's *An Unseen Enemy* (1912), he thought they were twins. According to Lillian's autobiography, he had to tie different colored hair ribbons on the girls to tell them apart and give them direction: "Red, you hear a strange noise. Run to your sister. Blue, you're scared too. Look toward me, where the camera is." Lillian and her sister Dorothy were once offered the chance of buying the whole Sunset Strip in Hollywood for $300. The Gish sisters considered the purchase for a while, and then went down to Bullock's department store, and each bought a dress instead. After her amicable parting with D.W. Griffith, Lillian Gish joined MGM in 1925, but was unceremoniously dumped when Greta Garbo emerged as a star. Considered a "sexless antique," she turned to radio and her first love, the theater. Ironically, MGM had Garbo on the set of *The Scarlet Letter* (1926) every day to watch Gish work as part of her apprenticeship. Her first love was theater; she left her entire estate, which was valued at several million dollars, to Helen Hayes. Lillian and Mary Pickford were childhood friends, but Mary tried to never be left alone with Lillian--remembering her mother's superstitious belief that "the good die young," Mary was in constant fear that Lillian would drop dead at any moment. On 11 June 1976, the Dorothy and Lillian Gish Film Theater was dedicated on the Bowling Green State University campus in Bowling Green, Ohio, USA.

Lillian Gish's list of lovers includes: Charles Duell, George Jean Nathan, and Douglas Fairbanks Jr. Dorothy Gish's list of lovers includes: Robert Harron, and James Rennie.

- **James Murray: From a leading and dashing star to a beggar in the street.**

This is a sad story about a star who became victim of alcohol. At one time, he was almost on the top of the world, a few years later, he was at the bottom of the shadows of poverty and homeless life.

By a stroke of luck, an extra by the name of James Murray was chosen by director King Vidor to play the lead in the 1928 film "The Crowd", a major picture by MGM. He did well, and starred again in the "Big City". And once again, he was chosen to co-star with Joan Crawford in "Rose Marie". Unfortunately, the filming stopped because of Murray's heavy drinking. Scratched off by the studio, Murray faded in total obscurity. Showbiz is unmerciful. Murray vanished from the face of the earth. Years later, in 1933, and by a pure coincidence, Vidor was sopped in the street by a beggar begging for food; he was James Murray. Vidor gave him ten bucks, and on the spot offered him a lead in his new picture "Our Daily Bread". Murray turned him down by saying, "I am finish, I can't act anymore," and faded away in the crowd of beggars and bums. Vidor was a loving man, and a very compassionate director; Murray's horrifying and helpless situation broke his heart, and here he is offering Murray a chance to redeem himself, but alcoholism has already destroyed his mind soul. Approximately, three years later, the police found his corpse floating in the Hudson River. Decades later, and still haunted by Murray's tragic life, King Vidor wrote "The Actor", a screenplay about his life, but it was never produced.

James Murray and Eleanor Boardman in "The Crowd", 1928.

King Vidor, fresh from the triumph of his last film "The Big Parade" and in favor with the studio, was looking for someone to portray the lead in his next film, originally titled, "One Of The Mob", later titled "The Crowd". One day, on the lot at MGM, he caught a glimpse of someone with just the right look, the exact look he needed for the lead role of "Johnny Sims". It was James Murray.

Photo: Jim (James Murray) is a trapper wanted for murder and Rose-Marie (Joan Crawford) is the belle of the trading post in "Rose-Marie" (MGM, 1928.)

According to Vidor, he started to approach James, but James was leaving the lot and was moving quickly. Vidor flagged him down and asked him his name. "Murray" was the reply. Vidor asked what he did at the studio. "Extra", another terse reply. This guy was clearly in a hurry. Vidor offered him his card and said "My name is Vidor. I'm a director here. Please come out tomorrow and see me. I may have some work for you." But, James never showed up.

In his autobiography, "A Tree Is A Tree", Vidor wrote: "I waited for three days but, my man failed to show up. By then, I had forgotten his name, so in desperation, I went to the casting office and looked at the long lists of extras who had worked on that day. When I finally came upon the name 'James Murray', I recognized the name I had been given so briefly on the street. I asked the studio to call Mr. Murray, but word came back that he was too busy!" "Well, it was certainly unusual for an actor to ignore a director. I asked the studio to call him and pay him a day's pay for the interview. This tactical move got results. Next day when Mr. Murray arrived at my office, I was curious as to why he hadn't shown up before"

'I didn't believe you'
'Didn't believe what?'
'Didn't believe you were a director or, if you were, that you were going to give me a job'
'Wasn't it worth a chance?'
'But bus fare to Culver City costs money' was the laconic reply.
'Can you act?', I asked.
'I don't know.'
'Will you take a test?'
'If they pay me', he said."

"I was now quite sure of my instincts about him so we paid Mr. Murray to take a test, an un-heard of procedure. When I showed the test to Irving Thalberg, we both agreed that James Murray, Hollywood extra, was one of the best natural actors we had ever had."

His performance as "Johnny Sims" in "The Crowd" remains one of the single finest performances of the silent era.

Nominated for two Academy Awards (the first year of the Academy Awards), "The Crowd" is generally acknowledged by film critics and historians to be one of the top one hundred films in the history of motion pictures. "The Crowd" was unusual and somewhat daring for its time in that it was not a happy or uplifting picture. Projecting a message of the futility of ambition, and undermining the American dream, it was downright depressing at a time when the American public flocked to the movies for much needed weekly shot of sunshine. The critics loved it and the film was a moderate success but certainly not the smash hit it might have been. It was a masterpiece before its time.

Photo: Joan Crawford, James Murray, Jerry Miley, and Carmel Myers from the adventure-melodrama "Understanding Heart". MGM, 1927.

Lawrence Murray, Jr., wrote, but, talent alone isn't enough and James continued to sabotage his career with alcohol.

Considering his self destructive patterns, it's a wonder he enjoyed the success he did despite his best efforts to thwart it. He couldn't, or wouldn't hold down a job, although after "The Crowd," he was offered many fine roles including the leading role opposite Marian Davies in Vidor's next picture, "Show People".

In fact, he accepted the role but never bothered to show up for the shoot and Vidor had to replace him. Years later, he was offered the lead role in the Our Daily Bread, the sequel to "The Crowd," on the condition that he get back in shape and stop drinking. He refused, rather rudely. One version of the episode suggested that he thought he was being given a handout and wouldn't accept charity, while another suggested that he simply had no intention of changing his lifestyle. No matter really; both versions have him heading in the same direction.

James' death was shrouded in mystery with a hint of scandal. Many people thought he committed suicide brought on by depression caused by his portrayal of Sims. Others, thought his addiction to alcohol brought about the depression. Still others speculated that he was simply a drunk who fell off a pier. Hollywood loves a mystery and a scandal. No matter which theory you subscribe to, here, was both. The truth, while tragic, is less melodramatic and is revealed further below. One thing that cannot be argued is that James was an advanced alcoholic with a classic pattern of self-destructive behavior. If we knew in the nineteen twenties and thirties what we know now about alcoholism and depression, James might have lived a long and fruitful life. In fact, his brother Harry, who originally started out with James for Hollywood, and who found work in films as an extra and some small speaking parts, found steady work as a stand-in for John Gilbert. An alcoholic himself, Harry Murray managed to escape his brother's fate by embracing the principles of Alcoholics Anonymous. He went on to entertain in Vaudeville and then on Broadway as a member of a dancing troupe known as "The Debonaires". Until he retired in 1968, he was a producer for CBS Television City in New York, producing such shows as "To Tell The Truth" and "Password". Harry lived to the ripe age of 98, spending his last 27 tears as a volunteer at a local hospital in Carmel New York, beloved by all who knew him, all in all, a very fulfilled life.

However, like a former day John Belushi, James Murray was a bundle of talent out of control and unable to overcome the demons of depression and substance abuse. Unlike Belushi, he did not self-destruct suddenly at the height of his fame and talent. Quite the opposite, in fact. He arrived on the scene with a flash at the top of the game and descended tortuously in a tragic downward spiral. Like a nova, he shone brightly and burned up quickly. Lawrence Murray Jr., wrote: "We remember my Great Uncle James through his films, pictures, memorabilia, and stories told and retold by aunts and uncles who knew him. He was an interesting character. I wish I could have known him, but I was just born a little too late."

Photo: James Murray with Wally Albright Jr., Frances Morris and Lon Chaney in the lost film "Thunder" (MGM, 1929).

Murray's classic movie "The Crowd" (1928) was so unrelentingly sad and bitter that MGM executives, fearing box office disaster, tried to force Director King Vidor to tack on an upbeat Hollywood ending. Of the seven different endings Vidor shot, it came down to two.

In the final alternate movie ending, the down-on-their-luck family wins a fortune and lives happily ever after. Fortunately, preview audiences laughed and balked at this absurdity. King Vidor got his way and the movie went on to become a cinematic masterpiece!

King Vidor recounts in his autobiography that he received a letter from one of James' friends, who was with him at the time of his death, relating the events. He said that according to the letter, James and a few cronies were hanging out by the Hudson River on New York's west side. They convinced a bunch of tourists and onlookers that they were shooting a picture for MGM, that James was an MGM star (which he had been) and that they were waiting for the camera crew and director to show up. They told the onlookers that they had left their money in their clothes back at the studio and asked if some of the people standing by could front them $20 or so for drinks, they'd pay them back as soon as the production crew arrived. One or more of the crowd obliged and they bought some liquor and were passing it around and they got drunk. Of course the film crew never arrived. In the meantime, James was clowning around trying to amuse the people with some slapstick humor. He pretended to slip and fall in the river and everyone laughed. But, after awhile, when he didn't return, they went over and looked, to find him floating face down in the river. When they pulled him out, he was drowned. That was July 11, 1936.

When James' body was recovered from the river, the police found a wallet in his coat and the only piece of identification was a business card for J. Christopher Murray, Attorney at Law (James' brother). The police mistakenly assumed that the body was that of Christopher and called his home. Christopher's daughter Patricia was at home that day and she recounts the events. "I took the call and gave the phone to my mother. The call was confusing because as far as we knew, Papa wasn't supposed to be in New York at the time. After speaking with the police for a few tense minutes, Mom realized their mistake and told the police whom they had. Papa (Christopher) was out of town for a few days and my mother said she'd contact him. He was up at our summer house in Penn Yan (a small town on the shore of Lake Keuka in the upstate New York resort area known as the Finger Lakes-LM) for a few days and was not easy to reach. There was no phone at the house back then, so Mom called someone in town and they sent someone out to see Papa to tell him what had happened. He rushed back to New York to attend Uncle James' funeral." Harry Murray, James' younger brother, made the arrangements for the funeral. James was buried in the family plot at Calgary Cemetery in Queens. It was not a happy year for the Murray family. James' father, Christy, had passed away on January 31st of that same year. Sadly, although buried next to his father and mother, James' name was never added to the headstone.

- **Tom Mix: A Hollywood's phony hero, a horse thief, and a deserter.**
  Photo: Tom Mix

Is Arnold Schwarzenegger the most highly paid actor in the history of American motion pictures as he has claimed? No! The most highly paid actor in the history of American motion pictures is the western/cowboy superstar Tom Mix. In 1920, he used to earn as high as $20,000 a week plus a big cut. He was the "model for the dandyish, squeaky-clean movie cowboy that was much parodied in later years." Signing on with the Fox Film Corporation in 1917, the studio found for him the role that would catapult him to stardom: The Untamed. In other words, Mix was a role model. Really? On screen or in real life? Well, Mix was neither a role model, nor a hero, or the clean cut All-American specimen. The studio marketed him as a great horseman, a valiant soldier, a bona-fide hero. In reality, Mix was a deserter, not an exceptional horseman, and a horse thief. The studio presented him as a former Marshall, a Texas Ranger, a hero in the Spanish American War, an intrepid who charged up San Juan Hill with Roosevelt's Rough Riders and a rider with Pancho Villa. All these claims were false. They are the fabrication of Hollywood. In fact, Mix deserted his military post at Fort Hancock, New Jersey, he was court martialed, and sent to prison when they caught him stealing horses. He was as phony as Rudolph Valentino.

*** *** ***

139

Chapter 4
Hollywood's Biggest Scandals: Suicides

---

1. Charles Boyer's suicide:

According to Hollywood USA, Charles Boyer (Left) is best known for his role in the 1944 film *Gaslight* in which he tried to convince Ingrid Bergman that she was going insane. Some years earlier, it was Boyer's role in Algiers (1938) that caused many to credit him with the never-heard line "Come with me to the Casbah." In 1948, Charles Boyer was made a chevalier of the French Legion of Honor. He continued to act until a few years before his death, his last major film role being that of the High Lama in a musical version of *Lost Horizon* (1973). For his contribution to the motion picture and television industries, Charles Boyer has two stars on the Hollywood Walk of Fame. Two days after his wife, British actress Pat Paterson, died from cancer, Charles Boyer committed suicide with an overdose of Seconal. He was interred in Holy Cross Cemetery, Culver City, California, alongside with his wife and son Michael Charles Boyer, who had committed suicide in 1965 at the age of 21.

As stated by Classic Film Stars, Boyer's marriage to British actress Pat Paterson, his first and only wife, was as romantic as his movies. It was love at first sight when they met at a dinner party in 1934. Two weeks later, they were engaged. Three months later, they were married. The marriage would last 44 years.

2. George Sanders' suicide: According to IMBD, Sanders told David Niven in 1937, that he intended to commit suicide when he got older. In 1972, he fulfilled his promise, leaving this note: "Dear World, I am leaving because I am bored. I feel I have lived long enough. I am leaving you with your worries in this sweet cesspool. Good luck." After being convinced by a woman he had taken up with, George Sanders sold his beloved house in Majorca. Soon after, he checked into a hotel in Barcelona, and two days later, his body was discovered next to five empty tubes of Nembutal. Sanders was one of two stars of *The Pink Panther* series to commit suicide. Capucine, who played Inspector Clouseau's wife in *The Pink Panther* (1963), killed herself in 1990. Sanders first got involved in acting when a secretary in the same advertising firm suggested it. That secretary was Greer Garson.

3. Capucine's suicide: On March 17, 1990 Capucine committed suicide in Lausanne, Switzerland.

4. Suicide of Bobby Harron: In September 1920, another suicide occurred, but because of the hype over Olive Thomas' death it went practically unnoticed. Bobby Harron, who played the sensitive lad in the film "Intolerence", shot himself in a New York hotel room. His death occured on the eve of the premiere of Griffith's new film, *Way Down East*. Harron who thought he would be hired for the film was passed for Richard Barthelmess.

5. Peg Entwistle's suicide: Hollywood's First Suicide
Photo: Peg Entwistle

Hollywood is filled with actors who crave stardom. Every once in a while I gaze up at this sign and ponder the short and very sad life of Welsh born actress Peg Entwistle. She was never a star. Not even a minor star. One tiny, non-speaking role in a movie called *Thirteen Women* makes up her entire filmography. And Peg wasn't even invited to the film's premiere. Such a slight in Hollywood can be devastating to a young and vulnerable actress. I've seen it time and again.

Peg Entwistle achieved fame, well, notoriety, by being the first suicide off this famous landmark. Her suicide note read: "I am afraid, I am a coward. I am sorry for everything. If I had done this a long time ago, it would have saved a lot of pain. P.E." Seraphic Press and Wickipedia stated that two days later, in an ironic twist, Entwistle's uncle opened a letter addressed to her from the Beverly Hills Playhouse; it was mailed the day before she jumped. In it was an offer for her to play the lead role in a stage production—in which her character would commit suicide in the final act. Peg Entwistle was just 24 years old when she died.

The Hollywood movie colony came into existence thanks to a group of eastern film makers and businessmen who saw a good thing in the nickelodeons which were springing up all over America. They were lured to the west coast by the promise of that fabled southern California sunshine (which was said to appear 355 days a year); low cost land; and by the opportunity to elude the process servers of Thomas Edison (who was filing lawsuits against anyone who copied his design of the early movie cameras). They settled into the city of Los Angeles and began building open-air stages and makeshift studios. It would be here where the early movie makers would begin cranking out primitive two-reelers, which would win over the hearts and minds of the American people. Soon, word trickled back to Hollywood that audiences across the country were flocking to see their favorite performers and at this point, the actors (who prior to this were seen as little more than hired help) suddenly gained importance as the sure way to sell tickets. The rapidly becoming famous faces took on new names and soon earned salaries to match their new status. Almost overnight, the once obscure and disreputable performers suddenly found fame and fortune, becoming America's royalty. Some of them managed to cope with this quite well... while others did not.

Throughout the 1910's, Hollywood re-created itself almost daily as the new art form of movies began to emerge. Money began to roll into studio coffers and then into the pockets of the stars. Cocaine became the drug of choice, or "joy powder" as it was called in those days. It is reported that the manic silent film comedies actually came about thanks to the drug and became known as the Triangle-Keystone "cokey comedy". In 1916, British drug expert and occultist Aleister Crowley journeyed to Hollywood and noted the locals as being the "cinema crowd of cocaine-crazed sexual lunatics". And that's quite a statement coming from Crowley!

In addition to drugs, sex was always plentiful in Hollywood and gossip mongers in the movie colony always had much to talk about. Was it true that famed director D.W. Griffith had an obsession, onscreen and off, with young girls?

Could it be true that Lillian and Dorothy Gish, up and coming young sisters, were actually lovers? Were the tales of Mack Sennett's "casting couch" actually true... and were some of Sennett's Sunshine Girls, like Gloria Swanson and Carole Lombard, really part of his hand-picked harem?

And what about Hollywood's sex goddess, Theda Bara, who was allegedly a French-Arab demon of depravity born beneath the Sphinx... was it true that she was in truth Theodosia Goodman, a Jewish tailor's daughter from Ohio? Oh, and there was more... much more! Within a few years of its founding, Hollywood would be the most maligned place to ever be spoken of from church pulpits across America. Preachers and evangelists would brand Hollywood as a place of legendary depravity and would call for boycotts of films and protests against theaters who would dare to show anything made in such a place. But the general public all but ignored the outcry and they continued to spend their hard-earned money at the movies.

The 1920's have been referred to as Hollywood's Golden Age and they were, in terms of both the number of movies made and in the amount of cash these films raked in. Unfortunately though, sometimes the golden ones fall just like the rest of us and when they do fall... they fall very hard.

*** *** ***

6. Olive Thomas: Hollywood's First Suicide of a Mega Star

There are certain figures from the silent era who are more famous for their unexpected deaths than for anything else: Thomas Ince, Virginia Rappe, Marie Prevost, Francis Boggs, and so on. Olive Thomas was one of them. She'd risen quickly from modeling jobs to the *Ziegfeld Follies*, and from there to a moderately successful film career, one that was abruptly snuffed out when she poisoned herself in Paris with most of a bottle of a bichloride of mercury solution.

The shocking news was first heard on the radio, on the night of September 10, 1920 but it would later make newspaper headlines:

OLIVE THOMAS DEAD FROM POISON

Olive Thomas, sprightly Ziegfeld Follies queen, Selznick Pictures Star and Mrs. Jack Pickford

Photos: 1. Jack Pickford. 2. Olive Thomas.

In Prairie Ghosts, Troy Taylor, wrote that the star was found dead in Paris, which makes her death an unlikely one for the first Hollywood scandal, but there was no denying the connections. On the morning of September 10, a Hotel Crillon valet used his passkey to enter the hotel's Royal Suite with a breakfast trolley. There, on the floor, was a sable opera cape and on top of it was the body of a nude young woman. In one of her hands was a bottle of bichloride of mercury.

The suite had been registered in the name of Mrs. Jack Pickford, known to millions of fans as Olive Thomas.

Olive was remembered as one of the most beautiful of the Ziegfeld girls and had become the darling of New York magazines like Vogue and Vanity Fair while only 16. She became the toast of the city and thanks to the assistance of Conde Nast, she appeared frequently in numerous fashion magazines. She also posed nude for the famous calendar artist, Alberto Vargas, and illustrator Harrison Fisher called her "the most beautiful woman in the world".

It came as no surprise to anyone when she decided to depart for Hollywood.

Photo: Olive Thomas. She was the Marilyn Monroe of the twenties.

She caught on in the movie colony right away and was cast as a young girl in light comedies like "Betty takes a hand", "Prudence on Broadway" and "The follies girl". In 1919, Myron Selznick began his own movie company and signed Olive to a lucrative contract. In 1920, she was huge hit in "The Flapper" and that same year, she married Jack Pickford, another screen idol and the brother of star Mary Pickford. Her place among the royals of Hollywood was assured.

The fact that Olive committed suicide just months later made headlines around the world and became the subject of much controversy. She was only 20 when she died, plus she had wealth, beauty, fame, and the adoration of not only millions of fans but that of her young husband as well. Newspapers and magazines had referred to them as the "perfect couple". So, what went wrong?

The Selznick Studio was deluged with letters from around the world and both the American Embassy and the French police promised full investigations.

Unfortunately, what the investigations revealed did not go along well at all with the public image of Olive Thomas!

Jack Pickford was supposed to join Olive in Paris as soon as he completed work on his film "The little shepherd of kingdom come" to make up for the honeymoon their busy schedules had prevented right after their wedding. Olive had gone on ahead to do some shopping, but as the investigators learned, it was not in the salons where her shopping was being done. Rumors and sources soon reported that Olive had been spotted in a number of clubs, while in the company of some of the more notorious figures in the French underground. A story began to circulate that Olive was desperately trying to purchase a large quantity of heroin for her husband, Jack, who was a hopeless addict. When she failed, it was said that she committed suicide.

When this story appeared in the press, Jack was undergoing treatment for nervous collapse following Olive's death and he was unable to refute the charges. However, his sister Mary issued a statement which denied the charges as "sickening aspersions" on her brother's good name. A short time later, a separate investigation, conducted by the U.S. Army into the activities of a Captain Spaulding, led to the arrest of a soldier who was dealing in large quantities of cocaine and heroin. On his list of steady customers was the name of Olive Thomas. Now, Olive was no longer known as the "Ideal American Girl", but as "Olive Thomas, Dope Fiend", and watch societies began to speak out against this new menace to American maidenhood. In the 1920's, the film colony lured young would-be stars from across the land and many warned these hopefuls against the dark allure of drugs and fast living.

Olive's death provided good newspaper copy for a year after her death, until finally, her suicide was crowded out of the headlines by the death of another Hollywood hopeful. This new girl was just a minor actress, but she was linked to a man who was known as "America's Funnyman"... Roscoe "Fatty" Arbuckle. She would also go on to become one of Hollywood's first lingering ghosts.

Olive Thomas

Portrait of Olive Thomas.
Alberto Vargas painted Olive Thoma's portrait in 1920 for Florenz Ziegfeld. The model was Olive Thomas in the flesh. In 1920, she was a household name, a movie star. In "Sunshine and Shadow, 1955, and Comcast; Mary Pickford's Autobiography, it was said, in 1915 she had met Ziegfeld who hired her first for the "Follies" and then for the "Frolics," a much racier revue put on after hours in the roof garden of the New Amsterdam Theatre for a mostly male audience. Olive proved a sensation. Then Hollywood called, first in the form of movie offers and then in the person of Jack Pickford, Mary's younger brother. Jack and Olive married, secretly.

Later, Olive would tell an interviewer that she kept the marriage secret for the first year because she did not want to trade on the Pickford name.

Leslie Coquette stated that only when she was an established star, she went on, did she disclose the union.

Mary Pickford's autobiography, a far from reliable source, suggests another reason: "I regret to say that none of us approved of the marriage at that time. Mother thought Jack was too young, and I felt that Olive, being in musical comedy, belonged to an alien world. Ollie had all the rich, eligible men of the social world at her feet. She had been deluged with proposals from her own world of the theater as well, which was not at all surprising. The beauty of Olive Thomas is legendary. The girl had the loveliest violet-blue eyes I have ever seen. They were fringed with long dark lashes that seemed darker because of the delicate translucent pallor of her skin. I could understand why Florenz Ziegfeld never forgave Jack for taking her away from the Follies. She and Jack were madly in love with one another but I always thought of them as a couple of children playing together."

Apparently Olive was the darling of Conde Nast's *Vogue* crowd at this point. She was also pursued by wealthy, powerful, and important men from all over the world; German Ambassador Bernstorff, for example, gave her a pearl necklace valued at $10,000.

In France, Olive might well have achieved famein the *Folies Bergère*. Rich men might have competed for her favors. There was a well-established niche for women like her in the *demi-monde*. Some even married the aristocrats who kept them. Céleste Mogador became the Duchess of Chibrillon in the 1850s and Liane de Pougy became Princess Ghika in 1910. The new princess was forty-one; her husband twenty. Beyond marriage, there was the possibility of becoming a serious actress. Sarah Bernhardt is the most famous case in point. Léonide LeBlanc is another. Still other courtesans wrote books, detailing their amours and adventures. Indeed, the upward mobility of notorious women out of the demi-monde into society became a serious preoccupation of male authors during the Second Empire and the Third Republic. Such movement threatened class, gender, and moral barriers.

- **7. Carole Landis, Rex Harrison and her suicide.**

Carole Landis was a superb actress and a wonderful human being. She appeared, and or starred in 52 films. Carole has a "star" on Hollywood Walk of Fame. She was also presented with a distinctive award, recognizing her as the "all-American girl who has done the most for the war effort." In 1937, Carole Landis met her future husband, Busby Berkeley, while auditioning for a role in a Varsity Show.

Photo : Carole Landis' suicide note.

Busby was the one who got her a contract with Warner Brothers. Irving Wheeler, Landis' first husband sued Berkeley for "alienation of affection", but lost his lawsuit. On March 14, 1943, Carole Landis was voted the best-dressed screen star by the Fashion Academy of New York. On July 4, 1948, Carol Landis wrote two unforgettable letters; one addressed to her maid, Fanny May Bolden asking her to take her cat to the vet because the cat had a sore paw. The second letter was a suicide note addressed to her mother.

In thatnote, Carole Landis wrote:

"Dearest Mommie: I am sorry, really sorry to put you through this. But there is no way to avoid it. I love you darling...everything goes to you. Look in the files and there is a will which decrees everything. Good bye my angel. Pray for me—Your Baby".

The stunning Carole Landis

On July 5, 1948, Carole Landis took a lethal dose of Seconal barbiturates. She died at the age of twenty nine in Pacific Palisades, California.

Rex Harrison who had dined with her the previous night, discovered her body the day she committed suicide. Her older sister, Dorothy stated that Carole did not kill herself. She claimed that Rex Harrison murdered her.

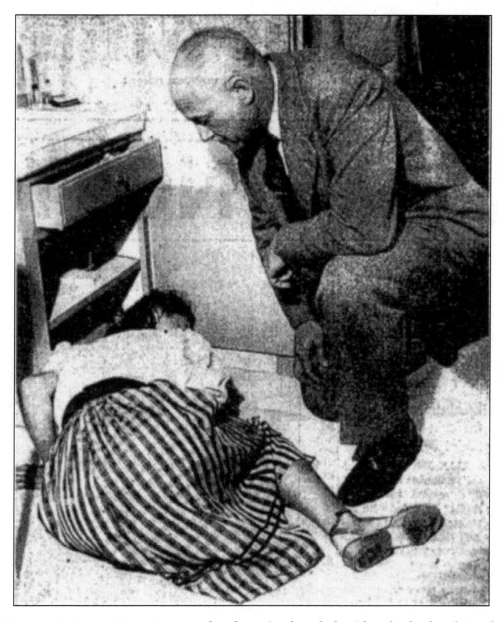

Captain Emmet E. Jones, West Los Angeles detective kneels besides the body of Carole Landis, found dead in her kitchen.

A rare photo of Marilyn Monroe with Bob Kennedy and President John Kennedy; both slept with her.

8. The Marilyn Monroe Suicide and the Kennedy's Factor

The Kennedys

Sex-addict US president John F. Kennedy had a burning ambition - to bed every woman in Hollywood. In the week when long-sealed documents revealed details of JFK's affair with a teenage intern, a scorching new book by Frank Sinatra's butler shows that when it comes to philandering, Bill Clinton couldn't hold a candle to Kennedy.

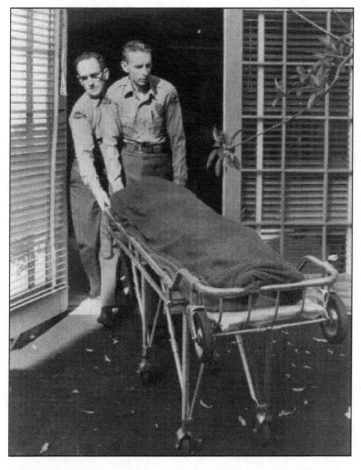

Photo: The famous shot of police wheeling away the body of Marilyn Monroe.

According to Kennedy Scandal 2: JFK wanted sex with every woman in Hollywood; MGN Ltd; ProQuest Information and Learning Company, ironically, these revelations also came in the week Boston's John F. Kennedy Library and Museum unveiled an exhibit commemorating the upcoming 50th anniversary of JFK's wedding to Jacqueline Bouvier. The book - Mr S.: My Life With Frank Sinatra - Written by Sinatra's devoted personal valet George Jacobs, tells how Old Blue Eyes cemented his close friendship with the President by setting him up with a string of showbusiness beauties, including Marilyn Monroe.

"JFK and Mr S. got along great," reveals Jacobs in the book. "They had everything in common: charisma, talent and power.

Mr S. stood in awe of JFK and his Ivy slickness, his heroics, his acclaim - but JFK was far more in awe of Mr S because Frank Sinatra controlled the one thing JFK wanted more than anything else...women.

Rachel Bell stated that "Mr S. was the Pope of Poontang and JFK was honoured to kiss his ring. The pontiff could bestow a Judy Campbell (Sinatra's long- standing mistress Judith Campbell Exner) or - if he was feeling magnanimous - a Marilyn Monroe, such was his beneficence." One day when Jacobs asked JFK what he wanted, he replied with a grin: "I want to fuck every woman in Hollywood."

Photo: Marilyn Monroe's bedroom.

The "what the butler saw" book leaves little to the imagination and includes an extract recounting the day Jacobs saw the then- Senator John F Kennedy doing lines of cocaine with his brother-in- law Peter Lawford in one of the guest rooms. Jacobs writes: "'For my back, George,' Kennedy said to me with his bad-boy wink. "Peter was more direct. 'For God's sake, George, don't tell Frank'." Once, while Jacobs was giving Kennedy a massage, the president-to- be told him that Marlene Dietrich had performed a sex act on him in the ballroom of the Hotel du Cap on the French Riviera.

Photo: A policeman points to an empty Nembutal bottle on Marilyn's night stand, next to where she was found dead.

On August 5th 1962, Marilyn Monroe was found dead in the bedroom of her California bungalow. Beside her bed lay a number of empty pill bottles. Two weeks later, on August 21st, the Los Angeles Coroner held a press conference and announced to the world a verdict of 'probable suicide'. It seemed that the world's most famous actress had committed suicide by taking a massive overdose of barbiturates.

This verdict has never been considered satisfactory. For the past 40 years, debate has raged around the circumstances of Marilyn Monroe's death, spawning a multitude of conspiracy theories.

Conflicting witness statements, unreliable testimonies, disappearing evidence and a refusal to investigate the death thoroughly have combined to produce a widespread belief that something deeply sinister took place. (Source: History California)

Marilyn Monroe was tricked into killing herself by Bobby Kennedy. So says Dr. Jack Hattem, who, backed up by secret FBI files, says the Hollywood bombshell was somehow fooled into believing she would be revived in time as part of a plot involving Senator Robert Kennedy, the brother of JFK, who was gunned down. Instead, Monroe, who staged many fake suicide attempts throughout her life to gain sympathy, was left to die by staff and friends. It's all in Hattem's book *Marilyn Monroe: Murder By Consent*. While the official story is that Marilyn committed suicide, conspiracists have claimed this is impossible as it was a barbiturate enema which killed her, and this could not have been self-administered.

Did Marilyn Monroe commit suicide by barbiturate overdose over her broken relationships with the Kennedy brothers or was she murdered/assassinated to protect a future US presidential candidate?

Theories

1. Suicide: This is the official cause of death and probably the most widely believed. She had tried it four times previously and she clearly had significant mood swings. The problem with this theory is that too many forensic facts are at odds with it, unless one can imagine Marilyn making up a barbiturate enema and administering it to herself. Quite a number of forensic experts have discarded the suicide theory as inconsistent with the facts. Another problem with the suicide

151

theory is that she was in good spirits at the time of her death and had been making plans for future events and movies, and if Spoto is correct, her remarriage to Joe DiMaggio.

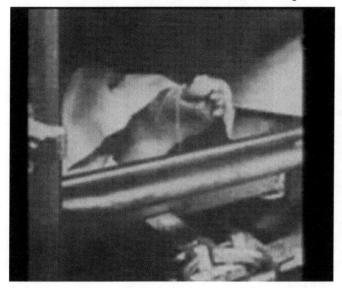 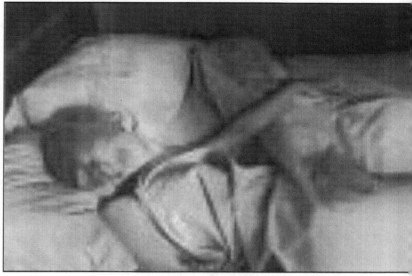

Photos: Left, The toe tag morgue photo of Marilyn Monroe, from Morbidly Hollywood.Right: Dead Marilyn in her bed.

2. Accident: If, in fact, Marilyn Monroe died from a rectally-administered barbiturate enema, the question is who prepared and administered it. It is not out of the realm of possibility that the overdose was accidental.

Spoto makes a very persuasive case for accidental death. Dr. Greenson had been working with Dr. Hyman Engelberg to wean Marilyn off Nembutal, substituting instead chloral hydrate to help her sleep.

Milton Rudin claimed that Greenson said something very important the night of Marilyn's death: "God damn it! Hy gave her a prescription I didn't know about!"

Dr. Engelberg was having serious marital problems and obviously didn't communicate well with Greenson on Marilyn's prescriptions. Spoto suggests that Greenson would not have given Marilyn a heavy dose of chloral hydrate the evening of her death if he had realized that Marilyn had been taking Nembutal capsules throughout the day. Spoto further suggests that after an exhausting full day with Marilyn that he arranged for Marilyn to have a chloral hydrate enema so that she would sleep through the night. Chloral hydrate significantly slows down the metabolism of Nembutal, but Greenson did not know that she had been taking Nembutal and Marilyn did not realize that Nembutal and chloral hydrate interacted adversely or she probably would have admitted to Greenson that she had taken Nembutals. If Spoto's theory is correct, then who administered the enema? Spoto believes that it had to be Eunice Murray, who, like Greenson, had no inkling that the sedative enema would be fatal. Any doctor might be loath to admit to himself or others that he had made such a significant mistake in such a high-profile patient, especially since Marilyn appeared drugged during the afternoon. Also, if Eunice was the person who administered the enema, it would be natural for her to try to protect herself and Dr. Greenson by pretending that no such procedure was given to Marilyn.

152

Photo: A Rolex given by Marilyn Monroe to JFK on the occasion of his 45th birthday.

3. Murder: Everyone loves a conspiracy. It is so much more exciting than accidental death or suicide. The celebrity status of the main characters in this drama lends itself heavily towards the romance of conspiracy. Look at the cottage industry that John F. Kennedy's assassination has generated. It's important to distinguish the cover-up of embarrassing information by powerful people from the commitment of a crime to eliminate people who can potentially create embarrassment. There are a number of credible people who claim that Marilyn Monroe had affairs with one or both Kennedy brothers. John Kennedy, at least, was known to indulge himself in extramarital adventures. So, it is not at all implausible that President Kennedy availed himself of the charms of one of the sexiest and most attractive women of that era. That Robert Kennedy was so inclined is not nearly as clear. According to Peter Lawford, Marilyn's unrealistic notions about becoming First Lady caused her to embarrass herself with both Kennedy brothers. Her letters and telephone calls to them had become both tiresome and very risky. It was one thing to cavort with anonymous girls, but quite another to be involved with a celebrity sex symbol like Marilyn Monroe. There was every good reason for JFK and RFK to break off the relationship with

153

Marilyn permanently. What allegedly became so troublesome was Marilyn's supposed rage at JFK's rejection of her and the fear that she was able to strike in both brothers. Donald Wolfe sums it up: "Marilyn Monroe was in a position to bring down the presidency. She was cognizant of Jack Kennedy's marital infidelities and other private matters. She had his notes and letters and was privy to Kennedy's involvement with Sam Giancana.

That the Kennedy brothers had discussed national security matters with the film star added to an astonishing array of indiscretions." It is not out of the realm of possibility that Robert Kennedy was the man appointed by his brother to deliver the rejection to Marilyn personally. It's not the kind of thing that one writes in a letter and it's unlikely that JFK was anxious to deliver the message himself. Did Robert Kennedy bring Marilyn the news of his brother's desire to break off his relationship on the night Marilyn died? After all, there are some witnesses, including a cop, who place Robert Kennedy near the scene that night. This information may never be known with any certainty, but if Robert Kennedy did somehow make an unannounced visit to Marilyn Monroe on the night of August 4, then it provides unexpected motivation for the suicide theory.

That is, while Marilyn may have been in good spirits that day and evening, a visit by Robert Kennedy shattering her notions about an enduring relationship with JFK could have abruptly changed her mood. Was there an attempt on the part of the government to cover up John Kennedy's indiscretions with Marilyn Monroe? It would be very surprising indeed if there were not such an attempt.

The alleged cover-up was believed to have extended beyond the phone records and police evidence found at the scene. Shortly after his phone call to the Naars before 11 p.m. on the night of Marilyn's death, it is believed that Peter Lawford and Pat Newcomb went to Marilyn's house. Purportedly in a state of panic, Lawford called brother-in-law Bobby Kennedy and explained what had occurred. However, destroying phone records and personal journals and scraps of paper are not in the same league with murder. To suggest, as some authors, have that Robert Kennedy was somehow complicit in the murder of Marilyn Monroe is to be ignorant of the character and integrity of the Attorney General. While mystery surrounds the death of Marilyn Monroe, mystery does not shroud the character of Robert Kennedy.

Robert Kennedy had a very fixed moral compass which was repeatedly documented in his crusade against organized crime. Was Marilyn murdered by the Mafia, eager to avenge itself on the Kennedys for Robert's strike against them and expose the Kennedys' philandering to the American public? The motive was probably there but with what is known about the individuals present in Marilyn's home on the night of August 4, 1962, it makes a mob hit with a rectal enema seem a bit unlikely and almost absurd. The actual events that surrounded Marilyn's death will probably never be known. What was known for certain was that a living legend mysteriously died before her time, in a mist of confusion, scandal and uncertainty. Following the autopsy, Marilyn's body was released to her family. Marilyn's mother, who was institutionalized, did not take custody of the body. Instead, Joe DiMaggio claimed her remains and arranged a small and quiet funeral for the woman he continued to love up until her death. Finally on August 8, 1962, she was laid to rest in Los Angeles' Westwood Memorial Park in the Corridor of Memories. On that day, thousands lined the streets and grieved for their icon and the world's movie legend, Marilyn Monroe.

Others have said:

a- Marilyn Monroe was having an affair with John F Kennedy and possibly Robert, and she was about to go public with what she knew. She was killed by 'government agents' to protect the president. Marilyn knew a lot about JFK: his marital infidelities (at the time hushed up) and other private matters. She had his notes and letters and was privy to Kennedy's involvement with Sam Giancana, the mob leader. The Kennedy brothers had discussed national security matters with

Monroe. It is reasonable for the Kennedy administration to try to cover up the liaison with Monroe, but did they?

b- Robert Kennedy, the president's brother, went to see Monroe the night she died to tell her that President Kennedy did not want to see her anymore. There are witnesses, including a policeman, who places Robert Kennedy in the area at the time of her death. It is possible after this rejection her good mood, seen earlier in the day, changed and she killed herself. It is also alleged that someobody removed a diary and an incriminating note from Monroe's home at 12305 Fifth Helena Drive, Brentwood.

c- Peter Lawford (Bobby Kennedy's brother in law) and Pat Newcomb went to Marilyn Monroe's house on the night she died. This is seen as further evidence of a Kennedy connection.

d- Bobby Kennedy himself murdered Marilyn Monroe. No, not likely at all. Robert Kennedy was a highly respected Attorney General with an unimpeachable integrity with little mystery surrounding him, as opposed to Monroe who had many secrets.

e- Marilyn was killed by the mafia as punishment to the Kennedy's for their attacks on them, and to expose Kennedy's philandering. Definite motive, but probably difficult to accomplish that night in view of the number of people about, as reported by Voice of Reason.

• 9. The suicide of Inger Stevens

In 1959, Inger Stevens moved back to New York, and on New Year's Day, 1960 feeling despondent after attending a party, she tried to kill herself, taking sleeping pills. She was found three days later, unconscious, with significant swellling in her legs, and remained blinded for two weeks, according to the news reports at the time. Her recovery from this incident was surprising: only two months later she was back at work, guest starring on several television series. Though Inger never subsequently discussed the reasons for this suicide attempt in any great detail, she would always claim that she was a stronger, wiser person as a result. In 1961, she was the last person to exit from a plane which exploded a few seconds later, in Lisbon, Portugal. On November 18, 1961 she married Isaac "Ike" Jones, an African-American producer/business associate of famed singer Nat King Cole, in Tijuana, Mexico. At the time, Inger and Ike decided to keep their marriage a secret, due to the potential negative backlash and damage to Inger's career. In hindsight, given the social climate of the time with the growing discontent regarding civil rights and that interracial marriage was not common and even deemed illegal in some states, Inger and Ike's decision to keep their marriage hidden seems prudent and certainly understandable, from a business perspective. However, this decision would have far-reaching consequences: Inger Stevens, the self-sufficient, outwardly direct and notoriously frank, up-and-coming actress had suddenly acquired a secret, double-life, one that she had to hide from the general public for the rest of her life. On the morning of Thursday, April 30, 1970, she was found lying unconscious in her kitchen by her hairstylist/houseguest, Lola McNally. Rushed to a nearby local hospital, she was declared dead on arrival at 10:30 a.m. From initial appearances and later confirmed by toxicology testing, the immediate cause of death was from an overdose of barbiturates. The Los Angeles County Coroner's office eventually ruled her death as a suicide. However, at the time of her death, her family and her friends would not accept the notion of suicide. There were no overt signs that she was depressed or despondent. On the contrary, she was excited about her return to weekly television, she had just purchased clothes she would wear for the show, and she had made a number of short term plans for the coming weeks (she had in fact made plans to attend the first MGM studio auction on the next Sunday, May 3, 1970). Immediately after her death, Ike stepped forward and identified himself at the Coroner's office as her husband to claim the body. A small memorial service was held in private a few days later on May 4th at publicist Ben Irwin's home. In keeping with her preference for small intimate gatherings, only a small number of Inger's family

and friends were invited. She was cremated and her ashes scattered over the Pacific Ocean. (Source: Stevens Memorial Site)

Inger Stevens and Walter Mathau in a scene from the "Guide for the Married Man", 1967.
Starring: Walter Matthau, Sue Ann Langdon, and Inger Stevens.
Directed by Gene Kelly.

- ### 10. Jean Harlow's husband, Paul Bern's death! Suicide or murder?

Photo: Paul Bern, husband of Jean Harlow.

Born Harlean Carpenter, Jean Harlow was a wealthy young socialite (she eloped at 16 with the heir to a fortune) when she got into movies on a dare using her overbearing mother's maiden name, Jean Harlow. Mama Jean liked the idea; she herself had tried to get into the movies shortly after divorcing Harlean's father in 1922. Now she could have a career through her daughter. Her early talkies are pretty rank, she most often looked like a whore and spoke with an affected upper-class accent, but audiences responded well even if the critics didn't. It wasn't until she joined the ranks of MGM that producer and star groomer Paul Bern made her drop the studied diction and cut loose with distinctive voice and pronunciation that would be her trademark.

Overnight she went from a siren to a babe in pre-Code sex comedies that packed in Depression audiences and went a long way toward keeping MGM afloat. On September 5, only two months after she married Paul Bern, he was found naked, shot through the head in their Benedict Canyon home. MGM suits descended on the house long before the police did, and when the coroner's jury returned with its verdict, it concluded his death was suicide. Nobody will ever know what really happened at the house that night; it's alleged that Dorothy Millette, Bern's deranged common-law wife shot him. The day after Bern's death, her body was fished out of the Sacramento River, a suicide. MGM fabricated a story that Bern had shot himself because he was impotent and unable to satisfy his hot young bride. Harlow never talked about it.

The story:

Photo: The Hean Harlow-Paul Burn wedding.

The gossip columns filled with news of Jean's activities and it soon became apparent that despite her many outings on the town, she never went out with other actors. All of her dates were either directors or producers. It was suggested that she was smart enough to realize this was her ticket to the top. One of the men she dated was an assistant to Irving Thalberg at MGM named Paul Bern. He had been the man responsible for getting Jean's contract purchased from Howard Hughes and for bringing her to MGM. It was apparent that he was attracted to the blond bombshell actress. It would have been hard to find two people more incompatible that Jean Harlow and Paul Bern. Most of Bern's contemporaries considered him a genius. He had been born in Germany in 1889 as Paul Levy, making him 22 years older than Jean. His formal education ended at age 14, but he went on to become one of the most intellectual men in Hollywood. He had come to the movie capital in 1926 after first working in both New York as a stage actor. He later took a job in Toronto with a fledging film company and then moved west to California when he realized the potential for movies. After landing in Hollywood, he worked as a film cutter and a script editor before directing a few pictures and ending up as a supervisor at MGM. It was here that Thalberg spotted Bern's ability and made him a general assistant.

While Bern may have been intellectually superior to Harlow, he certainly couldn't measure up in the looks department. According to a writer of the day, Herbert Cruikshank, Bern was described as "a slight man, insignificant in stature, slender of shoulder, only as tall as a girl." Apparently, not much to look at either. Regardless, he gained a reputation in Hollywood as a sensitive and compassionate person (a rare thing in Hollywood) and he began to be called "Hollywood's Father Confessor". Everyone took his troubles to Bern for advice, help and sympathy.

Bern was also never much for the public life. He was something of a mystery man, especially to those who craved the spotlight and the lure of Hollywood's legendary nightlife. So when he began appearing in local nightspots with Jean Harlow, no one thought much of it. They assumed that it could never last. Of course, that was what made the announcement of their marriage even a bigger surprise! Apparently, little planning went into the nuptials. In fact, Jean was not even able to purchase a real wedding gown. She simply went into a dress shop that she frequented and bought an off-the-rack white dress and a shawl. They gathered two days after Bern proposed with about 150 friends and relatives at the home of Jean's mother. They were married on July 2, 1932 but had to postpone their honeymoon because of their shooting schedules. They took one day off and then returned to work. According to Jean's friends, she looked "radiant" in the weeks that followed and the couple seemed very happy. But soon, that began to change. As the weeks passed, Bern looked less and less happy, becoming pale, distraught and almost haggard.

Photo: Paul Bern's body as it was found in the Bern-Harlow house.

He told no one what was bothering him, but that didn't stop the rumors from spreading. One of the rumors stated that they were having money problems. One of the arguments, it was whispered, concerned the house that Bern had given to Jean as a wedding present. The house was set in the midst of five acres of ground in Beverly Hills' Benedict Canyon. The problem was that Jean didn't like the house and wanted to sell it. Bern refused and argued that he wanted it to be their home together.

On September 5, 1932, just four months after his marriage to Jean Harlow, Paul Bern was found shot to death in the house. Bern's butler found his body in his wife's all-white bedroom. He was nude, sprawled in front of a full-length mirror and drenched in Jean's favorite perfume. He had been shot in the head with a .38 caliber revolver, which was still laying by his side. After finding Bern's body, the butler went running to find his wife. Then, instead of calling the police, he called MGM. The studio officer in charge that day immediately called MGM's security chief, W.P. "Whitey" Hendry, who was at home in Santa Monica, enjoying the Labor Day weekend. Hendry immediately called Louis B. Mayer and Irving Thalberg, who still did not notify the authorities. Instead, they both went straight to the Harlow's house.

Mayer arrived on the scene first, followed closely by Hendry and Thalberg. But it was not until two hours later that the Los Angeles police were notified of the death. Just what happened in those two hours will never be known, but we do know that Mayer took a suicide note that Bern

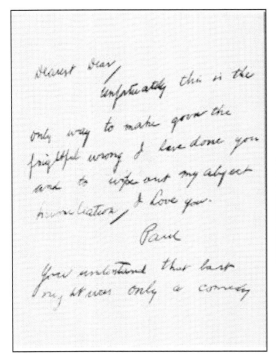

had left on a dressing table in the bedroom. He returned it to the police on the advice of Howard Strickling, the Publicity Chief for the studio. He was a neighbor of Bern's and insisted that Mayer give the note back to the detectives on the scene.

Photo: Bern's suicide note to wife Jean Harlow.

The note read: "Dearest Dear... Unfortunately, this is the only way to make good the frightful wrong I have done you and wipe out by abject humility. I love you.... Paul" A postscript had been added at the bottom of the note that said: "You understand that last night was only a comedy."

The detectives looked over the note but failed to understand the meaning of it. The case appeared to be a suicide and after speaking with the butler and the staff, they went to Jean's mother's house to talk with the actress. Her physician told them that she was "too hysterical to undergo questioning at this time." She later spoke to detectives but was not called as a witness at the inquest, which is unusual to say the least. According to the inquest, the following story was learned about Bern's final hours. Bern had sent Jean over to stay with her mother, who was alone on Saturday night. On Sunday, Jean returned to the house and had dinner with her husband. However, Bern sent her back to mother's, telling her that he would be along to pick her up after reading some scripts. When he didn't show up, Jean assumed that he had fallen asleep while reading and thought nothing more of it. Needless to say, the inquest brought many unanswered questions, such as why did Bern send Jean away again on Sunday night? Was he planning to meet someone later? And what was the motive for the suicide?

The official version of the suicide was that Bern had been suffering from a "physical infirmity" that made it impossible for him to have intercourse with his wife. The "comedy" referred to in the suicide note was Bern's attempt to overcome his impotence and carry out his marital obligations to Jean with a realistic, phony phallus. But why would a man with such an infirmity marry any woman, least of all a bombshell like Jean Harlow?

Surprisingly, this was not the most shocking information to come out of the inquest. It was learned that Bern had previously lived with another woman for many years. And, the day after Bern died, the other woman also died "under mysterious circumstances!" The woman's name was Dorothy Millette and she was a struggling actress when Bern met her in New York. They lived together in both New York and Toronto for many years and she often referred to herself as "Mrs. Paul Bern." Unfortunately, Dorothy fell victim to mental illness and she was institutionalized. Bern paid for all of her expenses. The love affair ended but Bern continued to provide for Dorothy, even after his marriage to Jean. After being released from the mental hospital, apparently cured, Dorothy moved into a room at the Algonquin Hotel in New York. She lived quietly, spending most of her time reading and walking in the park. Bern always visited her when he was in New York. His 1920 will, in fact, left everything he owned to Dorothy. However, this was changed in a later will, which bequeathed his estate to Jean.

On March 17, 1932, Paul received a letter from Dorothy stating that she was moving to San Francisco. He suggested to her that she stays at the Plaza Hotel, which offered an attractive rate, and that if she did decide to stay somewhere else, he would find some way of supplying her with funds in a manner convenient for her. Once this new information became public, Jean's stepfather, Marino Bello, issued a press statement saying that Jean knew nothing of Dorothy Millette. This was immediately contradicted by Paul's brother, Henry Bern, who said that Dorothy was common knowledge in Bern's circle of friends and that Paul had specifically discussed Dorothy with Jean prior to their marriage.

On September 6, the day after Bern died, Dorothy checked out of the Plaza Hotel and boarded a Sacramento River steamer that journeyed back and forth between San Francisco and Sacramento. An officer later found a woman's coat and shoes besides the ship's railing. Dorothy Millette was not on board when the ship docked at Sacramento. Her body was found two weeks later by fishermen. Her death was ruled a suicide. It was said that Jean Harlow loved Bern so much that when his body was discovered, she too attempted suicide. Even though her attempt was not successful, Harlow's days were numbered. Five years later, she died from kidney damage at the age of only 26. But that was not meant to be. A strange series of circumstances would shed new (and mysterious) light on the case a year after the inquest. At that time, a grand jury had been impaneled to investigate District Attorney Buron Fitts, who had handled the original Bern inquest. The jury foreman insisted that they were only interested in Fitts' expenditures in the case and yet new revelations came to light because of it. Important revelations came from Davis, the gardener and Miss Harrison, Bern's secretary. Davis thought it was a murder. "I thought so from the beginning", he said. He believed that the butler had lied about what happened. He testified that the butler told the police that Bern and Harlow were always hugging and kissing and that he sometimes overheard Bern talking of suicide. The gardener said that the opposite was actually true. He never thought that the couple got along that well and he had never once heard Mr. Bern talk about killing himself! He also said that he didn't believe the suicide note was even in his employer's handwriting.

Irene Harrison, Bern's secretary, confirmed this and she also added that Jean Harlow, not Bern, had been the pursuer in the relationship. She also added that she didn't think that Bern looked "particularly happy" at the reception after the wedding ceremony. The most exciting testimony came from Winifred Carmichael, Bern's cook. She stated that a strange woman had been seen by the household staff on Sunday evening. The cook stated that a woman's voice, which was unfamiliar to her, was heard. The woman screamed once. She also said that she later found a wet woman's bathing suit on the edge of the swimming pool and two empty glasses nearby. There is no record of whether or not the police ever "dusted" the glasses for fingerprints or whether or not they followed up further testimony from Davis the gardener who said that he told detectives of finding a small puddle of blood near Bern's favorite chair by the swimming pool. Even after all of this, Bern's death was still ruled a suicide. It remained that way until 1960 when writer Ben Hecht published an article that stated Bern's death was actually a murder. "Studio officials decided," Hecht wrote, "sitting in a conference around his dead body, that it was better to have Paul Bern as a suicide than as a murder victim of another woman." He wrote that it would be better for Jean Harlow's career that she not appear as a woman who couldn't hold a husband."

Paul Bern, noted producer, scenario writer and studio executive, with his wife, Jean Harlow.

The Los Angeles District Attorney got in touch with Hecht, who told him that director Henry Hathaway had told him about the tragedy. But Hathaway, who was living in New York claimed to have no first-hand knowledge of the case. He had no information to say that the suicide note was not real or that it had been planted by the studio heads. Still, many believed that Bern may have been murdered. But if he was, who killed him? Could it have been Dorothy Millette? There seems to be no reason for it and besides that, she vanished (to be found dead) the day after Bern's body was discovered. In those days, the fastest transportation between Los Angeles and San Francisco was the Southern Pacific daylight train or the overnight Lark. Either journey took almost ten hours. For Dorothy to have been able to catch the 10:00 pm train, she would have had to have called a cab to pick her up at Bern's home by at least 8:00. No trace of any such call or taxi driver was ever located.

But if Dorothy did kill Bern, was she the woman who was heard in the house and left a wet swimsuit behind? If so, why did she bother to go all the way back to her San Francisco hotel after a ten hour train ride, pack her things, board the river boat and after all of that effort, commit suicide? If this was a crime of passion, why didn't she just kill herself there, next to the body of her dead lover? And if not Dorothy, who did the wet swimming suit belong to? Whose blood was on the tiles near the swimming pool? Who did the second glass belong to? Why was it never dusted for fingerprints? These questions remain unanswered and for many crime buffs, the death of Paul Bern remains unsolved. Could this be why his ghost is still reportedly haunting the Harlow's house? Perhaps, but many believe that Bern's first otherworldly appearance in the house was actually a warning. It was an advance premonition for another beautiful blond actress that, if she had heeded it, might have saved her life. That woman's name was Sharon Tate.

In 1969, Sharon would fall victim to one of the most savage slayings in Hollywood's history. But three years before she was brutally murdered at the hands of the Charles Manson "family", she glimpsed a ghostly image of the horrific fate that awaited her. Could the glimpse into the future have been provided by the phantom of Paul Bern? Sharon was a struggling actress, hoping to make a name for herself, when she met Jay Sebring, who would soon become known as the premier men's hair stylist in Hollywood. The two dated for three years and even announced their engagement at one point, but Sharon broke it off with him in 1966, when she met her future husband, Roman Polanski. The break-up was not bitter and the two of them stayed very close friends. In fact, it was Jay who was keeping Sharon company at the Cielo Drive house while Roman was away filming. And it was Jay who died trying to protect her from the Manson clan.

Jay lived in Benedict Canyon in the former home of Jean Harlow. He loved the house but was always concerned about the fact that it was supposed to be "jinxed". He knew the stories about Paul Bern's death but he also learned that two people had drowned in the swimming pool as well. He shrugged off the idea that the house was "cursed" though, but perhaps he shouldn't have. One night in 1966, Sharon stayed alone at Jay's house. Unable to sleep, she lay awake in Jay's room with all the lights on. She was very uncomfortable, although she couldn't explain why. She felt "funny", she later told reporter Dick Kleiner, and was frightened by every little sound that she heard. Suddenly, a person that she described as a "creepy little man" came into the bedroom! She was sure that this man was Paul Bern. The man ignored her though and wandered about the room, apparently looking for something. Sharon put on her robe and hurried out of the bedroom. What happened next would be especially chilling in light of events to come. Sharon started down the stairs, and suddenly froze in shock. There was a figure tied to the staircase posts at the bottom of the steps. She couldn't tell if it was a man or a woman. However, she could clearly see that the figure's throat had been cut. Then, the apparition vanished. Shaken, Sharon went into the living room to pour herself a drink but she couldn't find where Jay kept the alcohol. She felt an inexplicable urge to press on a section of the bookcase and it opened to reveal a hidden bar. Not thinking, she tore away a piece of wallpaper at the base of the bar as she nervously poured herself a drink.

In the morning, Sharon was convinced the whole episode had been a terrible nightmare.... until she saw the wallpaper that had been torn away from the bar. She had indeed seen Paul Bern and at that time, had unknowingly seen a vision of her fate. (Source: Troy Taylor)

11. George Reeves' death: Murder or suicide?

Photo: George Reeves, the original Superman.

Superman died at 1:59 am on June 16, 1959. Even though the initial coroner's report listed Reeves' death as an "indicated suicide", after more than four decades there are many who do not believe that he killed himself. For years, we thought that Superman has committed suicide, but in fact, according to some Hollywood's insiders, Reeves was gunned down, because of his affair and juicy sexual relationship with Toni Lanier, the wife of MGM executive, Eddie Mannix. In fact, Reeves has left most of his estate to Lanier (She died from complications of Alzheimer's disease at the age of 77 on September 2, 1983 in Beverly Hills, California.) George's bruised, naked body was found in his bedroom by guests at his home.

Background:

George Reeves grew up as George Besselo. His mother, Helen, became pregnant in her hometown of Galesburg, Illinois, eloped and then moved to Iowa. Shortly after settling in, she divorced her husband, took baby George and moved to Pasadena, California. It would not be until George joined the Army during World War II that he would discover a number of parts of his life that his mother had hidden from him. She had concealed his true birth date, the identity of his father and the fact that his stepfather had committed suicide eight years after Helen divorced him. This so disturbed Reeves that he didn't speak to her through most of the 1940's.

Reeves loved the public and it was said that he loved the ladies as well. Many who were close to Reeves say that he was a womanizer, breaking the hearts of many of the actresses that he worked with. Rumor also had it that he became involved with a number of prominent married women like the wives of film executives and other actors. It is believed that one of these affairs may have led to his death!

In the three months before his death, Reeves was involved in three mysterious automobile mishaps that almost killed him. The first time, his car was nearly crushed by two trucks on the freeway. Another time, a speeding car nearly killed him, but he survived thanks to his quick, athletic reflexes. The third time, Reeves' brakes failed on a narrow, twisting road. All of the brake fluid, it was discovered, was gone from the hydraulic system, in spite of the fact that an examination by a mechanic found the system was in perfect working order.

"When the mechanic suggested that someone had pumped out the fluid, George dismissed the notion," said Arthur Weissman, Reeves' best friend and business manager. Weissman always remained convinced that his friend had been murdered. He tried to convince Reeves that he needed to be careful, but Reeves brushed off the warnings. About a month later, he began to receive death threats on his unlisted telephone line. Most of them came late at night, and there were sometimes 20 or more each day. Often, whoever was calling would simply hang up when he answered. They said nothing, but after a few graphic and detailed threats followed, Reeves knew it was the same person. Nervous after the near-misses in his car, Reeves filed a report with the Beverly Hills Police Department and a complaint with the Los Angeles District Attorney's office. He even went so far as to suggest a suspect, a woman named Toni Mannix.

It was never explained why Reeves openly pointed the finger at Toni. The Hollywood gossip columnists had linked the two romantically for some time, but their relationship was never a public one. They were a secret couple, as Reeves was engaged to Lenore Lemmon and Toni was married to a man named Eddie Mannix, the vice president of Loew's Theatres, Inc., and a former studio executive at MGM. According to Reeves' friend Arthur Weissman, it was no secret that Eddie Mannix was disliked by everyone and was an uncouth and despicable man. He also believed that Mannix was responsible for the threats and attempts on Reeves' life.

The D.A.'s office investigated Reeves' complaint and it was soon discovered that both Toni and George were receiving telephone threats and crank calls. When that was disclosed, many people assumed that it was Eddie Mannix who had instigated the calls through employees or hired thuds. Weissman believed that Mannix was behind Reeve's near-fatal auto crashes as well. In the film and theater business, Mannix had access to a lot of people outside of the general public. For a price, these men could maneuver two trucks close together on the highway, or could drain the brake fluid from someone's car. Furthermore, he was sure that Mannix also had access to someone who could arrange a murder too!

The Beverly Hills Police report of the incident states that while entertaining his fiancée and three others in his home, Reeves suddenly, and without explanation, left the room and impulsively committed suicide. He went up to his bedroom, they said, placed a pistol in his right ear and pulled the trigger. Even though he believed his friend was murdered, Arthur Weissman surprisingly did not dispute this sequence of events. He said that this was just how it happened but that Reeves did not intend to kill himself! He explained that Reeves was just playing his favorite game (although a morbid one, in his opinion), a practical joke he enjoyed with a gun that was loaded with a blank. All of Reeves' friends knew that when he was drinking, he would sometimes fire a blank at his head in a mock suicide attempt, making certain that his arm was far enough away so that he didn't get powder burns on his face! Weissman claimed that, unknown to Reeves, the blank was replaced with a real bullet by someone hired by Eddie Mannix.

Reeves' clandestine girlfriend, Toni Mannix, was an actress and former model who was 25 years younger than her powerful husband. She was also madly in love with Reeves and according to Weissman, their relationship was an open Hollywood secret. It continued for years and then came to an end when George announced that he was marrying Lenore Lemmon. Friends said that Toni was "enraged" over this new development and began bombarding Reeves with phone calls, making all sorts of threats. It was believed that both she and her husband, who was openly humiliated by Reeves over the affair, both had the perfect opportunity to seek revenge, especially since Toni possessed a key to the Reeves house. Many were unhappy with the findings of "indicated suicide", including Reeves' mother, Helen Besselo. She retained the Nick Harris Detectives of Los Angeles to look into the case. At that time, a man named Milo Speriglio was a novice investigator at the firm and played a small role in the investigation. "Nearly everyone in Hollywood has always been led to believe that George Reeves' death was a suicide," he said in a later interview. "Not everyone believed it then, nor do they believe it now. I am one of those who does not." And neither did Helen Besselo. She went to her grave in 1964 convinced that her son was murdered. The Nick Harris Agency, which had been founded in Los Angeles before the FBI was even in existence, quickly came to believe that Reeves death had been a homicide.

From L to R: 1. George Reeves, 2. Toni Mannix, 3. Eddie Mannix, 4. Lenore Lemmon.

Even based on the fact that many of the witnesses that night were intoxicated and incoherent, the detectives felt that they could rule out suicide. Unfortunately though, the Beverly Hills Police investigators chose to ignore their findings. A review of the facts seems to indicate the agency's suspicions were well-founded. To make matters more confusing, the detectives even managed to rule out Reeves' macabre "suicide game" as the cause of his death. The agency operatives believed that someone else was in the house at the time!

For one thing, the absence of powder burns on Reeves' face shows that he did not hold the gun to his head, as the police report stated. For the weapon to have not left any facial burns, it had to have been at least a foot-and-a-half away from Reeves' head, which is totally impractical in a suicide attempt. In addition, Reeves was discovered after his death, lying on his back. The single shell was found under his body. According to experts, self-inflicted gunshot wounds usually propel the victim forward and away from the expended bullet casing. Detective Speriglio made a careful examination of the police report and noticed that the bullet wound was described as "irregular". So, the agency reconstructed the bullet entry and exit. The slug had exited Reeves' head and was found lodged in the ceiling. His head, at the moment of death, would have had to have been twisted, making a self-inflicted shot improbable. Speriglio suspected that an intruder had entered Reeves' room and found his gun. A struggle had followed and Reeves was shot. The intruder then escaped from the house unnoticed. While interesting, this theory does not explain why the gun (normally loaded with blanks) had a bullet in it and how the intruder escaped from the house with other people inside. Regardless, there is another discrepancy with the police report. It stated that Reeves had pulled the trigger of the gun with his right hand. Prior to his death, Reeves had been in a terrible auto accident. His Jaguar had hit an oil slick in the Hollywood Hills and had crashed into a brick wall. Reeves later filed a personal injury claim in Los Angeles Superior Court asking for a half-million dollars in damages, because his right hand was disabled!

But just how disabled was it? If Reeves could fight Archie Moore in an exhibition match, then surely he could have pulled the trigger on a pistol. Regardless of whether or not he killed himself, it was obvious that Reeves' death was never properly investigated. Police investigators never even bothered to take fingerprints at the scene and people like Arthur Weissman believed that they were pressured to make it an "open and shut" case. George Reeves, according to the official findings, had committed suicide. But did he really?

165

We will never know for sure. In 1961, Reeves' body was exhumed and cremated, forever destroying whatever evidence was left behind. The death of George Reeves will always remain another unsolved Hollywood's mystery.

Could this be why ghostly phenomena has been reported at the former Reeves house ever since? Many believe that the ghostly appearances by the actor lend credence to the idea that he was murdered. Over the years, occupants of the house have been plagued by not only the sound of a single gunshot that echoes in the darkness, but strange lights and even the apparition of George Reeves! After Reeves' death, realtors attempted to sell the house to settle the actor's estate. Unfortunately though, they had trouble. Occupants would not stay long because they would report inexplicable noises in the upstairs bedroom where George had been killed. When they would go to investigate the sounds, they would find the room was not as they had left it. Often, the bedding would be torn off, clothing would be strewn about and some reported the ominous odor of gunpowder in the air. One tenant also reported that his German shepherd would stand in the doorway of the room and would bark furiously as though he could see something his owner's could not. There is also documentation of an extraordinary occurrence when two Los Angeles sheriffs were assigned to watch the house after neighbors reported hearing screams, gunshots, and lights going on and off during the night. New occupants moved out quickly, becoming completely unnerved after encountering Reeves' ghost, decked out in his Superman costume! The first couple who spotted him were not the first, nor the last, to see him either. Many later residents saw him too and one couple became so frightened that they moved out of the house the same night. Later, the ghost was even reported on the front lawn by neighboring residents.

In the 1980's, while the house was being used as a set for a television show, the ghost made another startling appearance. He was seen by several of the actors and crew members before abruptly vanishing, creating yet another mystery in this strange and convoluted case! said Troy Taylor.

Theories about the death of George Reeves:

1- Under the influence of some drug, he jumped off a building thinking he could really fly and fell to his death.

2- He was shot to death by someone hired by the husband of Toni Lanier.

3- He shot himself to death.

4- He went beserk, because there was some sort of "curse of death" on any actor who plays Superman.

The coroner's report stated that he was killed by a single gunshot to the head. The official ruling was suicide. However, the rumors back then were, that he shot himself, he leaped off a building to see if he could fly, etc. The suicide angle focused on how he had been typecast and couldn't get acting jobs. The night of June 15, Reeves and Lemmon and a few other guests were drinking and partying at his home until after 1 AM. Reeves went up to bed, a shot rang out, and he was found dead, sprawled nude on his bed, with a bullet hole in his right temple. The death was ruled suicide, largely since the houseguests all said there was no other explanation, and there was no sign of an intruder or forced entry. The high alcohol content in Reeves' blood (.27, well above the intoxication point), combined with narcotics (he was taking painkillers for injuries in a car accident), made this plausible. However, Reeves' mother and a few others thought the whole thing was suspicious and claimed Reeves was a victim of foul play. Thus, suspicions and questions started flying around, long before any Internet to spawn conspiracy theories.

The evidence (or lack of evidence) against suicide:

- No fingerprints were found on the gun.

- There were no powder burns on the head's wound, which would imply the gun was held several inches from the head at the time it was fired, pretty unusual for a suicide.
- His hands were NOT tested for gunpowder residue, so that's no help one way or the other.
- The spent shell was found under his body.
- The gun was found between his feet.
- The police were not called for at least half an hour after the death (although probably so the houseguests could sober up and get their stories straight).
- The supposed "slump" was over. His friends agreed he was happier than had been in years, looking forward to his marriage and to another season of the popular TV show. Money wasn't a problem either; he got residuals from the reruns.

The common theories:

1-Reeves was killed by Leonore Lemmon, (who lost him to another woman) in a fit of passion or argument, possibly over whether they would marry, but who knows. But why would the houseguests risk their own reputations to cover for her?

2-Reeves was murdered by Toni or Eddie Mannix, or by a mob killer hired by them.

3-It really was a suicide, as reported at the time, as reported by Straight Dope.

Bibliography/References:
Troy Talor, 2001
Straight Dope
Hollywood Babylon by Kenneth Anger (1975)
Haunted Places: The National Directory by Dennis William Hauck (1996)
Hollywood Unsolved Mysteries by John Austin (1970)
Hollywood Haunted by Laurie Jacobson (1994)
Haunted Houses of California by Antoinette May (1990)
The Hollywood Murder Case Book by Michael Munn (1987)
Ghost Stories of Hollywood by Barbara Smith (2000)

Undisputed facts:

Did George Reeves really have an affair with Toni Mannix, wife of the MGM studio mogul?

Yes. In real life, George Reeves did have an affair with Toni Mannix, who was the wife of MGM executive Eddie Mannix. George and Toni's affair lasted for over seven years. Eddie Mannix, despite his mob connections and fearsome reputation, didn't seem to mind his wife's relationship with Reeves. It helped him get Toni off his back while he carried on his own extra-marital affairs.

Did Toni, George, Eddie and his mistress really go on double dates together?

The movie about Reeves shows Toni Mannix and George Reeves having dinner with her husband Eddie and an Asian mistress. Strangely enough, according to friends these double dates did happen. Eddie openly approved of his wife and George. One friend recalled being at the Mannix Beverly Hills home when George strolled in the backdoor. Eddie was sitting in the kitchen eating his breakfast in his pajamas. Eddie and George said hi to each other, and George proceeded to the refrigerator and helped himself to a glass of milk, as stated by the New York social diary.

Is it true that Toni Mannix bought George Reeves a house?

Yes. This is true. In real life, Toni, unhappy in her own marriage, took a strong liking to George. She bought him a house up in Bendedict Canyon at 1579 Benedict Canyon Drive. George's bedroom (where his body was found) looked out over the backyard of the property. Toni also bought him a car and paid many of his bills. It has been disputed whether or not she helped him with his career.

Photo: The house Toni Mannix bought for George Reeves.

Photo: Lenore Lemmon.

However, it was not the car that Reeves drove as Clark Kent in *The Adventures of Superman* television series, as some have come to believe.

In fact, George did not drive any of his own cars in the series, according to Superman homepage.

Did Eddie Mannix murder his previous wife, as rumored?

Eddie Mannix was in fact accused of staging the murder of his first wife Beatrice. She died in 1937 in what many believe was a "make believe" high speed car crash.

The incident also raised questions because mobster Al Wertheimer was involved in the accident. As reported by The Desert Sun.

In real life, did George's relationship with Toni Mannix come to an end because he met Lenore?

No. George's breakup with Toni happened before he left California and met Lenore. Prior to George leaving to go on tour for Superman, Toni had wanted to build a house further up in the canyon. George liked the idea only if she would leave her husband Eddie and marry him. Toni refused, citing that Eddie was in poor health and did not have much time to live. George decided it was time to move on, as stated by Jim Nolte.

Was Toni Mannix really as distraught over the end of her affair with Reeves?

Yes. The movie *Hollywoodland* even downplays this somewhat. Reeves received up to 20 phone calls a day where the person on the other end, whom he believed was Toni, would hang up. Reeves

filed a complaint with the Los Angeles District Attorney's Office and suggested that the caller may be Toni Mannix. Some also believe that Toni Mannix was behind the abduction of Reeves' Schnauzer Sam. The dog was stolen from a car at 1627 Vine St (Google Map). The dog was under medical care for the loss of an eye as the result of an auto accident, according to Jim Nolte.

Photo: George Reeves with Toni Mannix

Could alcohol have played a part in George Reeves death?

Yes. On the night of his death, Reeves' blood alcohol level was .27, well beyond the point of intoxication. In addition, he was taking painkillers for injuries that he had sustained in a recent car accident, according to TV Party.

How did Lenore Lemmon explain the additional bullet holes found in Reeves' bedroom?

She told police that she had been "fooling around" with the gun at an earlier time, yet, these two additional bullet holes had been covered over with a rug on the night of George Reeves' death. according to Answers.com.

Did George's fiancée and the houseguests really wait forty-five minutes to call the police?

Yes. They waited approximately thirty to forty-five minutes before calling the police. They never gave an explanation for their delay. No one is entirely certain who was even at the house that night. George's fiancée Lenore Lemmon claims that in addition to George and herself, the only others at the house were Carol Von Ronkle, William Bliss, and writer Robert Condon. When the police questioned Lenore Lemmon and the houseguests, the group told the police that George Reeves had committed suicide. None of the houseguests have ever provided public testimony, according to TV Party.

What did Lenore Lemmon do after Reeves' death?

Approximately four days after George Reeves' death, Lenore left California never to return again. After learning that George left his entire estate to Toni Mannix, Lenore replied to the press, "Toni got a house for charity, and I got a broken heart". Though, it wasn't strange that George left his estate to Toni. She had paid for his house, his car, and many of his bills during their relationship.

Did Lenore Lemmon really take $5,000 from Reeves bedroom after his death?

Yes, Lenore took the $5000 in travelers checks originally intended for her and George's honeymoon. Lenore returned to the house with Gwen Dailey and they broke the police seal to get in. She claimed that she went in for the lunchmeat and the kitty (cat). This is most likely when she took the money. After the press reported that the traveller's checks were missing, Lenore turned them over to her attorney Leon Kaplan, who then turned them over to Reeves' estate. However, only $4,000 in traveller's checks were returned, which leads many to believe that Lenore kept $1,000 for herself. Hollywoodland screenwriter Paul Bernbaum said the following about the "take the money and run" theory, "I think she was a low-life for sure. I think she was probably told to shut up and get out of town. I think she stole money from him. I think she took five grand that was supposed to be for their honeymoon, and there was nothing really keeping her there..." according to Court TV, and Chasing the Frog.

169

Chapter 5: Hollywood's Biggest Scandals Murders and Crimes

Lana Turner's scandal: Lana Tuner and her teenaged daughter Cheryl stabbing to death Lana's boyfriend, hoodlum Johnny Stompanato.

Lana Turner was a statuesque blonde dubbed "The Sweater Girl", for the way wearing one would highlight her natural attributes. She was a gifted actress, appearing in such successful films as "Dr. Jekyll & Mr. Hyde" (1941), "The Postman Always Rings Twice" (1946) and "Peyton Place" (1957).

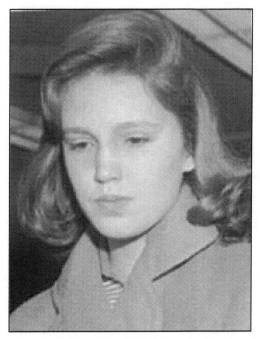

Photo: Cheryl Crane, daughter of Lana Trner.

But, as always with Hollywood, it was Lana's tumultuous private life which generated the most attention. She was married 8 times (twice to Steve Crane) and battled alcoholism throughout her life.

In 1958, her name was in the headlines in the worst possible way, when her then teenaged daughter Cheryl stabbed to death Lana's abusive boyfriend, Johnny Stompanato, a small-time hoodlum who had made a successful living as a gigolo.

Stompananto was very jealous and possessive of Turner and severely beat her on many occasions.

Turner attempted to end their relationship several times, but he always persuaded her not to do so. On the evening of April 4, 1958, Lana and Stompanato began a violent argument in Turner's house in Beverly Hills.

Fearing her mother's life was in danger, Lana Turner's 14-year-old daughter, Cheryl Crane grabbed a kitchen knife and stabbed Stompanato in the stomach, killing him.

The case quickly became a media sensation. It was later deemed a justifiable homicide at a coroner's inquest, at which Turner provided dramatic testimony. Some observers have said her testimony that day was the acting performance of her life. There have been endless rumors since 1958 that Turner was the actual killer. Her daughter supposedly took the blame because she was a minor and would face minimal judicial punishment under the circumstances. However, there is insufficient evidence to prove such claims. Today, Cheryl is a successful businesswoman. She recently helped produce a Lana Turner retrospective on cable television. Lana Turner's career, which hit a plateau before Johnny's death, was rejuvenated in 1958. She went on to make many more movies and starred on television in "Falcon Crest." She died in 1995, well-respected and honored till the end. The "Sweater Girl" proved to be a strong and capable survivor. (Source: Gunsock)

In Woodstock mythology, Johnny Stompanato's funeral features endless lines of black cars, gangs of swarthy mobsters, troops of undercover officers. Contemporary reports indicate an event far quieter than that. Around 75 friends and family, including Johnny's first wife, Sara, gathered at the small Merwin chapel. The Reverend Cecil C. Urch of the Presbyterian church told the mourners, "Our purpose is not to praise John Stompanato, but to give comfort and consolation to those who remain." Johnny lay in an open coffin, dressed in a tuxedo and ruffled shirt.

A larger crowd proceeded to Oakland Cemetery, accompanied by Woodstock's 22-man American Legion color guard. The legionnaires fired three volleys and blew taps. Johnny was buried in the family plot, beside the graves of his mother and father. "Johnny was the only child that she had; she didn't have any children of her own," says Erlene Wille.

The starcrossed couple **Lana Turner and Stompanato** share a close moment at a Hollywood's club in September 1957.

Mickey Cohen had announced that he would pay for Johnny's funeral, but he couldn't attend himself because he was on trial in Los Angeles for punching out a waiter. He came to pay his respects about a month later. Art Petacque of the *Sun-Times* caught up with him in Chicago at the Sands Motel on North Sheridan, where a squad car kept watch outside. Johnny "never did a bad thing in his life," Cohen said. "Whatever he did for me was legitimate—I was always in legitimate business as well as in the rackets." Cohen argued that Johnny should be pitied. "He was like a little baby, like a young kid. He got rushed into a falsely glamorous life too fast."

The next day, Cohen drove his new pink Cadillac to Woodstock. He put flowers on Johnny's grave and took Carmine and Verena to dinner at the Elks Club. Later, Carmine told Woodstock's police chief, Tiny Hansman, that the coffin Johnny arrived in from Los Angeles was cheap and too small. The family had to get a new one before they could bury him.

From left to right: Lana Tuner, her lover, the gangster/mobster, Johnny Stompanato, and Lana's daughter, Cheryl. In 1958, Lana Turner's 14-year-old daughter, Cheryl, stabbed to death Lana's boyfriend, Johnny Stompanato.
The slaying of the gangster was declared a "justifiable homicide", and Cheryl was sent free!

Carmine added that he was going to reimburse whoever had bought the cheap casket—the family didn't want to owe anyone anything. Despite the finding of the coroner's jury, the Stompanato family had trouble believing the accounts given by Lana and Cheryl. "I don't have any desire to prosecute Cheryl," Carmine said at one point. "I just want the truth to come out." In late April, the family sued Lana for $750,000 on behalf of Johnny's son. They built their case on the claim that Lana had negligently failed to control her daughter, but in fact they seemed to be searching for information about what happened that night. The suit kicked around the California courts for a few years and at one point the famed lawyer Melvin Belli represented the boy. In 1961, the parties settled with a $20,000 payment.

Just a year after the slaying, Lana scored a Hollywood success in *Imitation of Life*, playing another mother of a troubled teenager. Her career puttered on for several decades beyond that and then she became increasingly reclusive. In 1995, she died of throat cancer at 74. Cheryl couldn't escape her unhappy adolescence. Though she was removed only briefly from her family's custody because of the homicide, later troubles landed her in reform school and an asylum. As a woman, however, she straightened up and found success as a real-estate agent. In her book, she writes of her longtime, loving partnership with another woman, a relationship that continues to this day. In an e-mail, Cheryl said she had nothing to add to the facts in her book. Verena and Carmine Stompanato died years ago, and today the only Stompanato I could find in Woodstock is a retired schoolteacher who was married for a time to Carmine's son, who is also now dead. The barbershop stayed open into the 1970s, then became the Stompanato Barber Shop Lounge before it finally closed. Today, the space is again a tavern, D. C. Cobb's. I stopped in last summer, and the genial young man behind the bar had never heard of Johnny Stompanato. As I gathered information, I wondered whether Johnny's son, John III, might still be alive. He would be about 60 now, and I knew he had taken the name of his mother's second husband, Ali Ibrahim, like her, a Turkish immigrant.

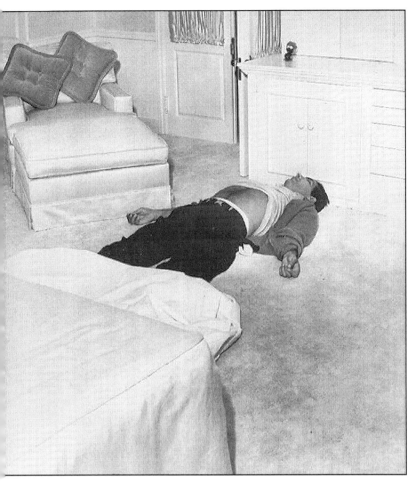

Photos, left, Stompanato, dead on the floor. Right, Lana Tuner testifying in court.

What had the son's life been like? Had he escaped the notoriety that touched his family?

Through an old Woodstock address book and some Internet sleuthing, I found John Ibrahim in California. Out of the blue, I called one day. He was understandably guarded, but as we were about to sign off on our first conversation, he asked me if I knew what day tomorrow was. I fumbled: An obscure religious holiday?

The date of a big football game?

I stared at my calendar. October 19th. The birthday of the father he had hardly known. Last January I flew to California to visit John Ibrahim. He and his wife, Lilly, live in a modest ranch house on a golf course in a flat, desert town east of Los Angeles. He is a handsome man who resembles his father, though he wears his graying hair short and he sports a trim salt-and-pepper beard. As we talk, he describes a productive life, with a close family. Ali Ibrahim adopted young John and raised him as his son. The two were close throughout the adoptive father's life. Sara, John's mother, is still alive and lives nearby. John himself has two children and five grandchildren. He served in the air force, then worked for years for the Defense Department, handling electrical systems on airplanes. Today, he is retired on disability, owing to lung damage from a career breathing in chemicals.

Only family and close friends know he is the son of Johnny Stompanato, and yet it's clear that his natural father has often been in John's thoughts. Sara sheltered the boy at Johnny's death and didn't let him go to the funeral, but John has read the newspaper clippings, the books. He doubts his father was as bad as portrayed. "How much do you believe in what you read?" he asks. Still, he has a theory about Johnny's character: A baby boy, left motherless in his first years, and a loving family tries to compensate. "He was spoiled," says John. "His family spoiled him." Today, John carries his father's marine dog tags, and he has seen all of Lana Turner's movies. He has even visited the house on North Bedford Drive in Beverly Hills. He wants to meet Cheryl. "I would like to sit and talk to her, just to find out, really, what is in the back of her mind is it true or false or whatever?" as told by Richard Babcok.

173

Virginia Rappe's Murder

Photo: Virginia Rappe

In what was one of Hollywood's first big murder scandals, huge (literally and figuratively) film star Fatty Arbuckle was accused of raping actress Virginia Rappe, who then died, allegedly of injuries she sustained during the rape. Arbuckle and Rappe were both guests at a party at the St. Francis Hotel. Rappe, who had a reputation for such things, became rip-roaring drunk and started tearing her clothes off and screaming. She somehow managed to stumble into Arbuckle's bathroom; he walked in and very unexpectedly found her vomiting in the toilet. She swore she was dying and loudly told anyone within earshot as much. And she was right – the next day she died due to a ruptured bladder. The friend she had been at the party with told police that Fatty had raped Virginia and police concluded that her bladder had ruptured under Arbuckle's immense girth. The problem is that it seemed completely out of character for him – people testified that he was a very shy man, especially with women, and was probably one of the chastest men in Hollywood. After three trials and more than seven months of sensational newspaper headlines, Fatty was unanimously acquitted by a jury who also issued a written apology to the actor. But the harm was done – his career was pretty much over, his marriage was ruined and he was too far in debt to his lawyers to recover. It was later thought that Virginia's ruptured bladder was the result of a recent abortion – one of many – gone wrong, stated Stacy Conrad.

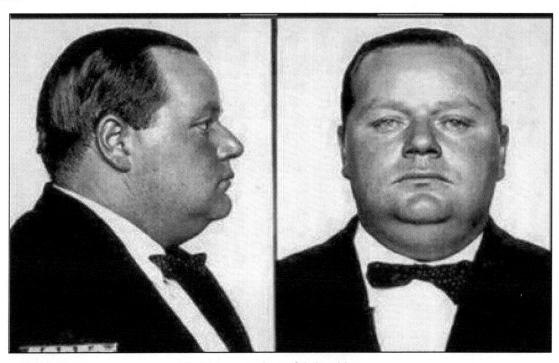

Police mug shot of Arbuckle.

174

Thelma Todd's Death: Suicide or Murder?

Photos, right and below: Thelma Todd.

Conrad continues, this comedic actress of the late '20s and early '30s was found dead in her car in the garage of another actress.

It appeared to be a suicide from carbon monoxide poisoning, but things didn't add up – she had no obvious motive to kill herself and had been in good spirits at a party just hours before her body was found. There are a few theories, including that she accidentally fell asleep in the garage. The first murder theory says that it was her ex-husband, whom she had had a public spat with earlier in the evening.

The second says it was Lucky Luciano, because supposedly she wouldn't allow her club to participate in his illegal gambling schemes. And a third says that her current boyfriend locked her in the garage to keep her from going on to another party and accidentally killed her with carbon

monoxide. Murder or not, the true reason behind Todd's death was never discovered because her body was very quickly cremated – another reason to suspect foul play, say conspiracy theorists. The reason listed on her death certificate is accidental poisoning.

Thelma Todd rose to fame as a comedic actress alongside the Marx Brothers, Laurel & Hardy, and Buster Keaton. Although well known in her day, she is now remembered for the manner and mystery of her death rather than for her achievements in life. Todd arrived in Hollywood in 1926 and over the next 9 years she made seventy films, mostly as a foil for comics such as Harry Langdon and Charley Chase, as well as six with Laurel and Hardy. Her best were two with the Marx Brothers 'Monkey Business' and 'Horse Feathers'. Her lively and flirtatious on-screen personality was more than matched by her riotous private life. She had so many drunken car crashes going from party to party, that the studio had to insist she have a chauffeur. Her marriage in 1932 to playboy Pasquale "Pat" DiCicco quickly degenerated into a series of drunken brawls and they divorced in 1934. In addition to her film career, Thelma was also involved in the restaurant business, where her path crossed that of Lucky Luciano, the New York mobster who was trying to gain a foothold on the West Coast.

In 1935, at the peak of her popularity, the 30-year-old actress was found slumped over the steering wheel of her Lincoln Phaeton Touring car. Her demise was first declared a suicide, then an "accidental death from carbon monoxide poisoning. The fact that she drank heavily and often passed out in her car after a binge supported this conclusion.

With blood at the scene, a high blood-alcohol content, and clean shoes (while the area outside the car was muddy), many believed it to be murder. While the theory was largely ignored by the LAPD, suspects ranged from Todd's highly possessive boyfriend, director Roland West (who was thought to have locked Todd in the garage to keep her from going to a party) to the most likely suspect, "Lucky" Luciano, who wanted to involve Todd's club in illegal gambling against her wish. Roland West was said to have later confessed the murder to a friend, but his only punishment was a closing of ranks by Hollywood's elite so he never worked in motion pictures again. Who killed Thelma Todd? Officially, no-one knows, but she did cross Lucky Luciano. When discussing with him the possible use of her restaurant by his mobsters Thelma once shrieked 'Over my dead body!

' 'That can be arranged', Luciano was heard to reply.

Another version of the story: On the morning of December 16, 1935, witnesses reported that she left the Trocadero nightclub about 3 a.m. in a chauffeur driven car, arriving at her café about 3:45 a.m. It was the last time she was seen alive. Her body was later found by her maid, Mae Whitehead, slumped over in the passenger seat of her brown 1934 Lincoln Phaeton convertible, which was parked in a two-car garage above her café. She was dressed in a mauve and silver evening gown and mink wrap. There were apparently no overt signs of violence.

Thelma Todd: The official story...as told by insiders

The 1930s had no shortage of blondes in film, but few were as memorable as Thelma Todd. She appeared in over 40 films and would have made more if she'd learned to stay away from creeps and garages, and especially creeps with garages. Her mysterious death at 29 in 1935 is one of old Hollywood's enduring mysteries. As a New England teenager she got good grades in school, liked boys, and didn't wear panties. In 1930 while on a yachting excursion to Catalina Island, she met director Roland West, known for his innovative film noir movies. West was married to actress Jewel Carmen, but began a long affair with Thelma shortly after their meeting. One year later, Thelma eloped to Arizona with slimy Pasquale "Pat" Di Cicco, an abusive playboy reportedly linked with Lucky Luciano. They brawled a lot.

After one beating, Thelma ended up in the hospital needing an emergency appendectomy. Their 1934 divorce was bitter. Thelma turned back to West, drugs, and drink for comfort, scoring so many drunken scrapes in cars that the studio had to give her a driver. Thelma and West went into business together, purchasing property facing the ocean on what is now Pacific Coast Highway and building Thelma Todd's Roadside Cafe. A restaurant was on the ground floor. Upstairs was Thelma and West's shared apartment, a private nightclub for film friends called Joya's, and a hexagonal third-floor ballroom with bandstand where guests could dance with a romantic ocean view. House specials included the *Thelma Todd Knockout, Thelma Todd Milk Punch* (with gin base), and the *Thelma Todd Rickey.*

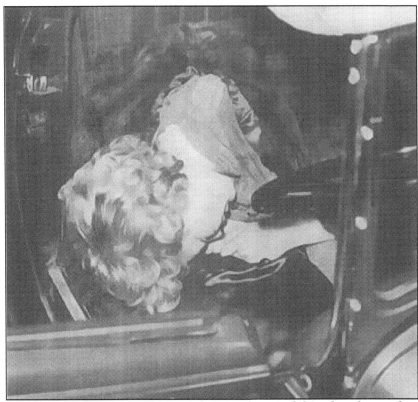

Photo: Thelma Todd, dead in her car.

One of the most sensational allegations (and easiest to dismiss for lack of evidence) emerging in the wake of her death was that Lucky Luciano had also become Thelma's lover, getting her hooked on amphetamines so he could control her while trying to muscle in on her restaurant by opening a gambling room upstairs to cheat wealthy film suckers.

One night over dinner at the Brown Derby, Thelma supposedly screamed, "Over my dead body!" to which Luciano replied, "That can be arranged."

On December 14, 1935, a Saturday night, British actor Stanley Lupino and his daughter Ida gave a party for Thelma at the Café Trocadero. Before she left for the night, West is supposed to have told her to be back by 2 A.M., or he was locking her out.

DiCicco had asked Thelma's friend Ida Lupino to seat him next to Thelma, but showed up at the nightclub with actress Margaret Lindsay as his date and joined another party inside the club. Several people saw Thelma confront DiCicco and accuse him of deliberately humiliating her. Just after midnight, DiCicco was seen making a phone call in the club foyer and left an hour later with his date. Thelma got drunk, and confided to Ida Lupino that she was cheating on West with a San Francisco businessman.

At 2 AM, West closed the cafe and locked up. Thelma left the Trocadero about forty-five minutes later with driver Ernest Peters, confirming to several guests that she would see them later that afternoon at a party Mrs. Wallace Reid was giving. Peters drove Thelma's Phaeton to the café between 3.15am and 3.30, and Thelma refused his usual service of walking her up the steps to the apartment entrance. It was revealed later that Thelma often got death threats in the mail from what would be classified as stalker fans today, so much that her maid routinely bundled them up and dropped them off at the police station. Peters allegedly noticed a brown Packard with its lights off, either parked or approaching, before he left. West claimed not to have seen Thelma, but that in the early morning hours he heard water running in the apartment. Later he said it might only have been the coolers in the bar below.

A druggist claimed that on Sunday morning at 9:30, Thelma had come into his store asking him to make a phone call, then disappeared when his back was turned. That afternoon, several witnesses (including Jewel Carmen) said they saw Thelma driving around with a dark-haired man. Around 4:30, Mrs. Wallace Reid said Thelma phoned her using her nickname *Hot Toddy*, apologized for being late, and promised to surprise her with a mystery guest. Thelma never showed up.

Monday morning, Thelma's maid May Whitehead arrived to clean the apartment above the café. At 10:30 she climbed the 300 steps to the garage, its door ajar and Thelma slumped dead behind the wheel of her Phaeton. Its ignition was on, but the engine wasn't running and there was still two gallons of fuel in its tank. Thelma was still wrapped in her mink coat and wore a tidy fortune in jewels. Her face was crimson, consistent with carbon monoxide poisoning. There was also coagulated blood on her mouth, in the car, and on her silver and mauve evening gown. A local service station operator and jack-of-all trades in the Palisades was the first person on the scene before the police, and claimed Thelma had been struck in the head. She was in the passenger seat and slumped over to the driver's side. Her makeup was intact, but her lip was bruised, her nose was broken, and a dental filling jarred loose. Her high-heeled sandals were pristine, yet when a policewoman of the same height and build attempted climbing the steps from the highway, her sandals got dirty. Thelma's blood revealed enough alcohol to have put her in a stupor, along with a 75-80% carbon monoxide saturation. Still more puzzling were the carrots and peas found in her stomach; none had been served at Ida Lupino's dinner. The time of death was fixed by the L.A. County Surgeon at between 5 and 8 Sunday morning. He explained the blood by suggesting Thelma had struck the steering wheel when she was overcome by the exhaust fumes.

The official theory was that Thelma, being locked out by West, turned on the engine to keep warm and fell asleep. Except that Thelma's maid stated she had given Thelma a key and it was found in her handbag. An alternate theory was that she had decided to go out again, turned on the engine, and passed out, suffocating. The café's cashier, who slept in a room above the garage, heard nothing.

After friends testified that Thelma sometimes got depressed and mentioned suicide, and the investigation revealed she was nearly bankrupt, a verdict of suicide was first returned, then overturned favoring accidental death. The LAPD dropped their investigation on December 21, just in time for Christmas. Thelma was filming *The Bohemian Girl* for Hal Roach when she died. Roach salvaged the Laurel & Hardy feature by cutting all of her dialogue, leaving only a few minutes of footage of her singing. Roland West was a man haunted for the rest of his life. He divorced Jewel Carmen in 1938 and married actress Rosemary Lane two years later. He rarely worked and withdrew into virtual seclusion. In the early 1950s, his health began to decline and he suffered a stroke and a nervous breakdown.

Before his death, West's good friend actor Chester Morris claimed that West had confessed to closing and locking the garage door without knowing Thelma was inside, until he discovered her later and left the garage door ajar for someone else to find. West died in Santa Monica in 1952, stated Claroscureaux.

Natalie Wood's death: Another "accident" that maybe wasn't so accidental.

On November 29, 1981, Natalie was out on a yacht with husband Robert Wagner and family friend Christopher Walken (yep, *that* Christopher Walken). Not much is known about exactly what happened, except that Natalie apparently left the yacht in a small dinghy in the middle of the night when waters were quite choppy. Some reports say Walken and Wood had been getting quite chummy, even going ashore without him while he slept, and that Wagner made no bones about his displeasure. Over the years, Wagner and Walken have given contradictory statements to the media, so what really happened that night might not ever be known, stated Stacy Conrad.

Who Killed Thomas Ince?

Thomas Ince
Photo: Thomas Ince

Gunsock stated that Thomas Ince has largely been forgotten now but he was an ambitious producer and director, and one of the early pioneers of silent films. He teamed up with D.W. Griffith and Mack Sennett in 1915, to form the company which became Culver City Studios.

In 1924, he died, supposedly of a heart attack, but in decidedly mysterious circumstances, during a birthday party in his honor aboard the yacht Oneida, belonging to William Hearst, the newspaper magnate.

The party guest list included Charlie Chaplin, film actress (and Hearst's mistress) Marion Davies, and gossip columnist Louella Parsons.

Ince and Hearst were in the middle of tense business negotiations and Chaplin was said to be romantically interested in Davies (a rumor of which Hearst was painfully aware), so the atmosphere aboard the yacht was not calm. Prohibition was in full swing but bootleg liquor was available on board Hearst's yacht and large quantities of it were consumed. Hollywood legend says that William Randolph Hearst shot Thomas Ince in the head by mistake. He really wanted Chaplin. As the story goes, Hearst suspected that Davies and Chaplin were secretly lovers. In order to keep tabs on the two, he invited them both on board the "Oneida."

Supposedly, he found the couple in a compromising clinch and went for his gun. Davies' screams awakened Ince who rushed to the scene. A scuffle ensued, followed by a gunshot and Ince took the bullet for Chaplin. An even more colorful account of the shooting came from Marion Davies' secretary, Abigail Kinsolving, who claimed that Ince raped her that weekend on board the yacht. Of course, things became even more interesting when, several months later, the unmarried Kinsolving delivered a baby, and died shortly after, in a mysterious car accident near the Hearst's ranch.

Two bodyguards, employed by Hearst, found her body, along with a suspicious looking suicide note. Her baby, a girl, was conveniently sent to an orphanage supported by Marion Davies. Charles Chaplin always denied even being on board the yacht. Published reports cited "acute indigestion" as the cause of death, but rumors began circulating immediately to the effect that Ince had been the victim of foul play. The fact that the body was cremated without an autopsy and no inquest was ever held only fuelled speculation about what "really" happened aboard the "Oneida" on November 15, 1924; speculation which continues to this day.

Birthday party with a circus theme for W.R. Hearst at Marion Davies' beach house is attended by (left to right) Irene Dunne, William Randolph Hearst, Bette Davis, Louella Parsons and Mary Brian.

Murder: Hollywood's Style, or The Magnate Did It?
All the story's versions and rumors
There were three versions of Ince's death

Photo: Hearst Movie Yacht

Thomas Ince was a film actor, director, and producer, sometimes called the "father of the Western." Born in 1882 to a family of stage actors, he began working in the infant film industry in New York in 1911. Ince is credited with inventing the concept of the "shooting script" and of planning out all aspects of production before shooting - at the time, movies were essentially made up as they were shot - and of redefining the producer's role as the overseer of production from start to finish, rather than just the financier of the film.

In 1915, he moved to Santa Ynez Canyon, not far from Hollywood, and founded his own studio, Inceville, where his organized and carefully thought-out system of film-making produced some of the finest Westerns of the silent era.

One of his greatest stars was the cowboy hero, William S. Hart. He also had a reputation for discovering and grooming new talents. The mystery surrounding his death begins in November 1924, when Ince and his wife Nell were invited for a weekend cruise aboard William Randolph Hearst's yacht, the *Oneida*, to celebrate Ince's 43rd birthday.

181

Photos: From L to R; Gloria Swanson, Charles Chaplin and Marion Davies at the premiere of *City Lights* in Los Angeles on January 30, 1931. The police found it hard to control the huge crowds.

Besides Hearst and the Inces, also on board for the festivities were Hearst's mistress, the actress Marion Davies, Charlie Chaplin, with whom Davies was rumored to be having an affair; the then-unknown columnist, Louella Parsons; the author Elinor Glyn; and assorted other hangers-on and wannabes who had somehow cadged a coveted invitation to hang out with Hollywood's high and mighty. The boat left San Pedro on Saturday, November 15. Thomas and Nell Ince joined the cruise in San Diego on Sunday for Ince's birthday celebration. By early Monday morning - or maybe Tuesday - Ince was dead.

What happened? Well, that depended on whom you asked.

The version that Hearst told and had printed in his papers was that Ince had fallen ill and was removed from the vessel on Monday morning, in the company of Hearst's own doctor, Dr. Daniel Goodman. Ince was taken by train to his own home, where he died of heart failure on Tuesday morning. Or wait, maybe he hadn't been on the boat at all. According to Marion Davies, Ince had actually been at the Hearst *ranch,* miles away from Hearst and Davies. And *she* had called Nell Ince to notify her of her husband's death on Monday afternoon, which was interesting, considering that, according to Hearst, Ince had died on Tuesday. Chaplin said he hadn't been on the boat either.

The stories, besides their obvious contradiction of each other, had other problems. First, the headlines in the Los Angeles' papers on Wednesday morning all contained variations of "Hollywood Producer Shot on Hearst's Yacht!" Second, lots of people had seen the Inces and Chaplin on the *Oneida*. Third, Charlie Chaplin's secretary, Toraichi Kono, reported that he had seen Ince removed from the boat on Monday morning, his bleeding head wrapped in bandages. Fourth, Hearst was known to keep a gun on the vessel.

Hearst was powerful enough to quell the headlines

Hearst was powerful enough to quell the headlines - headlines that, by the evening editions, had mysteriously disappeared, never to be seen again. Remember, this was the man who some believe engineered the Spanish-American War ("bring me the pictures, and I'll bring you the war"). The DA's office in 1920s Los Angeles was not above bribery and influence-peddling, either. Hearst also wielded, by virtue of his bottomless pockets, enormous clout within the movie community. He was a man to be reckoned with. What Hearst could not control, however, was the wagging of people's tongues. The murmuring got so loud that finally, reluctantly, the DA reopened the case.

What had happened to Thomas Ince?

According to the rumors, Hearst had invited Chaplin for the weekend cruise specifically to watch his interaction with Marion. He suspected them of having an affair. Which wouldn't have been surprising - not only was Hearst 34 years older than Marion, he was stodgy, controlling, jealous, and humorless. Marion, by all accounts, was friendly, funny, outgoing, and kind; she loved parties and good times, and had a wicked sense of humor. In fact, Chaplin, among others, was constantly urging Hearst to showcase Marion's natural wit and effervescence in comedies, rather than the stiff, slow, pretentious costume dramas he insisted she be featured in. Hearst wouldn't hear of it - he thought it was beneath Marion's dignity. Hearst, in any event, probably wasn't inclined to take any advice from Chaplin, who was suave, handsome, younger, fabulously successful and famously well-endowed, and whom he thought was sleeping with his girlfriend.

There were three versions of Ince's death

There were three versions of Ince's death circulating: One was that Hearst had caught Davies and Chaplin *in flagrante delicto*. Davies screamed; the passengers rushed to see what was the matter, and Hearst, in a rage, missed his aim and shot Ince by mistake. Version two had Marion and Ince chatting innocently in the galley. Hearst, according to this version, came into the galley, saw Marion with a man he thought was Chaplin, fired blindly, and struck Ince in the head. The final version was that somehow the gun had gone off accidentally in the deck below Ince's cabin. The bullet had traveled through the deck and struck Ince (although why this story would need a cover-up is not clear.)

Photo: Margaret Livingston

Responding to these rumors, the D.A. did indeed reopen the case.

However, his investigation consisted of interviewing Dr. Goodman and taking his story at face-value. Conveniently, Ince's body had been cremated almost immediately after he died, so there was nothing to examine.

The case was officially closed. Thomas Ince, according to the authorities, had died of heart failure in his own bed on Tuesday, November 19, 1924.

But the rumors wouldn't die. They were fed, in part, by events after Ince's death.

One was that Nell Ince immediately left for Europe, far away from the reach of the LA authorities.

Another was that Louella Parsons, prior to this a very low-level columnist from New York, was almost immediately taken under Hearst's wing as the authoritative syndicated gossip columnist of the stars and given a lifetime contract.

Under Hearst's aegis, Parsons became one of the most powerful and influential columnists in Hollywood, up until her death at age 91 in 1972. Was this, as some suggested, payment for her silence? Margaret Livingston, one of the no-name starlets also on board that weekend and perhaps not coincidentally Thomas Ince's mistress, saw her salary instantly jump from $1000 to $3000 a film, and she went on almost immediately to star in several quite successful pictures. And, as D.W. Griffith was reported to have said, "All you have to do to make Hearst turn white as a ghost is mention Ince's name. There's plenty wrong there, but Hearst is too big."

Marion Davies stayed with Hearst until his death in 1951, at one point writing him a check for a million dollars after his fortunes took a nosedive. Her movie career kept alive, with ups and downs, until the early 1950s, despite the effects of age and alcoholism. She died of cancer in 1961.

In the 1960s, Orson Welles, who had nailed Hearst forever in *Citizen Kane,* told Peter Bogdanovitch the story of Thomas Ince's death. (Welles also said that he was sorry that people thought the character of Susan Alexander, Kane's alcoholic and talentless wife, was meant to be Davies, whom he found to be an intelligent and gifted woman.) Bogdanovitch was so taken with

the story that in 2001 he wrote, produced, and directed the 2001 movie about the Ince affair, *The Cat's Meow*.

Edward Herrmann plays Hearst; Kirsten Dunst is excellent as Marion Davies, as is the fab Eddie Izzard as Charlie Chaplin. Cary Elwes plays the doomed Ince, stated Laura Orem.

Marion Davies secretly gave birth to Hearst's child in Paris.

Photo: Marion Davies on the "Oneida", waving at Ince.

For a long time, Davies' professional reputation was overshadowed by her long-running affair with newspaper tycoon William Randolph Hearst, trapped in the public perception of a gold-digger without any talent that was bolstered by Orson Welles in his masterpiece *Citizen Kane*.

By the time that film came out in 1940, Marion's film career was already a fading memory.

Born Marion Cecilia Douras in Brooklyn, New York in 1897, she followed the lead of her older showgirl sisters by taking the more English-sounding surname Davies and went on the stage, prancing around in some of Florenz Ziegfeld's annual Follies. For a young girl with Marion's luminous blonde beauty, the next natural step was film, and she made her debut in 1916. By 1918, she'd hooked up with Hearst who established Cosmopolitan Pictures to showcase her talents and put his arsenal of publications to work churning out nonstop publicity, a move Marion confessed in her memoirs had hurt her reputation more than anything else.

In the next ten years, she made 29 films (averaging almost three a year), but her acting over the decade was overshadowed by her relationship with Hearst -- whose wife Millicent refused to give him a divorce -- and a relentless social life mostly set at San Simeon, his over-the-top mountain retreat and Marion's ocean house in Santa Monica, said to be the largest house on the beach -- that was, the beach between San Diego and Vancouver.

185

In 1923, Marion secretly gave birth to Hearst's child in Paris. The girl, named Patricia, was passed off as her sister Rosemarie Van Cleve's daughter, and grew up believing Marion was her aunt.

During the early 1930s, Cosmopolitan Pictures was based at MGM, where Marion's dressing room bungalow was a Spanish mansion constructed, like all of Hearst's other confections, piecemeal with architectural relics plundered from Europe.

If you ever watch the brilliant 1932 comedy *Bombshell* with Jean Harlow, you can spot it in the scenes filmed outside Harlow's character's dressing room. It's the one with an arch and a statue of the Virgin Mary over the door, which allegedly led to the creation of one of Dorothy Parker's lesser-known poems:

Upon my honor
I saw a Madonna
Standing in a niche
Over the door
Of the whore
Of a prominent son of a bitch.

Parker always denied authorship, claiming she would never rhyme "honor" with "Madonna."

Despite her strong knack for comedy, Hearst preferred seeing his Brooklyn inamorata in epic historical dramas.

In the mid-30's, incensed that producer Irving Thalberg refused to give Marion the leads in two historical epics he was saving for wife Norma Shearer, Hearst pulled all newspaper support for MGM and had Marion's bungalow dismantled, moving it and Cosmopolitan Pictures to the Warner Brothers lot. Marion's final feature was completed at Warner Brothers in 1937. But there were still parties to throw, birthday masquerades at Ocean House and long stays at San Simeon hosting the cream of international celebrity.

In an upstairs sitting room across the hall from Hearst's bedroom, an antique sewing machine sits as if its owner just walked away, a pile of vintage dress patterns beside it. Yes, the guides will tell you, *Marion liked to sew in her free time*, presumably between nips of gin or vodka she hid in the water tank of her toilet. Liquor was verboten at San Simeon. Maids unpacking guests' bags had strict orders to confiscate any hooch sneaked in. To appear drunk during one's stay meant banishment. In the late 1930s, Hearst had a disastrous financial reversal that forced him to auction off the warehouses of antiquities collected over his lifetime. When it still wasn't enough, Marion sold $1 million of her own jewelry to keep him solvent. By 1951, Hearst's deteriorating health had forced him to abandon his beloved San Simeon when he died in Marion's Beverly Hills house. While she was sedated, Hearst's family spirited his body away for services and burial.

In his will, Hearst left 51% of his fortune to Marion, who reportedly sold it back to his family for $1 a year

In his will, Hearst left 51% of his fortune to Marion, who reportedly sold it back to his family for $1 a year, claiming she had loved Hearst and was not a gold-digger. On Halloween, 1951, ten weeks after Hearst's burial, Marion married Horace Brown in Las Vegas. Friends and the press enjoyed pointing out his resemblance to a younger WR Hearst, but looks were as far as they went. It wasn't a good match. Brown is supposed to have encouraged her drinking, and she filed for divorce twice, but neither was finalized. In 1952, she donated $1.9 million to establish a children's clinic at UCLA which still bears her name. A minor stroke in 1956 was followed by an operation for a cancerous jaw. On her deathbed in 1961, she revealed to her niece Patricia (married to Arthur Lake who played Dagwood in the Blondie film series) that she was in fact, Marion and Hearst's daughter. Marion left an estate estimated at over $30 million, said Claroscureaux.

Who killed William Desmond Taylor?
Photo: William Desmond Taylor

Taylor was well-known in Tinseltown, directing the likes of Mary Pickford, Wallace Reid and Mary Miles Minter. It was quite a shock when he was found shot to death inside his L.A. bungalow in 1922. The crime scene was shockingly sloppy; people traipsed in and out, items were removed and Paramount's general manager went in and destroyed evidence. It is speculated that this was allowed because the police were highly influenced by Adolph Zukor, then head of Paramount.

Because of all of the tampering, we don't know who shot Taylor to this day. Suspects include two of his lovers (Mabel Normand and Mary Miles Minter), Minter's mother, Taylor's valet *and* his former valet, and an actress named Margaret Gibson. The latter confessed to his murder on her deathbed in 1964, stated Stacy Conrad.

The story:
Photo: Mabel Normand

William Desmond Taylor was a very successful director of the silent era. In February of 1922, he lived in a bungalow on Alverado Avenue in the Westlake section of Los Angeles, then a favorite neighborhood for the movie community. Handsome, urbane, and courtly, Taylor was enormously popular with the actors he directed, who included Mary Pickford, Wallace Reid, and the up-and-coming young actress, Mary Miles Minter.

His past was somewhat mysterious; like that other icon of the Jazz Age, Jay Gatsby, he had reinvented himself into the life he dreamed of.

Born in Ireland in 1872, his real name was William Cunningham Deane-Tanner. In 1890, he came to America to pursue an acting career.

In 1901, he married Floradora Girl Ethel May Hamilton and had a daughter. One day in 1908, married life not agreeing with him in some way and after an affair with another actress, he walked out and never came back.

Apparently this was a family habit: his brother Denis did the same thing to his family and was never seen again. What happened to him remains a mystery. His wife obtained a divorce in 1912. By this time, Taylor was in Hollywood and meeting with some success in his acting career, although by 1914 he had switched to directing. He was known as an "actor's director," respectful, thorough, and quite successful. The acting community seems not to have known about his past life. In 1918, the final year of World War I, he enlisted in the British Army as a private and served so well that when he left the army in 1919, he had been promoted to lieutenant.

By 1922, he was an entrenched, well-respected member of the Hollywood film community. He had also re-established contact with his daughter, who, after seeing one of his films, had written to him; he started sending her a monthly allowance and named her as his legal heir. On the surface, Taylor's life seemed to be well-ordered and peaceful.

Until the morning of February 1, 1922. Taylor's valet, Henry Peavey, arriving for work at about 7:00am, stopped briefly to pick up a bottle of milk left on the front step, opened the door, and let out a shriek that woke up the rest of the neighbors in the little bungalow court. Taylor was sprawled on his back in the little entry room directly in front of the door, dead. Peavey's screams soon attracted a crowd, among them an executive from Taylor's studio, a cameraman, and Taylor's friend and colleague, Julia Crawford Ivers.

By the time someone thought to call the police, Taylor's friends had entered the house and removed what they considered items liable to tarnish Taylor's reputation, including letters from several women and a pink négligée hanging neatly in a closet.

When the police finally arrived, the crime scene had been hopelessly contaminated. What they did find was that Taylor had been shot in the side, probably about 12 hours earlier. There was no sign of forced entry. In his pockets, in addition to $78 in cash (a not-inconsiderable sum in 1922), were a gold pocket-watch, an ivory toothpick, and a cigarette case. He was also wearing a two-carat diamond ring. All of these were easily-pawned items, which seemed to rule out robbery as a motive. Later, Taylor's accountant claimed that Taylor had shown her a large roll of cash the day before. This cash was never found.

However, the accountant's claim was never substantiated. If robbery wasn't the reason, who would want to kill this well-known and well-liked man?

And why?

The first thing that the police wanted to do was to reconstruct Taylor's movements the evening before. According to Peavey, Taylor ate dinner at about 6:30pm, then made a phone call to his friend, the actor Antonio Moreno. While he was on the phone, the actress and comedienne Mabel Normand arrived. Taylor was also trying to help Normand kick a vicious heroin addiction. They were not romantically involved, according to those who knew them both.

After finishing his phone call, Taylor gave Normand a book of German philosophy he had been saving for her (he had called her house repeatedly that day, to see when she was coming to pick it up). At about this time, Peavey left work for the day. Taylor and Normand chatted for a few minutes, then Taylor walked Normand out to her car. He did not bother to close the front door. He teased her when he saw a copy of the "Police Gazette" on the back seat and peanut-shells strewn on the floor - despite her interest in serious literature, Normand like to read the scandal sheet while eating peanuts. They said good-bye, and as the chauffeur drove her off, Normand watched Taylor go back inside the house.

A few minutes later, a neighbor of Taylor in the bunaglow court, Faith MacLean (Wife of screen actor Douglas MacLean), heard what sounded like a shot and went to her front door to investigate. She saw someone in an overcoat, cap, and muffler (an odd get-up for Los Angeles, even in February) backing out of Taylor's door. The person did not appear in a hurry and MacLean thought the person must be speaking to Taylor, still inside.

Then the person turned, looked directly at Maclean, and walked slowly off. MacLean assumed what she had heard was a car backfiring. Questioned by the police, MacLean said the person was "funny-looking." The police asked her to clarify, and MacLean said it looked as if the person were in costume, and might well have been a woman dressed as a man.

Well, this was interesting. Especially since the coroner reported that Taylor had been shot in lower right side, toward his back, as if he had had his hands up -- or had his arms around someone who used the opportunity to shoot him with a concealed weapon.

More investigating soon uncovered a plethora of suspects. When the police finally got hold of some of the letters taken from Taylor's bungalow, they found several coded ones signed "Mary." The police discovered this was Mary Miles Minter, a beautiful 19-year-old actress whose career Taylor had encouraged (he had directed her in several films, including a very successful version of "Anne of Green Gables") and who, it turned out, was desperately in love with the director. The pink nightgown found at Taylor's home was thought to be hers, although sources differ on whether it was monogrammed "MMM" or not.

According to several sources, including Mary, Taylor had been trying to break off the romance, citing their 30-years' age difference. Others thought Mary's overbearing, toxically ambitious mother, Charlotte Shelby, might have had more to do with the director's desire to end things. Either way, Mary was openly distraught over the rejection.

Other suspects included, for a while, Henry Peavey, who was scheduled to go to court after a "lewd conduct" charge, possibly soliciting young boys. Taylor was planning on appearing as a character witness for Peavey, which seems to counter-indicate any reason the valet would have to murder his boss. Peavey also had an alibi for the night in question. (This story fed rumors of Taylor's bisexuality, never substantiated but certainly the topic of much discussion.)

Another shady character was Taylor's former valet, Edward Sands, a convicted embezzler and forger who had worked for Taylor until he made off with several thousand dollars in checks and belongings while Taylor was in Europe. He disappeared after the murder and was never heard from again, although it seems unlikely that a man with Sands' eye for the valuable would have left Taylor's diamond ring, money, and other expensive items behind.

A third theory was that Taylor was killed by drug dealers. It was well known that Taylor was desperately trying to help Normand kick her drug habit (drugs in Hollywood are nothing new). Maybe an angry dealer snuck in through the open front door while Taylor was saying goodbye to Normand and shot him when he came back inside. Again, though, why would someone like that leave the valuables behind?

Back to Mary and Charlotte. They both had alibis - each other. Mary, however, kept changing her story here and there; not enough to erode the alibi, but enough to arouse suspicion. On top of being heartbroken over the breakup, she was also known for being a bit unstable and prone to hysterics.

As for Charlotte - well, Charlotte, according to almost everyone who encountered her, was a beast, a nightmare of a woman who was known for making huge trouble on movie sets and with studio bosses whenever she felt her daughter was being slighted or not managed properly. Also, Charlotte and her other daughter were supported by Mary. Ostensibly Mary's business manager, Charlotte depended on Mary's earning potential to keep her in the lifestyle to which she had become accustomed. An affair with an older man certainly would not help the career of an actress known and loved for playing sweet innocent young girls like Anne of Green Gables. And finally, Charlotte owned a .38 caliber handgun, the same type that had killed Taylor. Surely, there was enough smoke here to do some serious looking for fire.

The District Attorney, Thomas L. Woolwine, however, seemed to feel Mary and Charlotte needed protecting. He refused to prosecute or even investigate further. He also managed to lose important evidence, including the love letters and the pink négligée that may or may not have been monogrammed with Mary's initials. Two other DAs in the years immediately after Woolwine reopened the case, but declined to prosecute or even continue the investigation. And ever since, people have been asking why.

One theory is that the DAs office bowed to pressure from studio bosses, who wielded enormous political power in the 1920s and who were determined to avoid yet another scandal like the Fatty Arbuckle case. By the time the studios had lost their political clout, almost all the evidence from the case was lost or destroyed.

In any event, whether they participated in a cover-up or not, the studio bosses were unable to prevent a public backlash against the perceived immorality and debauchery of the movie community. The drug and alcohol related deaths of actors like Normand, Olive Thomas (who gruesomely drank a flask of bichloride of mercury, prescribed as a topical treatment for her husband's syphilis, thinking it was gin), and Wallace Reid, combined with scandals like the Taylor and Arbuckle cases, brought about "morals" clauses in actors' contracts and oversight by the Hays office, which monitored actors' onscreen behavior and appearances.

By the 1930s, Hollywood's public persona had been tamed, although the bad behavior continued underground.

So who killed William Desmond Taylor?

Was it heartsick and unstable Mary?

Her jealous, controlling mother?

Someone else?

Theories abound, but we will never know for sure. Many of the people associated with the case had sad ends. Henry Peavey died in the early 1930s from tertiary syphilis. Mabel Normand died in 1930 of tuberculosis, complicated by her drug use. Mary Miles Minter's career was ruined. She and her mother were estranged after Minter sued her for money she claimed her mother had stolen from her.

At one point during an argument, Minter's younger sister is supposed to have accused Charlotte of murdering Taylor, but that's just hearsay. Charlotte died in 1960. Minter left the movie business and lived on in invisible but comfortable retirement in California, having invested wisely in real estate. She died in 1984.

In 1986, Connie Chung interviewed William Cahill, one of the first police officers on the scene of Taylor's murder. Despite being 100 years old, Cahill had a sharp memory of events and a clear opinion as to who killed William Desmond Taylor. He maintained his aplomb even after Chung, attempting to drop a bombshell, tells him Taylor might have been homosexual, stated Laura Orem.

***   ***   ***

Another version of the story, and new analysis according to Dina-Marie Kulzer

The Murder

Photo: The Alvarado Street Bungalow

It was February 1, 1922 and an unusually cold night for Los Angeles.

Despite the fact that this was during prohibition, director William Desmond Taylor and silent film comedienne Mabel Normand enjoyed the Orange Blossom Gin cocktails, and discussed Nietzsche, Freud and movies.

Mabel played comic riffs on the piano. At about 7:45 p.m. he walked her to her car leaving the door open or unlocked to his exclusive Alvarado Street bungalow. As her chauffeur drove off, they blew kisses at one another. With the exception of the murderer, Mabel Normand was the last person to see William Desmond Taylor alive.

Taylor went back into his apartment and at about 8:00 p.m. what was thought to be a car backfire was heard by the neighbors. Faith MacLean went to the window and saw what she at first believed to be a man in a long coat wearing a muffler or with his collar turned up and a plaid cap over his face. He looked at her and casually went back inside as if he'd forgotten something. Later she said this person had an "effeminate walk" and was "funny looking". More than a decade later during Grand Jury Testimony when pressed by the Sheriff and asked if she could be certain it was a man that she saw, MacLean answered she could not. Another neighbor Hazel Gillon stated that she just saw a dark figure after hearing the car backfire.

All was deadly quiet on Alvarado Street until 7:30 a.m. The next day when Taylor's houseman Henry Peavey arrived at the bungalow and found Taylor, 49, lying dead in the living room. Peavey screamed and ran out into the courtyard and chaos ensued as it was the studio that was called first and not the police. Originally, it was thought that Taylor might have died of natural causes but once he was turned over, it was noticed that he was lying in a pool of blood....shot once in the back.

Studio Cover-Up

Representatives from Paramount Studios, where Taylor was employed, came out and seized all the letters they could find (with the exception of some Taylor had hidden in his riding boots) and all the bootleg liquor. They even instructed Peavey to clean up the blood and the apartment. The fledgling motion picture industry was in peril as this was during the time of the rape/murder trial of comedian Fatty Arbuckle (who was finally acquitted after 3 trials, yet his career was ruined), There were also the drug addictions of actors Wallace Reid and Jack Pickford (Mary's brother) and the mysterious death by poison of Pickford's wife actress Olive Thomas. Women's Clubs and religious groups were up in arms against the film industry and were threatening to boycott films. By the time the Los Angeles Police Department detectives arrived, the Taylor's crime scene was severely compromised.

Mabel Normand - The Last Known Person to See Taylor Alive

Mabel Normand, the lovely doe-eyed, brunette actress, was never a serious suspect in the Taylor case, although she was very intent on getting letters back that she had written Taylor. She told officials that she had returned to the house to get the letters saying, "Not that they meant anything to any one but us, but I feared that they might fall into other hands and be misconstrued." While Mabel Normand may not have pulled the trigger, there is a theory that Taylor's death might have been a result of his trying to help Normand kick her addictions to cocaine and opium. Taylor arranged a stay for Normand at a facility which must have been one of the first cases of a celebrated film actor going into rehab. So intent was Taylor on keeping drug pushers away from the studios and actors including Normand, that he headed a commission against drugs of which he was Chairman of the Board. Normand alone is said to have spent about $2,000 a month (and this was the 1920s) on drugs. Taylor definitely tampered with the drug dealers' business which was and still would be a very dangerous thing to do. In Robert Giroux's book *Deed of Death* (1990), he theorizes that a professional hit-man killed Taylor because of his "take charge" opposition against drug dealers. Her body in a weakened state from past abuses of drugs and alcohol, Normand, by all accounts a warm and generous friend to many including William Desmond Taylor, died of tuberculosis in 1930. It's been said that one of her last statements was "I wonder who killed poor Bill Taylor?"

Mary Miles Minter - Suspect
Photo: Mary Miles Minter with William Desmond Taylor.

Mary Miles Minter, the golden-haired actress with astonishingly beautiful blue eyes, adored William Desmond Taylor. Just 20 years old at the time of the murder, she had written him letters professing her undying love. Some of these letters were made public after the murder but they were written in a schoolgirl crush fashion and were hardly lurid. Of course, these were only the letters made public. Who knows what letters were taken from the crime scene by the studio before the police arrived.

Even decades later she would refer to Taylor as "my mate" and claim they were engaged which was not true. Handkerchiefs embroidered with the initials MMM and a pink nightgown that was said to hers were found at Taylor's bungalow. Actually, the nightgown did not have any identification on it. At one point, Minter issued a challenge that she would give $1,000 to anyone who could produce this nightgown with her initials.

Photo: Mary Miles Minter

Given her strong feelings for Taylor, in a way she probably wished that it had existed. Minter had visited Taylor on more than one occasion slipping out of the house late at night after her mother Charlotte Shelby (who kept a very close watch of her), grandmother Julia and sister Margaret were asleep. She threw herself at Taylor while he reportedly tried to let her down gently explaining that he was old enough to be her father.

On the day of the murder a friend asked Taylor how Minter was, he answered wearily, "She's all tonsillitis and temperament."

Ed C. King, a special investigator with the Los Angeles District Attorney's office, stated in an article for *True Detective* magazine in 1930 that Taylor was troubled by Minter's unyielding infatuation. King interviewed Arthur Hoyt, Taylor's friend, with whom he worked out with at the L.A. Athletic Club in connection with the case. An excerpt follows: "Taylor swore Hoyt to secrecy, saying that if he would promise not to breathe it to a living soul, he would tell him something that was causing him a great deal of worry. Mr. Taylor then told Mr. Hoyt that the dearest, sweetest little girl in the world was in love with him, and that he was old enough to be her father. This little girl was madly in love with him--had been to his apartment the night before, coming at nearly 3:00 o'clock in the morning. She had insisted on remaining. He had insisted on her going home, whereupon this little girl had cried and threatened that if he tried to put her out, she would scream and cause a scene.

This, of course, Mr. Taylor wanted to avoid, as he had many friends in the neighborhood. He finally persuaded her to leave, driving her to her home. Mr. Taylor stated to his friend Hoyt that this little girl had become so infatuated with him that it was really becoming serious. He was worried and didn't know what to do about it.

She stated that she had not seen Mr. Taylor for a long time, the last time being on the streets of Los Angeles. Mr. Taylor was in his own car and she in hers. They merely waved to each other. This statement was not true. We were able to prove that she had been in his apartment many times, and had actually been there the night of the murder."

Three long blonde hairs were found on Taylor's jacket and were determined by the police to be those of Mary Miles Minter by matching them with hairs left in her brush at the studio. Taylor was meticulous about his clothes and had his jacket brushed every day. There are two versions of Taylor's seeing Minter while driving the day of the murder. One that they passed and waved while driving, and another that they stopped their cars and greeted each other. If it was the latter scenario, then Minter could have hugged Taylor and that would explain the hairs on his jacket.

Charles Higham, in his book *Murder in Hollywood: Solving A Silent Screen Mystery* (2004), theorizes that the backfire heard by the neighbors at Alvarado Court was just that and that the person seen leaving Taylor's bungalow was a visitor that Taylor got rid of quickly as he had planned on working on his taxes that evening. Higham believes that Mary Miles Minter visited Taylor late at night. She threw herself at him once again...this time threatening to shoot him or herself. He embraced her to calm her down and the gun accidentally went off.

The bullet hole in Taylor's jacket and vest were not aligned. The powder burns indicated that Taylor was shot at close range with his left arm raised as if in an embrace. The person who shot Taylor had to be just a little over five feet tall (which describes every female suspect in this case) or would have had to crouch on the ground and shoot Taylor at an angle.

There had been an incident in 1920 when Minter had a tantrum while locked in her room with her mother Charlotte Shelby's gun and shots were fired. Minter played "dead" when the family came in she jumped up and laughed. Higham believes she was using the gun to get her way with Taylor just as she tried to do with her family a couple of years before. In the rafters of the home where the Shelby family lived at the time of the "fake suicide" incident was found an unfired soft-nosed lead bullet which "was the same type and weight as the fatal bullet, which was extracted from Taylor's body," according to Detective Lt. Sanderson in 1937 Grand Jury testimony.

It's said that the reason that Minter or Shelby were never prosecuted at the time of the murder was that Shelby was a close friend of District Attorney Thomas Lee Woolwine. It's alleged that Shelby may have paid off not only Woolwine (accused of bribery in 1915) but successive District Attorneys Asa Keyes (later convicted of bribery in another case) and possibly Buron Fitts (indicted in 1934 for bribery and perjury in another case). In the Shelby/Minter family accounts there was $750,000.00 never declared to the IRS. Transfers beginning in 1922 were made to negotiable bonds and stock certificates with no written trail as detailed in 1931 litigation between Shelby and her accountant Les Henry. Henry claimed the money went for police and press protection. Henry was convicted of improper financial transactions but not of stealing the money. In addition, Woolwine had benefited from contributions from the studios during his campaign (and some say after) and wished to protect the studio at all costs. According to Higham's book, Woolwine didn't believe women on a jury would ever find angel-faced Mary Miles Minter or any other woman guilty of murder let alone sentence her to death. Woolwine was worried about his political future if he lost the conviction. More than one police detective stated that every time they got close to solving the case they were either told to "lay off" or "you're going in the wrong direction."

The one big hole in Higham's theory is that no one heard a gun shot late in the night. The gun shot was shortly before 8 p.m. If Minter did commit the murder, she had to have been hiding in the Taylor bungalow the entire time of Mabel Normand's visit or slipped in while the door was unlocked/open and Taylor had walked Normand to her car.

Charlotte Shelby – Suspect
Photo: Charlotte Shelby

In James Kirkpatrick's book *Cast of Killers* (1986), largely based on research and interviews conducted by Director King Vidor who was fascinated with the Taylor case, it is theorized that Charlotte Shelby, mother of Mary Miles Minter, killed William Desmond Taylor. The theory is that Shelby dressed as a man slipped into Taylor's bungalow, found Mary there and shot Taylor.

To say that Charlotte Shelby was possessive of her daughter Mary Miles Minter would be an understatement. In the classic tale of a stage mother, Shelby had wanted to go on the stage herself but lacked the talent to be a success. Instead, she lived vicariously through her daughter who began acting as a child. At all costs, Shelby wanted to protect her investment. When Minter was still a teenager she became involved with director James Kirkwood and reportedly became pregnant. Shelby paid for the abortion and is said to have threatened Kirkwood with the .38 revolver. Once when she caught Minter in a passionate embrace with actor Monte Blue she took out the revolver and said "If I ever catch you hanging around Mary again, I'll blow your goddamned brains out". And last but not least, in 1920 Charlotte Shelby showed up at Taylor's Bungalow late one night with her 1912 .38 Smith & Wesson blue steel revolver tucked in the long sleeve of her gown demanding to know whether Mary was there (according to testimony of Chauncey Eaton her chauffeur). Fortunately for Taylor, at least in 1920, Minter was not there. It wasn't until 1937 that Shelby was questioned in the Taylor case. This was a result of a civil lawsuit between Shelby and her other daughter Margaret Filmore who testified: "I protected her (Charlotte) against the Taylor murder case." This testimony spurred on the Grand Jury inquiry where Filmore stated that Shelby was not home the night of the murder and that she was afraid Mary would run off with Taylor. Strangely enough, Shelby insisted on the Grand Jury inquiry to clear her name after her daughter Margaret's accusation.

Shelby's non-family member alibi for the night of the murder was actor Carl Stockdale who it has been alleged in Higham's book accepted a lifetime income for saying that he was with Shelby between 7:30 p.m. and 9:30 p.m. Charlotte Shelby paid Carl Stockdale $200.00 a month for life....why?

Shelby's mother and Minter's grandmother, Julia Miles, is said to have taken the infamous revolver and thrown it in a bayou near her plantation in Louisiana in August 1922. In *Cast of Killers*, an interview between Detective Lt. Sanderson and director King Vidor reveals that the gun was later retrieved from the bayou. In 1973 former District Attorney Buron Fitts killed himself with an identical .38 Smith & Wesson Revolver which hasn't been seen since.

In 1926, District Attorney Asa Keyes questioned Mary Miles Minter asking if she ever heard her mother threaten to kill William Desmond Taylor. While Minter said she did not believe her mother was the murderer, she did answer, "Not definitely. She may have said, "I'll kill him....I'll kill him....she was like that. She was always going to kill somebody."

Edward Sands - Suspect
Photo: Sands and in early Navy photo.

William Desmond Taylor had the misfortune of hiring sociopath Edward Sands a.k.a. Edward Snyder as his houseman in 1920. Sands pretended to be British, a cockney, actually he was born in Ohio. In the days before employee background checks, how was Taylor to know that Sands had deserted from the Navy and re-enlisted using different names? Sands was charged with fraud and embezzlement in 1915. He was dishonorably discharged after one year of hard labor in 1916. Later he enlisted in U.S. Naval Reserve in 1917 and stole an automobile and wrecked it. He got off saying he'd pay for the damages and then deserted saying they could come after him if they wanted the money. In 1919, he enlisted in the Navy again and was assigned to the finance office of all places. He forged a check payable to himself for $481.53 and then forged his own discharge papers!

The first year of Sands' employment with Taylor was relatively smooth. He, in fact, seemed to adore his employer even offering himself as a slave for life. However, in 1921 when Taylor took a trip to Europe, Sands forged $5,000 in checks and stole and wrecked Taylor's car. Sands also stole jewelry and Taylor's Russian gold-tipped cigarettes. A few months later, Taylor came home and found the distinctive cigarettes crushed and smoked on the porch indicating that Sands had come back to the bungalow. Sands had also mailed the pawn tickets for the jewelry back to Taylor under his real name William C. Deane-Tanner with a note: "So sorry to inconvenience you even temporarily. Also observe the lesson of the forced sale of assets. A Merry Xmas and a happy and prosperous New Year. Alias Jimmy V." Handwriting analysis confirmed the note was written by Sands. This also shows that Sands knew Taylor's true identity.

In a Los Angeles Times article from 1922, Taylor's friend Julia Crawford Ivers said: "There never was a more devoted man serving another than this man Sands during the first year and a half of his service for Mr. Taylor. Mr. Taylor trusted him with everything. Sands read everything he could find. He used to study into the late hours of the night and when Mr. Taylor told me of the various actions attributed to Sands, we all decided the man must have become deranged..."

Before the murder, Taylor had been troubled with phone calls. Someone had been calling him late at night and would hang up. It seemed as if they were checking to see if he was home. The night before Taylor's murder he had shown his tax preparer Marjorie Berger, $5,000.00 in cash that he kept. The $5,000.00 was not found after Taylor's death. Yet on his body was $78.00 and his diamond ring. No other valuables were taken.

It would seem that Sands was the murderer, with the exception of the fact that he signed in for work at a lumber yard in Oakland, California on the day of the murder. The fact that Taylor didn't do more to find Sands, indicates that Sands may have been blackmailing him. Also, Taylor's bank accounts were surprisingly low considering his salary, at the time of his death.

It has been reported that Sands was found dead from a suicide in Connecticut, and that District Attorney Woolwine knew this and kept it a secret from the press to throw suspicion away from suspects in the movie industry. Woolwine continued a man-hunt for a dead man.

Margaret Gibson a.k.a. Patricia Palmer/Pat Lewis - Deathbed Confession
Photo: Margaret Gibson

Bruce Long, the foremost Taylor historian, who has written the book *William Desmond Taylor: A Dossier* (1991) and runs the excellent Taylorology website received an email in 1996 from Ray Long (no relation). Long had been a neighbor of a reclusive little old woman who didn't leave the house often and had her groceries delivered. This woman, who he knew as Pat Lewis, was a widow and a friend of his mother's. One day in 1964 the poor woman, who had converted to Roman Catholicism, was having a heart attack and asked for a priest to confess. No priest being available, she began to make her deathbed confession anyway saying that she had once been a silent film actress and that she shot and killed a man named William Desmond Taylor. At the time, Long didn't know who William Desmond Taylor was. Long's mother revealed that one evening, she and Pat Lewis were watching *Ralph Story's Los Angeles* on television. When a piece on the Taylor murder aired, Lewis became hysterical and blurted out that she'd killed him and thought it was long forgotten.

"But mother never once said a word to any of us about this incident", wrote Ray Long.

Margaret Gibson, the exquisitely beautiful actress, and Pat Lewis were one in the same person. At the time she was a silent film actress, Gibson had trouble of her own having been arrested for vagrancy connected with opium dealing in 1917. She was in what was then called a "disorderly house"; translation: A house of prostitution. At the time she said she was picking up "local color" for a movie role. Gibson was acquitted. After this incident, she changed her name to Patricia Palmer. In November 1923, she was arrested again on federal felony charges involving a blackmail and extortion ring. The charges were dropped by the District Attorney.

Margaret Gibson did indeed work with William Desmond Taylor before World War I.

They worked together in theater in Denver in 1910 and then in Hollywood films. Other than the fact that they worked together as actors years before the murder, there is no known connection between them. However, Gibson, as Patricia Palmer, was working at Paramount in 1921. Undoubtedly, she would have seen Taylor on the lot.

Did Gibson have some kind of romantic obsession with Taylor as did Mary Miles Minter?

Was Gibson somehow involved with a group of people in blackmailing Taylor? Given her arrests concerning blackmail and drugs, this could be a possibility. Despite women coming and going through Taylor's bungalow as if through a revolving door. There is some speculation that he might have been a bisexual. If that fact came out, Taylor's career would have been ruined. Could the mysterious man who was seen leaving Taylor's bungalow the night of the murder have been Denis Deane-Tanner, his younger brother? The trail on Denis Deane-Tanner ends in 1930.

During his lifetime, William Desmond Taylor was described as an individual who enjoyed his solitude, good books and most of all his work. His intelligence, sophistication and gentlemanly manners made him a sought after guest at gatherings where Hollywood personalities were not usually invited. Taylor was a three-term President of the Motion Picture Directors Association and tried valiantly to keep drugs out of the film industry. Unfortunately, he employed unsavory characters and became involved with emotionally unbalanced women. One of these associations, his mysterious past or his fight against drug dealers led to his murder. For all the notoriety of his death, the gravestone of William Desmond Taylor reads very simply:

William C. Deane-Tanner

Beloved Father of Ethel D. Deane-Tanner

Died February 1, 1922

A loving tribute from the daughter he once deserted and then reunited with. (Source: Dina Di Mambro)

- **Horrible death and body's mutilation of aspiring actress "The Black Dahlia."**

Photo: Beth Short "The Black Dahlia"

When it comes to the study of murder cases, nothing tops the case of the aspiring actress, "The Black Dahlia." It has stumped Hollywood's thriller writers and readers for more than half a century. She often dressed in all black, and attempted to woo various types of men.

She had an affair with George Knowlton, father of Janice Knowlton, the author of "Daddy Was the Black Dahlia Killer." Born July 29, 1924, in Hyde Park, Mass., Beth Short was daughter of Phoebe and Cleo Short. They soon moved to Medford, Mass. Her legal name was Elizabeth Short (no middle name). While a child, many called her Betty, and as she matured, she preferred to be called Beth. In 1929, Cleo disappeared, many believing he had committed suicide, as his empty car was found near a bridge. He later sent a letter to his wife, apologizing for leaving. Phoebe refused to allow him to return. Beth matured quickly. She grew up to become a beautiful teenager - she looked older and more sophisticated than others her age. At age 19, Beth ventured to Vallejo, California, to live with her father. The stay did not last long, however. Her father asked her to leave because he said she was lazy and stayed out late. Near Santa Barbara was Beth's next stop. It was here where she was arrested for underage drinking. After her arrest and fingerprinting, police instructed the young woman to return home to Medford. At one time she had gone home for a visit, but Beth was determined to be in movies, and returned to Hollywood. It was mid-January, 1947, when Beth was last seen alive at the Biltmore Hotel. It was reported that she was to meet a gentleman. After leaving the hotel, she was never again seen alive. Her body was found severed, in the Crenshaw District, January 15, 1947.

Photo: On January 15, 1947, a passerby spotted the body of Elizabeth Short in a vacant lot near Hollywood.

The Black Dahlia murder; discovered January 15, 1947

The murder of Elizabeth Short has intrigued, mystified, even disgusted the city of Los Angeles for more than half a century. Elizabeth Short, a 22-year-old wannabe actress, spent several years moving around, gaining odd jobs. Her passion for servicemen and aspiration to be famous made her a "different" woman of her time. She *reportedly* hooked up with a variety of men and women (one reported to having been Marilyn Monroe). Her name evolved from her black hair and black attire. Some say she was named the Black Dahlia before her murder in January of 1947, others say the name was applied by journalists to sensationalize the crime. On January 15, 1947, a passerby spotted her nude body in a vacant lot near Hollywood. Her body, cut in half, was bruised and beaten. Grass had reportedly been forced into her vagina, and she had reportedly been sodomized after death. Rumors of henna in her hair and BD carved into her body, as of yet, have not been verified. Upon the release of the news of the murder in the press, several men and women admitted to the crime. But the police could not validate anyone's story, as stated by Dahlia Site.

Chapter 6: Hollywood Biggest Sex Scandals

At a dinner in Paris, Capucine told me:
"They (Hollywood's actors/actresses) fucked each other so much...women began to smell semen and men perfume..."

Photo: Peg Entwistle.

According to the Hub Pages, Hollywood has always been a highly sexed town full of attractive young people with plenty of money or needing plenty of money.

The idea of hitting it big in Hollywood has always been a powerful draw, and young innocents from all over America and the world flocked to the West Coast from 1915 onwards. Once there starstruck young hopefuls fell prey to established actors, agents, directors and producers who promised a big break in exchange for their souls or bodies. Tragedy was often the result and the situation was ripe for scandal.

Hollywood needed a huge publicity machine and the studios created stars whose public image was completely different to their real selves. Innocent young virgins were actually fast-living sex kittens with a taste for drugs and alcohol. Lovable family men were known for their sexual conquests and more than one hero who made the ladies swoon secretly found young men more to his liking.

Photo, right: Peg Entwistle jumped to her death from the letter 'H' in 1932.

There is a tendency in all of us to look at the past through rose colored spectacles so it is easy to think of Hollywood scandal in terms of modern stars like Michael Jackson or Hugh Grant. However, the glittering facade of the so-called Golden Age of Hollywood contained enough juicy scandals of its own. Rape, adultery, alcoholism, drug addiction, murder and suicide, as in the tragic case of failed actress Peg Entwistle all featured heavily in the supposed innocent days of early Hollywood. Over the decades, the names and faces have changed, but the habits and hungers have always been around. Here are some of the main scandals. (Source: Gunsock)

It may be near the top on the "ick" meter, but the trial of Michael Jackson on charges of molesting a 13-year-old boy is hardly unique, or even unusual, really. It's simply the latest installment of that beloved American sit-com, the Hollywood sex scandal. Sex scandals, of course, have been with us ever since Sodom and Gomorrah. And while notable figures throughout history got themselves entangled in hangups over sex — Pope Alexander VI had an illegitimate daughter, who grew up to be Lucrezia Borgia, for example — the sex scandal as thrilling public entertainment didn't come into its own until the 20th century and the birth of the movies.

The original tabloid victim

Photo: Fatty Arbuckle, in a publicity photo with two unidentified actresses at Coney Island in 1917, was the loser in the first enormous Hollywood sex scandal. He was also innocent.

Roscoe Arbuckle was one of the most popular comic actors of the silent film era.

Better known as Fatty Arbuckle for his 266-pound frame, he was the original star of the Keystone Kops. He's credited with discovering Buster Keaton and with making the pie in the face the apotheosis of film slapstick. Hollywood legend has it that it was a pair of Arbuckle's enormous pants that Charlie Chaplin put on, giving him the inspiration for the Little Tramp. He's generally believed to be the first Hollywood star to win a million-dollar contract, and the first to be given complete artistic control over his films. In September 1921, however, Arbuckle was arrested in a San Francisco hotel and charged with rape and manslaughter in the death of a minor starlet named Virginia Rappe.

Prosecutors said Arbuckle, whom they portrayed as a lecherous drunk, tried to force himself on Rappe, whom they painted as the ultimate flower of chaste virtue. Arbuckle's enormous bulk caused internal bleeding, they charged. Rappe, 26, died three days later of peritonitis. The newspapers ate it up — the biggest star of the day was charged with killing a beautiful young actress in their alleged love nest. And they were spoon-fed the scandal, thanks to details freely distributed by the prosecutor, Matthew Brady, who was known to aspire to higher office and thought he could get there on the back of Fatty Arbuckle.

Big, fat injustice.

Biographers and film historians agree that it was a bum rap. The first two trials ended in hung juries, but Brady was driven to win. His eagerness to convict Arbuckle was so immense that more than 30 years later, when it came time for the authors of the play "Inherit the Wind" to give a fictionalized name to the obsessed prosecutor modeled on William Jennings Bryan, they chose "Matthew Brady." The third jury took six minutes to acquit, releasing a statement, which is reprinted in Stuart Oderman's biography "Roscoe 'Fatty' Arbuckle: A Biography Of the Silent Film Comedian." It said: "Acquittal is not enough for Roscoe Arbuckle. We feel that a great injustice has been done him."That didn't matter. The Hays Office, Hollywood's censor at the time, banned Arbuckle from films, and while the ban was soon lifted, he was not able to return to the screen except for a few token appearances almost a decade later. By then, silent film slapstick was dead. Arbuckle was a broken man, making ends meet by directing minor comedies under the assumed name William Goodrich. For the movie history "Hollywood: The Pioneers," actress Louise Brooks told author Kevin Brownilow that Arbuckle "made no attempt to direct this picture" — "Windy Riley Goes Hollywood," which was released in 1931, a year before he died. "He sat in his chair like a dead man," she said.

Kissing cousins.

Arbuckle's tale illustrates how a sex scandal can destroy a person, even if he's innocent. You have to be a particularly ornery cuss to survive such things. Especially if you did it. Jerry Lee Lewis couldn't understand what all the fuss was over about his marriage to Myra Gale Brown. When he arrived in England for a British tour in 1958, he found out. Myra was Lewis' cousin, and when they married in 1957, she was only 13 years old and he was still married to his second wife. The British tabloids did what they do, and in the ensuing frenzy, Lewis' tour was canceled, his record contract was torn up and his songs disappeared from the radio. He had to return to small clubs and detour into pure country music to make his comeback, and even then it took him almost a dozen years to resume making hit records. But he did it. Often the scandal — like Lewis' and Jackson's — explodes because the object of a star's affection (or alleged affection) is just a kid. Over the years, many celebrities have been hounded by the press and the cops because of their involvement with sweethearts young enough to be in high school:

- Elvis married 22-year-old Priscilla Ann Wagner Beaulieu in 1967. They began dating, however, when she was 14, and she moved into Gracelannd, at 17.
- Salvatore P. Bono never would have hit the big time had he not fallen in love with and married 16-year-old Cherilyn La Pierre in 1963. They were better known as Sonny and Cher.
- Chuck Berry spent a year and a half in jail for transporting a 14-year-old girl across state lines in 1961.
- Roman Polanski became a fugitive when he was convicted of the statutory rape of a 13-year-old girl in 1979, when he was 42. While living in Europe, he was linked to actress Nastassja Kinski, who was 15 at the time.

Then there was Errol Flynn. The movie hero who buckled more swashes than any real-life pirate was tried on charges of statutory rape involving two teenage girls in 1942. He was acquitted — not so much by arguing that he was innocent, but by arguing that he was Errol Flynn, and what redblooded American girl could resist?If anything, the scandal only added to his reputation as a devilish ladies' man, so much so that the phrase "in like Flynn" was coined, for all the reasons you would think.

The rich are different.
There was one famous man, however, for whom scandal was never a real obstacle. William Randolph Hearst lived perhaps the most remarkable American life of the 20th century: congressman, press baron and movie mogul (in fact, he hired Arbuckle to direct a film after Arbuckle's descent). His story was told in "Citizen Kane," only thinly disguised. One of the characters in that film, Susan Kane, was based on Marion Davies, Hearst's mistress. It is a testament to the sheer power Hearst wielded that he could openly live with a former showgirl for more than 30 years — installing her as hostess at his palatial San Simeon estate and starring her in dozens of his films — while remaining married to his wife until his death in 1951. The notoriously combative Hearst never bothered to respond to gossip about his very public affair, the sort of gossip that could be professionally fatal in the 1920s. He was so rich and so powerful that it didn't matter. Hearst eventually lost most of his fortune, but it was not his affair with Davies that did him in; indeed, Davies bailed Hearst out on more than one occasion, once with a $1 million check. And while Davies' career was sometimes ridiculed as being the product of her relationship with Hearst, the affair certainly didn't hurt her: Among those attending her funeral was former President Herbert Hoover, stated Alex Johnson.
Note: Marion Davies — a shrewd, talented actress unfairly lampooned as Susan Kane in "Citizen Kane" — lived with William Randolph Hearst for more than 30 years even though he was married. She was Hollywood's most famous hostess and once wrote a $1 million check to save Hearst from bankruptcy.

The MGM Rape Scandal
It Happened One Night, at MGM: The Rape of Patricia Douglas.
As told by David Stenn, word for word, and unedited.

Photo: Patricia Douglas identifies her attacker, David Ross, from a stack of photographs.

When Patricia Douglas was raped by an MGM salesman at a 1937 studio party, the 20-year-old dancer filed charges, taking on Hollywood's most powerful institution. Today, as Douglas breaks a 65-year silence, the author exposes the perjury, bribes, and smear tactics used to destroy her.

April 2003

'What," asked Jacqueline Onassis, "are we going to do next?" It was September 1993. She had just edited *Bombshell: The Life and Death of Jean Harlow,* in which I solved the long-standing mystery of how Metro-Goldwyn-Mayer's beloved Blonde Bombshell died suddenly and inexplicably at 26. (Unbeknownst even to herself, Harlow had been suffering from kidney failure since she was 15.) Now, over lunch at the Peninsula hotel in Manhattan, I told Jackie of an intriguing topic I'd stumbled onto in my Harlow research.

Photo: Ross at the time of a grand-jury inquiry, June 16, 1937.

A month before the star's death, in 1937, a dancer named Patricia Douglas had been raped at a wild MGM party thrown by Louis B. Mayer. Instead of bartering her silence for a studio contract or cash, Douglas went public with her story and filed a landmark lawsuit. One person I interviewed told me, "They had her killed."

I didn't believe that, I told Jackie, because, though MGM was then the world's most powerful movie studio, with its own railroad and in-house police force, it would never have gone to such an extreme. Jackie smiled and said, "Well, why don't you find out what *did* happen? You're the only person who can, David."

It has taken a decade, but the story is astounding. Absent from all reference works, presumed by participants to be buried forever, the Patricia Douglas case is probably the biggest, best-suppressed scandal in Hollywood history. I managed to find old newspaper coverage, previously unseen photos, damning studio documentation, long-forgotten legal records, privately shot cinematographic evidence hidden in an MGM film vault, and, most amazing, Patricia Douglas herself. I tracked the reclusive invalid down and eventually persuaded her to break her 65-year silence.

In the spring of 1937, Patricia Douglas was a chunky, chestnut-haired 20-year-old with porcelain skin and perfect teeth. Born in Kansas City, Missouri, she had migrated to Hollywood with her mother, Mildred Mitchell, who was determined to design gowns for screen queens. Instead, she became a couturière for high-end call girls; in the meantime, she neglected her teenage daughter. Patricia dropped out of convent school at 14; she did not drink, date, or dream of film fame—an appealing rarity for the half-dozen male stars for whom she soon became a platonic mascot. She had lemon Cokes at drive-ins with Dick Powell ("When the waitress saw him, she almost fainted"), barhopped with Bing Crosby and pre–*I Love Lucy* Bill Frawley ("The three of us used to go to this dive on Sunset Boulevard; Bing would sing, and the drunks didn't even care"), dined at the Brown Derby with Jimmy Durante ("His daddy wanted him to marry me, and I was all of 15"), played kid-sister confessor to George Raft ("He couldn't get it up, but he had to keep that manly reputation, so the studio manufactured a big romance with Betty Grable"), and learned "truckin'," the Cotton Club's latest hep step, from Larry Fine, one of the Three Stooges ("What a blue tongue! Even at the dinner table, you should've heard him: 'Pass the fucking potatoes!'"). A natural-born dancer, Douglas drifted into movies "just for something to do." By 15 she had already appeared in two classics: *So This Is Africa,* a pre–Production Code comedy that climaxed with the wedding of its two leading men, Bert Wheeler and Robert Woolsey, and *Gold Diggers of 1933,* a Busby Berkeley extravaganza, in which Douglas hoofed behind Ginger Rogers.

Since she was supported by her mother, Douglas had no need to work. So when a casting call came on the afternoon of Sunday, May 2, 1937, she demurred at first, but later agreed to show up. "They never mentioned it was for a party," she recalls. "*Ever.* I wouldn't have gone! Oh God, oh God, I wouldn't have gone."

MGM had much to celebrate that year. To battle the Depression, which had already sent rivals Fox, Paramount, and RKO into bankruptcy or receivership, MGM sales executives had devised a radical scheme to re-structure film rentals: rather than charge exhibitors on a sliding-percentage scale of box-office receipts, which declined with each booking, the studio would set fees on a per-film basis, calculated on first-run grosses in 30 key cities. That way, a success in select, urban markets could command higher rentals once the film went into wide release.

The new sales formula relied on hits, and MGM quickly supplied three all-star blockbusters: *San Francisco,* with Clark Gable, Jeanette MacDonald, and Spencer Tracy; *Libeled Lady,* with Tracy, Jean Harlow, Myrna Loy, and William Powell; and *The Great Ziegfeld,* with Powell and Luise Rainer, which won an Oscar for best picture. (*San Francisco* and *Libeled Lady* were also nominated.) The combination of socko box office and adjusted film-rental fees spiked MGM's profits to $14 million, almost double those of the prior year. While other studios struggled to stay solvent, MGM was in fiscal heaven.

Bowing to the sales force that had engineered this miracle, Louis B. Mayer decreed that MGM's annual five-day sales convention would, for the first time in a decade, be held in Culver City, on the studio's home turf. Mayer promised salesmen "a super-special production," and from its start that Sunday, as 282 conventioneers arrived in Pasadena by private railcar (and Patricia Douglas received her fateful casting call), a freewheeling and foreboding tone was set. Emboldened by three days of binge drinking, detraining delegates groped starlets assigned to pin carnations on their lapels. "The Santa Fe is not on the job," one salesman cracked. "We ran out of scotch last night!"

From a makeshift stage at the Pasadena station, which was festooned with red-white-and-blue MGM banners, Mayer welcomed his honored guests: "Our fine Chief of Police [James] Davis remarked to me a moment ago [that I] must think a lot of these men to have sent the beauty that he sees before him." The allusion was not to local sunshine or orange groves. "These lovely girls—and you have the finest of them—greet you," continued the purportedly puritanical Mayer. "And that's to show you how we feel about you, and the kind of a good time that's ahead of you.... Anything you want."

That night there was a dinner at the Ambassador Hotel, and the next day, Monday, motorcycle police escorted the salesmen to Culver City, where cigar-chomping, bulldog-faced MGM general manager Eddie Mannix, known and feared as "a fucking gangster"—during one tantrum he broke his wife's back, and an ex-mistress, actress Mary Nolan, endured 15 abdominal surgeries after his beatings—presented Mayer with a key to ceremonially open the main gates of the 117-acre lot. As a marching band played "The Gang's All Here" and 4,000 MGM "family members" hurled confetti, dazzled delegates were paraded through the "world's greatest film studio" to a swank luncheon with some of Hollywood's biggest stars, including Clark Gable, Jean Harlow, Joan Crawford, Norma Shearer, Charles Boyer (in costume as Napoleon for *Conquest,* opposite Greta Garbo), Rosalind Russell, and Sophie Tucker.

To a bunch of starstruck Babbitts, hobnobbing with Hollywood royalty was a once-in-a-lifetime thrill, and MGM understood the effect it would have on them. "We want you to go back to your respective territories," a studio bulletin exhorted the salesmen, "firmly convinced that Metro-Goldwyn-Mayer, under the leadership of Louis B. Mayer, is bending every effort to back up the men who provide the one connecting link with the exhibitor, and through him, the public."

Bending every effort. Anything you want. After three days of "strenuous business activities," delegates were rewarded with a down-home respite. "Yippee! Get Set for Wild West Show at Roach's," announced the convention schedule for Wednesday, May 5, 1937. "It will be a stag affair, out in the wild and woolly West where 'men are men.'" This "typical California celebration" would be hosted by producer Hal Roach, whose Laurel and Hardy and *Our Gang* shorts were distributed by MGM.

At four p.m. that day, 120 young female dancers, plus several girls who had answered a small classifed ad for MGM party hostesses, reported to the Hal Roach Studios on Washington Boulevard in Culver City, just up the block from MGM. Summoned by casting assistant Vincent Conniff, these fetching unknowns with marquee-friendly names—Teddie Blue, Dona Dax, Iris Gaye, Maren Marlin—were outfitted in felt cowboy hats, belted bolero jackets, leather-studded cuffs, short suedette skirts, and black boots. If the results seemed less Annie Oakley than Gypsy Rose Lee, to hungry hopefuls that was beside the point: here was not only their best shot at stardom but also a hot meal and $7.50 for the day. After applying thick camera makeup, the girls were bused to "Rancho Roachero," a remote, eucalyptus-lined studio property several miles away. Herded into a large banquet hall, they were ordered to sit at tables and wait. Two hours passed, but Patricia Douglas stayed patient. Had she possessed a savvier nature, she might have noted a disturbing detail: though an orchestra and bar were being assembled, this "location set" lacked any sign of a crew, lights, or cameras.

At seven o'clock Mayer, Mannix, Roach, assorted MGM bigwigs and male stars, and almost 300 revved-up conventioneers appeared at the ranch. Given that they had been promised a stag affair, the salesmen's lust-at-first-sight response to a bevy of young, over-made-up beauties makes sad and terrible sense. Delegates mistook the professional dancers for party favors and treated them accordingly; without telephones or transportation, the young women had no means of escape. Tricked into attendance, then trapped into service, they were left to fend for themselves.

"You'd never think they'd pull anything like that," says Douglas, seething as she recalls the scene. "You're *trusting* with the studios. You're not expecting anything except to work in a movie. That's what you're *there* for." At first the Wild West party seemed tame. Though the open bar featured only scotch and champagne—500 cases for 300 men—other, inoffensive diversions existed:

barbecue was served cafeteria-style in a large mess tent, and there were exhibition boxing matches to enjoy in an adjacent arena. Laurel and Hardy tipped off delegates on the upcoming Kentucky Derby ("Bet on Dellor!" said Hardy of the horse that would take the Trial Purse). The Dandridge Sisters, 13-year-old Dorothy included, performed in a live revue. David Ross, a roly-poly, 36-year-old Catholic bachelor from the Chicago sales office, had eyes only for Patricia Douglas. When he saw her truckin' on the dance floor, he approached her and demanded a lesson. Douglas obliged, but she says she found Ross "repulsive. He was slimy, with eyes that bulged like a frog." Accustomed to her chivalrous star cronies, Douglas had no clue how to handle "an annoying creep doing his best to cop a feel." After their dance, Douglas ducked into the ladies' room. "I've got a man, and he's really sticking," she fretted to the attendant.

By 10 p.m. the party's polite veneer had vanished. "The men all became intoxicated," Oscar Buddin, a waiter, would later testify under oath. Buddin heard "filth in conversation" and saw "girls get up and move from the tables because the men were attempting to molest them."

"The party was the worst, the wildest, and the rottenest I have ever seen," said Henry Schulte, another waiter, in his affidavit. "The men's attitude was very rough. They were running their hands over the girls' bodies, and tried to force liquor on the girls." Ginger Wyatt, an 18-year-old ex–Miss Wichita, begged the actor Wallace Beery for help. "I'm tired of being mauled," she told him. Beery rushed her from the premises and "socked a couple of men" in the process.

Patricia Douglas had no such luck. Spurned by a nobody who, he presumed, was there for his pleasure, David Ross decided to retaliate. "He and another man held me down," she says, shuddering. "One pinched my nose so I'd have to open my mouth to breathe. Then they poured a whole glassful of scotch *and* champagne down my throat. Oh, I fought! But they thought it was funny. I remember a lot of laughter." As soon as her tormentors released her, Douglas fled to the washroom and threw up.

Still woozy, she stepped outside the banquet hall to get some air. Before her lay a freshly tilled field, covered with studio Ford sedans; from behind, a hand clamped over her mouth. "Make a sound," hissed David Ross in her ear, "and you'll never breathe again." Ross dragged her to a parked car and pinned her onto the backseat. "I'm going to *destroy* you," he boasted. When Douglas started to black out, he slapped her with the back of his hand and snapped, "Cooperate! I want you *awake*." At approximately 11:30 p.m.—almost seven hours after the dancers' arrival at the ranch—parking attendant Clement Soth heard screams and then saw Douglas staggering toward him. "My god," she moaned, her eyes swollen shut. "Isn't anything sacred around here?" As Soth approached, he saw David Ross run away.

A hysterical Douglas was taken to Culver City Community Hospital, across the street from MGM, where she vomited again. Since childhood, Douglas says, she had not undressed "around *anyone,* not even my mother." Intensely modest, she now suffered more torture: "I was given a cold-water douche. *Then* the doctor examined me. It's no surprise he didn't find anything. The douche had removed all evidence." Dr. Edward Lindquist, who treated Douglas, co-owned the hospital, and his practice was largely dependent on MGM. "For us, he was 'the family doctor,'" one old studio employee explains. A botched exam gave Lindquist room to equivocate. He claimed that while he could not prove his point, he believed there had been no intercourse.

Douglas was driven home in a studio car. Despite the presence at the Wild West party of 11 officers from four different police departments (California, Los Angeles, Culver City, and MGM)—one of whom, Culver City motorcycle cop Tom Lindsay, accompanied Douglas to the hospital—no crime-scene report was ever filed. Douglas was in a state of collapse for 14 hours. When she awoke, she recalls, "I was *so sore* down there, and my face was still swollen." She did not seek medical aid. "I would've been too embarrassed," she says. "Someone would've seen me naked."

Two days later she returned to the Roach Studios. "You ought to know what happened to me," Douglas said to the cashier, Maude Van Keuren, "so it doesn't happen to anyone else." Instead of receiving sympathy and compassion, Douglas was handed her $7.50, just like everyone else, as if her nightmare had been a bona fide movie call.

Another victim might have exploited the cover-up for advancement, demanding hush money or an ironclad contract. Douglas had no desire for either. "I wasn't trying to get anything," she insists. "I just wanted somebody to *believe* me." But she heard nothing from MGM, and her rapist returned to Chicago scot-free. Douglas's anger led her to make a momentous decision. Chaperoned by her mortified mother—"I don't remember any words of comfort from her, no 'Too bad this happened to you,' *nothing*"—Douglas appeared at the Los Angeles County district attorney's office to swear a complaint against David Ross. Since Douglas was still a minor, Mildred Mitchell signed the document as a court-appointed guardian.

In an era that branded rape victims as damaged goods, the Douglas complaint was unique and historic. No woman had ever dared to link a sexual assault to a Hollywood film studio, especially the almighty MGM. Even if a victim were to win her case in court, the stigma would wreck her name and her career. Patricia Douglas was undaunted. "I guess the Irish in me came out," she says. "You knew you'd be blackballed. Me, I didn't care. I just wanted to be vindicated, to hear someone say, 'You can't *do* that to a woman.'" If she imagined the D.A. to be that special someone, Douglas could not have been more mistaken. Six months earlier, Buron Fitts had been elected to a third term in spite of an indictment for perjury in a rape case involving a 16-year-old girl (his acquittal caused a furor). Fitts counted Louis B. Mayer as a close friend; MGM had been the top contributor to his campaign. "There was a strong bond between them," concedes Fitts's daughter today.

Budd Schulberg is much more blunt. "Buron Fitts was completely in the pocket of the producers," says the son of Mayer's former partner B. P. Schulberg and the Oscar-winning screenwriter of *On the Waterfront,* his own rallying cry against organized corruption. "The power MGM had is unimaginable today. They owned *everyone*—the D.A., the L.A.P.D. They *ran* this place."

Patricia Douglas trusted the system and waited. Weeks passed without any word from Fitts. Most women would have given up, but Douglas was quickly proving to be unlike most women. She sought advice from a Mob-connected acquaintance ("He looked just like James Gandolfini"), who contacted attorney William J. F. Brown. Described by his son, Kelly, as "a larger-than-life character, the Johnnie Cochran of his day," Brown wore double-breasted suits, drove custom Packards, and indulged in controversial but effective courtroom theatrics. When his ex-wife shot her next husband four times, Brown's impassioned appeal saved her from the gallows. "He always went for the underdog," says Kelly Brown, "and took cases no one else would touch." After offering to represent Douglas pro bono, Brown fired off an ultimatum to Fitts: either the D.A.'s office would investigate his client's complaint or she would share it with the press.

Fitts dismissed the threat as a bluff, but once again he was underestimating Patricia Douglas.

Probe of wild film party pressed, headlined the William Randolph Hearst–owned *L.A. Examiner* on June 4, 1937. Douglas's sensational story pushed ahead of accounts of the Duke of Windsor and Wallis Simpson's wedding and Jean Harlow's mortal illness. Since "rape" was still ruled a four-letter word, reporters had to resort to prudish euphemisms: Douglas had been "attacked," "outraged," or "ravished" at a "studio orgy." In an ominous sign of MGM's clout, the studio went unnamed in the newspapers, which published not only Douglas's name and photo but also her home address.

The unidentified studio released a brief statement. "We have read with astonishment the alleged charges of the girl," it began. "It is difficult to make any real comment as to a situation which appears so impossible and as to which we know nothing."

Behind its gates, MGM was in a panic. Except for Paul Bern's bizarre suicide (two months after his 1932 wedding to Jean Harlow, the revered producer had stood nude before a full-length mirror and put a .38 to his temple), the studio had managed to steer clear of scandal. Now a nobody had MGM at her mercy, for, even if her rape charge could be refuted, Douglas's disclosure of a "stag affair" costing $35,000 ($440,000 today), with free-flowing liquor and teenage girls, would not only horrify the stockholders of Loews Inc., the corporate parent of MGM, but also tarnish both the studio's squeaky-clean image and the moral sanctity of Louis B. Mayer himself.

So began a blame-the-victim smear campaign unparalleled in Hollywood to this day. Operatives of the Pinkerton Detective Agency, the nation's oldest and largest security-services company, were deployed to track down every girl on the "guest list" and strong-arm her into toeing the party line. In studio-sponsored interviews, 19-year-old Virginia Lee assured reporters that the alleged orgy was actually "a jolly affair, with lots of good clean fun."

Grace Downs, a bottle blonde from Pittsburgh, portrayed Douglas as an "unrefined" lush who had swigged scotch "from a quart bottle" all night. Sugar Geise, a 27-year-old chorine whose stage mother socialized with Buron Fitts, described a prior sighting of Douglas "passed out" in the Knickerbocker Hotel bar. "Anyone who knew me knew I didn't drink," counters an indignant Douglas. "And since when is getting raped 'good clean fun'?"

Pinkerton detectives also shadowed Douglas in order to dig up dirt. "Douglas must have attempted to proposition men," read an internal Roach Studios memo. "Many of them must have turned her down but can testify to her solicitation." When the Pinkerton men returned with the truth—that before her rape Douglas had been a teetotaling virgin—studio efforts to besmirch her grew desperate, especially after Dr. Wirt Dakin, a urologist who had previously treated a cyst on Douglas's bladder, stood firm and declined a request from Hal Roach himself to re-diagnose it as a genital urinary infection, a discreet term at the time for gonorrhea. Meanwhile, in the face of scandal, Douglas was abandoned by all her celebrity pals. "My name was mud, and they couldn't get dirty," she says without rancor. "They had their careers to think about."

Front-page coverage of the Wild West party intensified when Buron Fitts showed Douglas photos of two dozen MGM salesmen and she—as the D.A. reluctantly told reporters—"without hesitation" identified David Ross. "That's the man," said Douglas. "I can never forget that face." Left with no choice but to convene a grand jury, Fitts summoned Ross (who called the charge against him "absurd" and "ridiculous") from Chicago on an overnight flight. Upon landing, Ross went into immediate conference with Mendel Silberberg, Louis B. Mayer's personal attorney.

Held in the Los Angeles Hall of Justice on June 16, 1937, the grand-jury hearing traumatized Douglas all over again. Of the 120 dancers present at the party, only 2, Ginger Wyatt (whose rescue by Wallace Beery was now denied in the actor's MGM-scripted statement) and Paula Bromley, dared to testify on her behalf. Forced to recount her rape in detail, Douglas had to watch Lester Roth, a Silberberg law partner representing Ross, point at her with withering scorn and say to the jurors, "*Look* at her. Who would want *her?*" Exiting the courtroom, Douglas found herself face-to-face with her rapist. She froze. He calmly smoked a cigarette as photographers shoved them together, shouting to Douglas, "Look at Mr. Ross!"

"I can't. I just *can't,*" she cried, and ran down the hall to a window. "I was going to jump through the glass," she confesses. "To get away from everything and everybody ... so I couldn't be hurt anymore." Douglas was restrained by her mother and her lawyer as flashbulbs popped. Wire services picked up the photos, which ran nationwide the next day. Back in the grand-jury room, Lester Roth called Clement Soth, the parking attendant who had discovered Douglas. Soth had originally said that he had seen David Ross flee the scene, but now he recanted that crucial detail. "The man was much thinner," Soth said under oath. "Mr. Ross's face is fat." When I contacted Soth's daughters, they confirmed that, in exchange for their father's perjury, MGM offered him "any job he wanted." Soth joined the studio "family" as a driver and remained there for the rest of his life.

The grand jury did not indict David Ross.
Douglas's oppressors considered the case closed, but again they had misjudged her. A month later, with her mother still acting as guardian, Douglas filed suit in Los Angeles County Superior Court against David Ross, Eddie Mannix, Hal Roach, casting assistant Vincent Conniff, and "John Doe One To Fifty" for their "unlawful conspiracy to defile, debauch, and seduce" her and other dancers "for the immoral and sensual gratification of male guests." She asked for $500,000 in damages.

This salvo made even more headlines. Although MGM issued no public statement, in private memos the studio lawyers nicknamed Douglas "our girlfriend," and they rewarded perjurers with jobs. "I just had another talk with [bit player and gossipmonger] Bobby Tracy, one of our star witnesses in the Douglas case," reported Roach Studios attorney Victor Ford Collins to general manager S. S. Van Keuren. "He seems badly in need of work, and was very much in the hopes that somebody could phone Mr. Mannix direct about him getting a few days at M-G-M.... It is highly imperative that we keep these people in good humor, and get them some kind of work. May I again say—it is really important!" It certainly was: the studio had just been notified by its insurer that it would be wholly liable for any damages awarded to Douglas. This made MGM lawyers stall the proceedings, and, although David Ross was the main defendant, process servers never contacted him. Finally, on February 9, 1938, a superior-court judge dismissed the case.

Douglas seemed to have exhausted all options, yet just 24 hours after the judge's dismissal—again with her mother as guardian—she filed an identical suit in U.S. District Court. In an apparent legal first, a female plaintiff made rape a federal case, based on its violation of her civil rights.

The timing of Douglas's suit was most unfortunate for Mayer and Mannix. By then, as movie-theater attendance hit 85 million people per week—two-thirds of the entire U.S. population—and MGM remained first in grosses, Mayer's annual income had soared to $1.2 million, making him the highest-paid executive in the United States. Only three weeks earlier, he and Mannix had signed new five-year contracts with Loews Inc. that guaranteed them both a percentage of MGM profits. A federal rape case would jeopardize their jobs. Patricia Douglas had to be stopped.

The best means to this end was her press-hungry attorney, and here MGM had a huge stroke of luck. Enraged by Buron Fitts's bungling of the Douglas case (the "subservient" D.A. had allowed rape "without reprisals to the rapers"), William J. F. Brown had vowed to challenge his nemesis in the next election. And since no campaign could be won by a candidate who was in litigation with MGM, the largest employer in L.A. County, Brown sacrificed Douglas to his political race, failing to appear in court three consecutive times, until a federal judge finally dismissed the case "for want of prosecution." Since counsel for the defendants also skipped each hearing, Brown appears to have illegally apprised MGM of his plan.

Douglas had been betrayed yet again, this time by her lawyer and, worse yet, her mother. As court-appointed guardian to a minor, Mildred Mitchell had sworn to protect her charge's best interests; had she done so by exposing Brown's brazen malpractice, another attorney could have taken the case. Instead, she ignored the flagrant misconduct of Brown. Six decades later, one question lingers: Were Douglas's lawyer and mother bought off? No smoking gun survives to confirm it, but, if so, any ill-gotten gains became losses: Fitts trounced Brown in the 1940 primary election, and Mildred Mitchell married an alcoholic gambler who blew through her life savings and then disappeared.

Douglas's quest had been doomed from the start. "I never sued about money," she stresses. "That's not me. And it wasn't for glory; it was just to make them *stop having those parties*.... And, besides, money can't cure a broken heart." Before Eddie Mannix died in 1963—six years after Louis B. Mayer succumbed to leukemia, 10 months after David Ross was ravaged by rectal cancer, and a decade before the gunshot suicide of Buron Fitts—he was asked what ever became of "that girlie" who took on MGM. "We had her killed," Mannix allegedly retorted. Though in hindsight his meaning was metaphorical, the insinuation remains chillingly clear: post–Patricia Douglas, no rape case on record would implicate MGM. And so successfully did the studio expunge its Wild West party from history that, though it was national news at the time, not a single published source since that I could find—on MGM, Mayer, Mannix, Hal Roach, or Hollywood—mentions the once notorious event.

A one-reel short commemorating the convention (complete with Mayer announcing the festivities, star cameos, and a glimpse of delegate-rapist David Ross), which MGM shelved in the ensuing scandal, now sits in a studio film vault, its historical importance unrealized. After requesting a screening (without revealing my motive), I stared slack-jawed at the on-camera, incontrovertible proof—Mayer pimping starlets, conventioneers consorting with Harlow and Gable, a brazen plug for the Wild West party. An archivist on duty informed me, "Only useful stuff here's the candid star footage. The rest of it has no value at all."

A similar fate befell Patricia Douglas. A page-one story and a legal pioneer in 1937, "that girlie" was never heard from again.'It ruined my life. It absolutely *ruined my life,*" says Douglas. She is 86 and a great-grandmother, housebound by glaucoma, emphysema, and fear. "They put me through such misery," she murmurs. "It took away all my confidence." She has not spoken of her rape since the case was dismissed. Until now, not even her family knew about it.

Douglas has agreed to go public again because she realizes this could be her last chance. "When I die, the truth dies with me, and that means those bastards win." Her need for vindication remains as strong today as it was back then. She can still feel that freshly tilled field underfoot moments before David Ross raped her, she says, adding, "And to this day I can't stomach the smell of scotch." Such sense memories come at a cost. After the dismissal of her federal case, she tells me, "I went from 'Little Miss Innocent' to a tramp. I did it to demean myself. I was worthless, a 'fallen woman.'" Douglas married three times in five years, and two of her husbands were exposed as bigamists. "All washed up with fellas" at 37, she has gone without relationships or sex ever since. "I've never been in love," she states flatly. "And I've never had an orgasm. I was frigid."

Douglas fled Hollywood to settle first in Bakersfield, a desert town she terms "hotter than hell," and later in Las Vegas, where she subsists on Social Security with a bullterrier named Magdalene. She likes to be called Patsy now, and won't even answer to Patricia. All her recollections of herself are laced with self-laceration: she says she was "naïve," "stupid," "a lousy mother," "a walking zombie who glided through life." And because she never shared her deepest secret, which was also the defining event in her life, Douglas can say with confidence, "There's nobody in this world who really knows me."

In 1937, burying her past for self-preservation made sense. But even now, in this Oprah era of confession as catharsis, Douglas still lives under self-imposed house arrest, oblivious to her historic status. "What was it I accomplished?" she wonders. "What's so special about my story?"

When I tell her what I've turned up, including corroboration from fellow Wild West–party girls and an apology from the children of Clement Soth, whose perjury helped exonerate David Ross, the truth begins to dawn on Douglas. "Pretty gutsy, wasn't I?" she says.

"Before you found me," she confides during one of our many long conversations, "I was getting ready to die. I'd buy less food; I wasn't planning to be around long. Now I don't want to go. Now I have something to live for. And for the first time I'm *proud* of myself."

The lion raped, but Patricia Douglas was—and still is—the mouse that roared. Her heroic cry was once cruelly silenced; 66 years later, the last word is hers, stated David Stenn.

Mary Astor's Diary: Sex and lust...lovers and multiple orgasms...

Photo: This picture from the 1936 trial over the custody of Marilyn Astor Thorpe. Mary Astor charged that her ex-husband, Franklyn, wasn't a fit parent (he allegedly had women spend the night while his daughter was in his custody and was supposedly abusive to the girl) and he made similar accusations; citing passages in her diary describing her affair with playwright George S. Kaufman. From left, Attorney Joseph Anderson, Franklyn Thorpe, attorney Ethel M. Pepin (that's the lady in the hat), attorney A.P. Michael Narlian, attorney Roland Rich Woolley and Mary Astor. Ruth Chatterton is in the audience between Thorpe and Pepin.

In Mary Astor's diary, she had a list of her lovers, including the principal player, George Kaufman, and Gene Fowler, who was at the top of the list of her skilled lovers, and "Fuckers"; a term, Astor used in her diary. Allegedly, 16 lovers featured in the diary, and largely detailed host sex scenes and encounters were described. Astor's diary was so erotic, and so extremely sexually charged, which made the judge presiding over her trial, confiscate the diary, and later ordered to be incinerated. Astor's diary earned her the infamous reputation of being "The greatest nympho-courtesan since Madame Pompadour."

Juicy erotic excerpts from Astor's diary describing her extramarital affairs and love-making. In her own words and writing:

- "Sexually I was out of control."
- "Ah desert night with George's body plunging into mine, naked under the stars..."
- "We played kneessies during the first two acts, my hand wasn't in my own lap during the third...It's been years since I've felt up a man in public, but I just got carried away..."

- "His (George Kaufmann) powers of recuperation are amazing, and we made love all night long...and we shared our fourth climax at dawn..."
- "He went down on me, and I exploded..."
- "Was any woman ever happier? It seems that George is just hard all the time...I don't see how he does it, he is perfect."
- "He tore out of his pajama and I never was undressed by anyone so fast in all my life."
- "It was wonderful to fuck the entire sweet afternoon away...I left about 6 o'clock."

Her most famous sexual partners were (To name a few):
1. John Barrymore
2. Humphrey Bogart
3. Gordon Wheelock
4. Manuel Campo
5. George Kaufman
6. Gene Fowler

One would assume that these revelations would destroy an actress' career, but they did not, far from it. Au contraire mon cher ami, au contraire, Mary Astor scored high on the chart of fame and success. She became one of Hollywood's most bankable stars after the scandal. C'est la vie, Hollywood has a double-standard!

Previously, Mary Astor had many many steamy sexual affairs with Hollywood's leading men, like Humphrey Bogart, and the sex-maniac John Barrymore who deflored her at the age of 17 in his dressing room. The decadent Barrymore taught her how to please a man at multiple levels. He told his friends how fascinated he was with her "sexual naivete." But Astor grew up to become an expert in sex and extra-marrital affairs. But her husband, Dr. Franklyn Thorpe was not a saint either. He fooled around quite a bit; his favorite dish was young and stupid starlets like Norma Taylor, and his greatest satisfaction came from threesome with the "Bathing Beauties", and Busby Berkeley showgirls, and those who were called "Extras", then, another word for Hollywood harem and beautiful girls hired by studios for sexual acts and orgies scenes; hores! The master of these orgies ceremonies was none but Erich von Stroheim.

(Author's note: I wrote at length about von Stroheim's orgies in book 2: "Hollywood's Most Horrible People, Stars, Times, and Scandals: From The Stars Who Slept With Kennedy To Lavender Marriages And The Casting Couch."

*** *** ***

There was a rare opportunity for mass keyhole-peeking into the private lives of public figures when, in 1936, the personal diary of popular screen actress Mary Astor was used against her in a legal battle concerning custody of her daughter. In a courtroom drama with a script worthy of Hollywood, Astor and her ex-husband, Dr. Franklyn Thorpe, exchanged exposés in an attempt to prove each other unfit to raise a child. The doctor's major source of ammunition was a diary which had been kept by Astor from 1929 to 1934, containing many intimate portraits of her friends and lovers and recording events and hearsay of the film colony.

George Kaufman's headlines were more usually found in the drama reviews for plays like The *Band Wagon, Dinner at Eight, The Man Who Came to Dinner, Night at the Opera,* and others of the more than 60 he eventually wrote alone or with collaborators; or for first-run Broadway plays that he directed, like *My Sister Eileen, Front Page, Of Mice and Men,* and *Guys and Dolls.*

AFFAIR WITH PLAYWRIGHT ADMITTED BY MARY ASTOR

Actress Asserts Spouse Condoned; Judge Calls for Her Diary; Barrymore Subpoena Due

Associations with George S. Kaufman, which were condoned by her husband, Dr. Franklyn Thorpe, were admitted on the witness stand yesterday by Mary Astor, screen actress, in the sensational battle between mother and father for their 4-year-old child, Marilyn.

That, coupled with disclosure that most of the 200 pages of intimate secrets concerning Miss Astor's private life, written painstakingly in lavender ink by the actress in her diary, have mysteriously disappeared, was the principal evidence adduced at the close of yesterday's sessions of the trial.

SAYS MATE AWARE

That Dr. Thorpe was aware of this affair between the red-haired screen actress and the Broadway playwright six months before he filed suit for divorce, and that during those six months Mary Astor and Dr. Thorpe lived together as man and wife, was declared by Miss Astor under the cross-examination of Attorney Joseph Anderson.

"You know George Kaufman has nothing to do with this divorce," Miss Actor said she told her husband at the time he brought the divorce action. "You've known about him since last September (1934) and you've condoned it. Now you bring it up in order to threaten me and obtain the custody of my baby."

the actress said she knew her husband wanted to "shame" her.

At least a month before Dr. Thorpe is said to have threatened her, Miss Astor said she had consulted an attorney about a divorce.

"I did wish to be free from Dr. Thorpe because of his constant association with Lillian Miles," she blurted before Attorney Anderson could stop the witness.

But at that time she did not know that her former husband intended to put up a fight for baby Marilyn and name Kaufman in the action.

As for the divorce action, she repeated again and again that she had instructed her attorney to do exactly as Dr. Thorpe ordered.

CHARGES THREAT

"He said he would blacken my name," declared the actress, "plaster my name and that of my prominent friends over the front pages of every paper in the country, wreck and ruin my career as an actress. I told him it was a horrible thing to do and that, if he wrecked my career I wouldn't be able to earn money for my child's care— a thing which he can't or won't do."

The screen player was accompanied to court by Ruth Chatterton, also dressed in white, and by Miss

Headlines in the newspapers

213

Although married and sharing a close relationship with wife Bea, he maintained an apartment on 73rd Street for his many affairs. The Kaufmans were at the center of the sophisticated, always interesting people who met around a table at the Algonquin Hotel; who played croquet by special permit in Central Park; and whose parties introduced the young and hopeful to New York. It was to this sparkling atmosphere that a California-weary Mary Astor came in the summer of 1933. She had been working hard at her contract roles in the film capital. Her marriage of three years was ending. A friend suggested a New York spree to cheer her up, and George Kaufman as someone to show her around. She "fell like a ton of bricks" for George and found New York exhilarating-the theater; parties where Gershwin could be found previewing *Porgy and Bess*; new ideas exchanged by some of the country's most intelligent people. Mary Astor, one of Hollywood's most flawless beauties, was accepted without question. She had not yet won her Academy Award for the part of Sandra in *The Great Lie,* and was still to be kissed by Bogart as Brigid, the fascinating bad woman in *The Maltese Falcon.* She was most often walking through nothing roles in nothing films to fulfill her contract. Now she was offered a play, asked for ideas, treated for once, not as a product, but as a person. The romance continued when George visited Hollywood as scriptwriter or went to Palm Springs with collaborator Moss Hart to write a musical.

The newspaper version of the diary read: "Ah desert night-with George's body plunging into mine, naked under the stars..." Dr. Thorpe discovered the diary carelessly tossed in a drawer. Shortly afterward he visited his wife's lover, but was so incoherent that George was at a loss as to the real purpose of the doctor's visit. After warning Mary that her husband had discovered their 16-month relationship, he fled to his wife and New York. Bea Kaufman thought it would blow over. In 1935, the doctor sued Mary for a divorce. One of Mary's friends, hearing of the circumstances, suggested lawyer Roland R. Woolley, who accepted the case. Mary did not contest the divorce but filed a countersuit to prevent giving the legal custody of their daughter to Dr. Thorpe. The first press coverage appeared in the entertainment section. Soon, even the conservative New York Times acknowledged the impact of the story. The courtroom theme wandered from child neglect to bedroom habits, as Dr. Thorpe's penchant for young blond actresses and Mary Astor's eventful past were explored and distorted. Readers were delighted to hear that John Barrymore was to be summoned. The man who had been 17-year-old Mary Astor's first lover was by this time undone by alcoholism. He had retreated to the quiet of a sanitarium.

The scandal touched other prominent figures-most often with only the slightest excuse. The diary was at the core of the accusations and was the cause of the innuendos. Suddenly, after attempting to keep the diary out of court since the trial began, Woolley called for it to prove that its contents were harmless. A group including Goldwyn, Thalberg, Warner, Cohn, Mayer, and other industry leaders asked the actress to keep the book out of court. They quoted $12 million as the amount tied up in names involved in the diary. If these stars were dragged into the scandal, their films could be banned from distribution by the censors. Mary Astor refused. Sam Goldwyn, whose film *Dodsworth* stood to lose most surely, was encouraged to use the morality clause in the actress's contract to fire her. He didn't. "A mother fighting for her child....That's good!" he observed.

Lawyer Woolley knew that pages had been torn from Mary Astor's diary, and when it was brought into the courtroom, he was able to have it excluded as evidence because it was a "mutilated document." By that time, however, no one really needed the original diary. Finally, George S. Kaufman was subpoenaed to appear in court. He didn't. A chase resulted through Beverly Hills backyards and all the way to Catalina Island, where Kaufman had fled on Irving Thalberg's yacht.

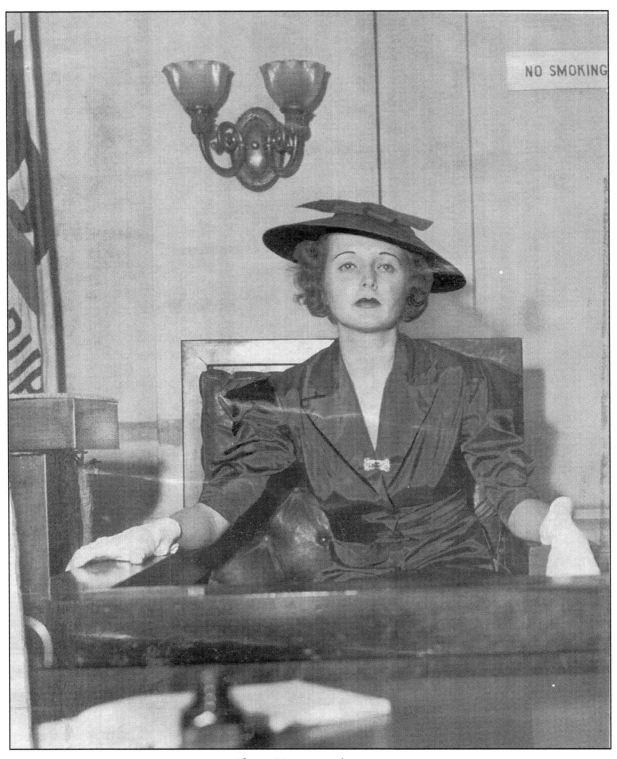

Photo: Mary Astor in court.

Photo: Mary Astor, Roland Richard Woolley and Ruth Chatterton.

Versions differ: Either Moss Hart or the Marx brothers anticked for the bailiffs while Kaufman escaped out the back door; or he was smuggled to New York either in the guise of an English naval officer-thanks to a studio costume department-or wrapped mummy-like in bandages. The press loved it. Finally the story hit the front pages of The New York Times. A national event, just like the New Deal and the drought: "Warrant out for Kaufman." The tolerance of the court was worn very thin. After a public rebuke to both lawyers, Judge Goodwin Knight-soon to be elected governor of California-called for an early settlement. With the strong encouragement of the film industry, the case was decided. Custody was to be split between Mary Astor for nine months, Franklyn Thorpe for three. A distraught Kaufman finally emerged in New York. "I do not keep a diary," he apologized to the press. (Source: David Wallechinsky & Irving Wallace) But Mary Astor was a loving and a generous woman, with a heart made out of gold. Mary Astor might be one of the first child stars to be taken advantage of by her parents. When she was only 14, she started making movies with some big name people, including John Barrymore, and earned $500 a week. She moved from Paramount to Warner Brothers to Fox, who increased her salary to $3,750 a week. Her parents bought a mansion in the Hollywood Hills and lived the good life on Mary's money. She escaped her parents when she married Kenneth Hawks in 1928, but the happiness wouldn't last long: he was in a fatal plane crash in 1930, just about the time her movie career started going under because her voice didn't translate well to "talkies". She had a nervous breakdown and ended up marrying the doctor who attended to her. By 1933, she was pretty broke and had to get the Motion Picture Relief Fund to pay her bills. Her parents didn't have much sympathy – they sued her in 1934 for more financial support. She testified that all of her money had gone directly to their bank accounts even after her first marriage. It wasn't until Hawks died that Mary decided she needed to look out for herself. She did, however, give them the home that they had purchased with her earnings. She also gave them $1,000 per month. When she hit hard times in '33, she told her parents she couldn't afford to support them unless they moved to a smaller house – the house they lived in was bigger and more expensive than the one Mary lived in with her family.

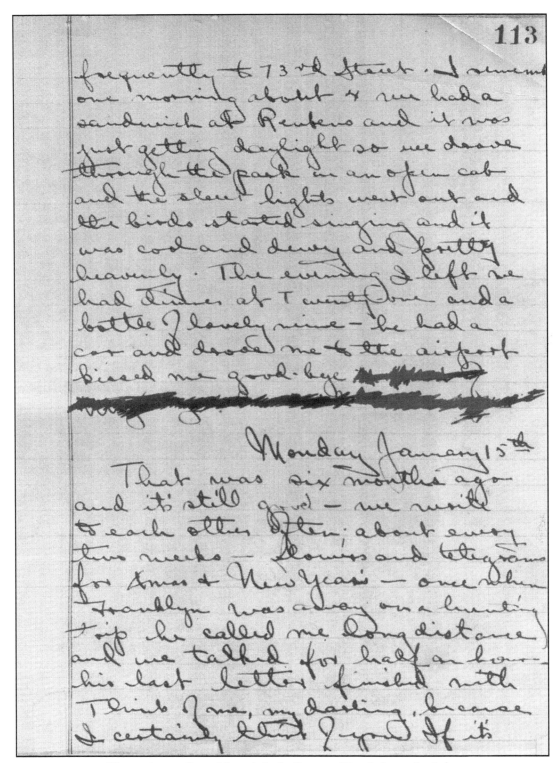

Photo: A page from Mary Astor's diary, written in lavender ink.

She also offered them $100 a month, plus food and utilities, but they refused to leave the mansion. Mary said in her memoirs that in 1947 she sat with her delirious mother on her deathbed in the hospital. Because of dementia, her mother spent hours complaining to Mary about her selfish, horrible daughter Lucile (Mary's real name). Mary read her mother's diaries after she died and said she was surprised to know how much her own mother hated he, reported Lacy Conradt.

The Charlie Chaplin and Joan Barry Affair--1943

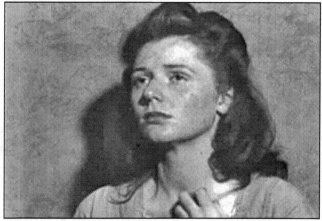

Photo, left: Fingerprinting Charlie Chaplin, like a criminal. Right, femme fatale, Joan Barry.

Hedda Hopper was working on her popular Hollywood gossip column when an excited red-haired young woman rushed into the office.

She said that her name was Joan Barry, that she was pregnant, and that the father of her unborn child was 54-year-old millionaire movie star Charlie Chaplin. Hedda might well have whooped for joy.

It was 1943.

People were still titillated by the Hollywood marriage-divorce-remarriage cycle. As for documented fornication, that was hot stuff.

Hedda understood this culture perfectly. She had made a career of pandering to it, trading in innuendos just this side of libel--"At the Brown Derby last night, what happily married leading man was snuggling up to?" So a real live bouncing baby on the way was a scoop. Moreover, Hedda Hopper hated Chaplin. Already long at the top, he did not need her. And he had never clowned or groveled--every gossip columnist's price for a good press.

He also had a long history of relationships with young girls (gossip writing was as priggishly moralistic as it was leering); and he was emotionally sympathetic to a number of left-wing causes. Like most other successful gossip columnists of the time, Hedda was a red-baiter. She printed the story and thus launched a series of trials which were not over until 1946, and which led to an extended estrangement between the U.S. and its greatest film comedian.

Chaplin admitted that he had been intimate with Joan Barry. Indeed, at 22, she was one of the eldest in a long list of his tender-aged Hollywood protegées. Like Errol Flynn, he had a weakness for teenagers. Twice, in 1918 and 1924, he had married 16-year-olds just a step ahead of statutory rape charges. During the Barry fracas, he wed Oona O'Neill, then 18. Joan, a pretty but by no means stunning starlet, had come into his life in June, 1941. This was in the wake of Chaplin's divorce from Paulette Goddard, and it was no cooing love match. Charlie and Joan were not seen together. The affair was totally unpublic until Hedda Hopper's expost facto "exclusive." It sounded like the familiar Hollywood flesh-market story: Joan trading her favors for a teeth-capping job, acting lessons, and the promise of a movie role; Charlie able and happy to pick up the bills. It is impossible to say whether the two were still having intercourse late enough to conceive the child which was born on Oct. 3, 1943.

Photo: Oona Chaplin

Chaplin claimed they had gone their separate ways more than a year before. Joan insisted otherwise. She related a tantalizing incident in which she had forced her way into Chaplin's posh house, held a gun on him, and so aroused both of them that they had promptly gone to bed together. This was around Christmas, 1942, an inauspicious date.

Even more damaging: Joan said that in October, 1942, she had gone to New York City at Chaplin's expense, had been followed by him, and had had relations with him in his hotel room. This meant that Chaplin could be prosecuted under the Mann Act, a federal law which made it a serious crime (up to 25 years in prison and a fine of $25,000) to transport a female across a state line for immoral purposes. Originally aimed at organized prostitution ("white slavery"), the Mann Act was also used as a sort of "interstate intercourse act," a way of prosecuting people the authorities wanted to "get" for some other, not necessarily criminal reason. With public opinion whipped up by the gossip columnists, Chaplin became such a person. He was prosecuted in federal criminal court as well as sued for child support in a paternity case.

In the Mann Act trial, Chaplin was acquitted. His lawyer was Jerry Giesler, already famous for defending Errol Flynn in similar circumstances. Among other convincing arguments, Giesler scored points with his remark that Chaplin had no need to spirit Miss Barry from California to New York City for sex; he could have had it with her in Los Angeles "for as little as twenty-five cents carfare." Further, in a real-life Perry Mason-style defense, Giesler all but put the finger on a more likely sugar daddy, oil tycoon Jean Paul Getty. Although the judge prevented Giesler from pursuing the point, it looked very much as if Getty had financed Barry's eastern swing as well as a Mexican trip or two.

The paternity case ended less happily for Chaplin. Assuming it was routine, he dismissed Giesler and relied on his regular, less expensive attorney. This was a mistake. Giesler may have been more ham than legalist, but he was exactly what was called for. The anti-Chaplin atmosphere was so intense that Charlie was declared the father of the infant and ordered to pay substantial support despite a blood test showing that his fatherhood was scientifically impossible. Chaplin had in effect been found guilty of behavior offensive to conventional morality. As Joan Barry's lawyer put it in his summing-up: "There has been no one to stop Chaplin in his lecherous conduct all these years--except you. Wives and mothers all over the country are watching to see you stop him dead in his tracks. You'll sleep well the night you give this baby a name--the night you show him [Chaplin] the law means him as well as the bums on Skid Row." Chaplin's film career was finished. Monsieur Verdoux (1947) was widely boycotted, and it flopped commercially. Limelight (1952) was well received by the critics but failed to appeal to the mass audience which had made the Little Tramp the best-known and best-loved character in the history of the cinema. In September of 1952, Chaplin left on the Queen Elizabeth for a European vacation. Almost as soon as the ship was out of American waters, the U.S. attorney general rescinded Chaplin's reentry permit (Charlie was a British subject), and virtually no one but a few leftists, liberals, and film buffs protested. Chaplin settled in Switzerland, bitter but mostly silent about the country which, if it had given him much, had also taken much. Only in 1972, when he was over 80 years old, did Chaplin return to receive Hollywood's homage and the overt acceptance of the American public. His death in 1977 prompted a widespread display of respect and affection. Joan Barry had been committed as a schizophrenic to a California state hospital back in 1953. Of the innocent cause of it all, the child legally named Carol Ann Chaplin, nothing is known, as it was reported in People's Almanach; David Wallechinsky & Irving Wallace.

Joan Barry was a convicted felon

When she hopped the Santa Fe Limited for the West Coast after graduating from high school in 1938, Joan Barry (born Mary Louise Gribble) was a would-be actress with no professional acting experience or training. An impulsive, temperamental redhead with a voluptuous figure, the flamboyant 18-year-old planned to take Hollywood by storm. Instead, while struggling to support herself by waiting tables, she was arrested twice by the LAPD for upgrading her wardrobe by shoplifting dresses from swanky department stores. In search of a less risky way to outfit herself, she became the mistress of a wealthy and prominent Los Angeles business man who paid the rent and kept her in style for the following two years.

During the zig-zag course of psychologically unstable Barry's check-bouncing, pill-popping, wrist-slashing, binge-drinking, emotional blackmailing progression from harlot to starlet, she briefly became the luxuriously pampered playmate of the richest oilman in America, John Paul Getty. Finally, in June 1941, she signed a contract to become the $75/week salaried protégé of the wealthiest star in Hollywood, Charlie Chaplin, after making a successful screen test for the Chaplin Studio. (Getty had given her a Cadillac; Chaplin gave her a fur coat).

At the time, 52-year-old Chaplin signed Barry to the renewable six-month studio contract complete with acting lessons at the classy Max Rheinhardt School, and swanky Beverly Hills dentistry to cap her teeth—he considered her a gifted and promising actress. Looking back with regret twenty-five years later, the dignified septuagenarian awkwardly alluded to other characteristics of the young starlet that had also caught his eye. "Miss Barry was a big handsome woman of twenty-two, well built, with upper regional domes immensely expansive which...evoked my libidinous curiosity," he stiffly recalled in *My Autobiography*.

The basis for Chaplin's hindsight chagrin over his breast fixation was that his torrid love affair with this histrionic drama queen with a borderline personality disorder (she employed theatrical temper tantrums, suicide gestures and pistol-packing threats of violence to get her way) turned out to be an even more disastrous personal fiasco than his marriage to Lita Grey had been. The Grey affair had cost him a tidy sum and some unwelcome publicity (which later inspired his film *The Circus)* and then blew over. But the public relations aftermath of the tawdry Barry affair eventually lost him the good will of the American people and resulted in his permanent political exile—as well as the immediate public rejection of his very next film, *Monsieur Verdoux*. Not surprisingly, *Monsieur Verdoux* was a self-referential black comedy about the sensational public trial and execution of a lady-killer.

Chaplin based his fictional character Henri Verdoux on Henri Landru, a cold blooded Parisian blue beard who married and murdered ten women for profit. But the trial scenes in this movie echoed Chaplin's time in the court room with Joan Barry. His first trial was criminal. The second two were civil. A crass seductress who lacked nuance, primitive Joan Barry was not in the class of the seductresses of his childhood imagination, Josephine de Beauharnais, Lillie Langtry or Nell Gwyn.

Her manipulative and explosive emotional outbursts undoubtedly provoked simmering feelings of murderous rage in many of her emotionally exasperated and exhausted former patrons and admirers over the years, including Charlie. Chaplin was of course, the only one of her former lovers in an artistic position to sublimate creatively the feelings Joan provoked by filming a witty, sardonic, semi-autobiographical black comedy about the trials and tribulations of a cold-blooded lady-killer (which he told sympathetically from the killer's point of view). Either despite or because of Joan Barry's borderline personality disorder, she exerted an extraordinary attraction over Chaplin—the irrational basis of which he surely did not fully understand.

Although he was in the dark about why he found this erratic young woman so fascinating and alluring, she probably reminded him unconsciously of that other status-seeking, slightly crazy, grasping and materialistic, emotionally flamboyant *femme fatale*-actress, Lillie Harley. "When I behaved myself he was bored," Barry recalled.

FBI's J. Edgar Hoover personally authorized Chaplin's frivolous prosecution

The most striking similarity between Chaplin's actress mistress and his actress mother was their shared history of mental illness. In Barry's case, she would later be hospitalized in a California state mental hospital and diagnosed with schizophrenia (in the 1950s). The FBI exploited this already borderline psychotic young woman years earlier as their prize witness and poster child in a cynically trumped-up white slavery case whose covert agenda was to neuter Chaplin politically for his outspoken support of the Soviet Union during World War II.

But their own FOIA files clearly indicate that the L.A. Bureau agents investigating the case alerted the home office even then that slightly crazy Joan Barry was an unreliable witness. The priceless opportunity, however, that their carefully orchestrated courtroom media circus provided to discredit Chaplin politically (with a lurid photo as he was finger-printed like a common criminal spread gratis across the front pages of the nation's newspapers) was more than worth the time and money J. Edgar Hoover spent when he personally authorized Chaplin's frivolous prosecution on lurid charges of transporting a young woman across state lines for immoral purposes. The graphic "pimp shot" of Charlie even made "Picture of the Week" in the February 28, 1944 issue of *Life* magazine. At the time, Chaplin actually was a happily married man and expectant father (having wed Oona O'Neill on June 16, 1943). Ironically, Joan Barry's patently obvious emotional instability also seemed to be the unconscious inspiration for which Chaplin had been searching, for an uncompleted film project, *Shadow and Substance*.

Contrary to the Hollywood grapevine, Charlie did not place Joan under contract simply to sleep with her. Barry's screen test had revealed that apart from her nasal New York accent, which Chaplin planned to correct with elocution lessons, she had a remarkable ability to project convincingly his protagonist in that film, a spiritual young woman who has visions of the Virgin Mary, communicates directly with her namesake Saint Brigid, and experiences a deeply personal connection to the Saviour.

If Joan Barry's temperament had much in common with Lillie Harley's; Chaplin's martyr-like screen heroine in Shadow and Substance, Brigid, evoked powerfully Hannah Chaplin's own deep spiritual connection to Jesus Christ, even before Hannah lost her mind and began to experience religious visions during her floridly psychotic episodes at the Cane Hill lunatic asylum. But the uncanny similarities between Joan Barry's instability, and Chaplin's childhood memories of his mother's, did not end there. Returning to court after his white slavery acquittal for a series of civil trials over the hotly disputed paternity of Joan Barry's out-of-wedlock child, Chaplin found himself in his father's shoes. Like Charlie Chaplin Sr. who protested bitterly in a London courtroom the unfairness of his being obliged legally to financially support a child who was not his biologically (Sydney Chaplin), Chaplin soon found himself in a Los Angeles courtroom protesting an identical injustice. Despite the fact that scientifically incontrovertible but legally inadmissible blood group testing evidence conclusively demonstrated that the child in question could not have been his, Chaplin lost this jury trial (eleven to one) and, like his father before him, was instructed to pony up.

Vilified by the American press: While he felt as morally outraged as Charlie Sr. had in the face of that earlier miscarriage of justice, Chaplin paid the child support. But he abandoned the *Shadow and Substance* project which glorified and idealized a religious martyr figure like his mother and started instead to work on his courtroom drama, *Monsieur Verdoux* , which bitterly satirized the Kafkaesque legal injustices he and his father had suffered. Conceived as an ironic comic indictment of modern capitalist society, which had driven Henri Verdoux into his financially motivated career as a lady-killer, Chaplin's film failed to win the sympathy of American moviegoers for his new martyr villain/hero, whose cynical morality, urbane manners and fastidious dress seemed the antithesis of the lovable *Little Tramp*, whom everyone had seen as a chivalrous rescuer of damaged and fallen women). Having been vilified by the American press as an arrogant symbol of elitist wealth and privilege, and made to look like an unfeeling monster in his relationships with women throughout the course of the Barry trials, Chaplin was unable to win back the enormous public sympathy which he had previously enjoyed (and mistakenly assumed he could take for granted). Not only did *Monsieur Verdoux* flop at the box office, but two months after its release an irate Republican congressman in the House of Representatives called for his deportation by the Truman administration. Charlie Chaplin, he declared, was un-American, reported Stephen Weissman.

The Bergman-Rossellini Affair—1950: On March 14, 1950, Sen. Edwin C. Johnson of Colorado took to the floor of the U.S. Senate and delivered an extraordinary and impassioned harangue. Extraordinary, for in this instance the good senator wasn't rallying against the red peril or his political rivals, but against a movie actress. The actress was Ingrid Bergman, and during Johnson's blistering tirade she was labeled a "free-love cultist" and a "powerful influence for evil." The unusual episode was typical of heated public reaction in 1950. For Ingrid Bergman, Hollywood's favorite embodiment of saintliness and virtue, had given birth on Feb. 2 to Renato Roberto Gisuto Giuseppe Rossellini. Little "Robertino" had been conceived, not in sunny Hollywood, but in far-off Italy, and the child's illustrious father wasn't Ingrid's husband, Dr. Peter Lindstrom, but Italian film director Roberto Rossellini. Senator Johnson wasn't alone in his righteous wrath. Hell hath no fury like a public scorned, and Bergman and her lover Rossellini had quite literally managed to inflame their public with a passion. Sermons rang from pulpits, women's clubs sniffed through their blue noses, and pickets paraded around theaters showing Bergman films. Producers--already hurt by the infant television industry--cringed, and Hollywood moralists, led by gossip columnist Louella Parsons, raved in indignation at the adulterous activities of the virginal star of Joan of Arc and The Bells of St. Mary's. When idols fall, they land with a crash. The noise was still reverberating a week later when Bergman secured a quick Mexican divorce from Lindstrom and married Rossellini by proxy in Juarez. Mexico. The whole brouhaha had begun quietly enough with a letter.
Bergman, who had come to the U.S. from Sweden in 1939 to refilm her Swedish success Intermezzo for David O. Selznick, had allowed herself to be talked into a long-term contract.

Unhappy with her subsequent film roles and with no challenging roles in her immediate future, she had let her contract lapse and had begun looking around for opportunities elsewhere. Some of her friends had introduced her to the films of Italian neo-realist Roberto Rossellini, and after seeing his Open City in 1948, she wrote Rossellini, modestly offering him the use of her talents. The brilliant but little-known Rossellini was delighted and cabled back enthusiastically: "I have just received with great emotion your letter.... It is absolutely true that I dreamed of making a film with you and from this very moment I will do everything to see that such a dream becomes a reality as soon as possible." Rossellini's "dream" may have included more than merely making a film. The 43-year-old director had developed a reputation as a playboy and, although married, was keeping several mistresses. Elated, Bergman arranged to meet with Rossellini in Paris in 1949 while she was filming Hitchcock's Under Capricorn in England. Her husband, acting as her manager, also flew in from the States to offer his advice. The meeting went well, and Rossellini, visiting the U.S. later that year, spent some time as the Lindstroms' houseguest. He and Ingrid began discussing plans for a motion picture together. The Bergman-Rossellini romance apparently began during this period. Bergman would later write to Lindstrom from Rome, where she had gone to film Stromboli for Rossellini: "You saw in Hollywood how my enthusiasm for Roberto grew and grew, and you know how much alike we are, with the same desire for the same kind of work and the same understanding of life." Whether Lindstrom had seen or not, he had not discouraged his wife's trip to Rome. A somewhat stiff and humorless man, Peter Lindstrom had always encouraged his wife's career, and had pursued his own career ambitiously, making an unusual switch from successful dentist to respected neurosurgeon. In any event, the Lindstrom marriage had been shaky for a number of years, and the couple's divergent professions had often kept them apart. The film in Italy might have been just another Bergman film. The way Rossellini saw it was another matter. Returning to Rome after his first meeting with Bergman and her husband in Paris, he told friends, "Swedish women are the easiest in the world to impress, because they have such cold husbands." And the following January, back home after his stay in the U.S. with the Lindstroms, he proudly announced, "I'm going to put the horns on Mr. Bergman." Although Ingrid's enthusiasm "grew and grew" in Hollywood, the affair obviously hadn't been consummated there. Within a week after filming had begun, Bergman wrote Lindstrom asking for a divorce. The ebullient Rossellini displayed the letter around Rome, presumably as proof that the horns had finally been put on Bergman's husband. Dr. Lindstrom refused to consent to the divorce, and the heated Bergman-Rossellini romance began making the gossip columns. Always painfully honest, Bergman didn't try to keep her love a secret. Rossellini flamboyantly reveled in the notoriety. By the time little Robertino was born, Bergman's career had already slipped. The newspapers, loudly critical of the affair, pontificated on the birth of the child. "St. Joan" had committed adultery. It would take 10 years of exile before the American public would forgive her. In the sixties, with her rocky marriage to Rossellini annulled and back in public favor after winning an Academy Award for Anastasia--which she ironically had had to film in England--Bergman told the press: "I have had a wonderful life. I have never regretted what I did. I regret the things I didn't do." What Bergman had done was to shatter a myth she hadn't wanted created in the first place, but it was a blow from which Hollywood never completely recovered. "Times have changed...," she ventured to reporters several years ago. "No one objects to the Beatles having a holiday with their girls, perhaps because everyone is so pleased they are not taking boys with them." In 1975, Hollywood gave her a "best supporting" Oscar for her work in Murder on the Orient Express, in which she portrayed a mousy matron. As Bergman said, times have indeed changed. In June, 1977, Rossellini suffered a heart attack and died at his home in Rome. He was 71, according to People's Almanach; David Wallechinsky & Irving Wallace.
Read more on page 227.

Sex: The Key Players

Photo, above: Douglas Fairbanks

Silent Screen Star Scandals: Sex, insanity, Substance Abuse and So On...

The murderous, sexual, economic, political, and generally diverse scandals of the silent film era were torrid, sorrowful, and more extreme than many movie star scandals of the talking picture era.

Before the days of censorship and codes within Hollywood, the stars of the silent silver screen created several scandals.

Douglas Fairbanks

Douglas Elton Ullman (1883-1939) is famed for his acting and athletic ability in silent swashbucklers. Not only a screen star, he also jointly formed United Artists, but he is perhaps most remembered as the husband of silent screen sweetheart Mary Pickford. Although wed to the daughter of wealthy industrialist Daniel J. Sully, Fairbanks and Pickford began a discrete affair soon after meeting in 1916. Finally, obtaining a divorce in 1919, Fairbanks and Pickford married in 1920. The marriage of the two stars made them the first celebrity couple of Hollywood. However, Fairbanks eventually left Pickford to marry Sylvia Ashley, who would later wed Clark Gable, as stated by Classic Films. Fairbanks has slept with more than 30 stars and starlets in Hollywood.

Lillian Gish (Left)

In an acting career stretching seventy-five years, Lillian Gish (1893-1993) was one of America's most popular silent screen stars. Gish never married or had children, but her romantic involvement with producer Charles Duell resulted in a tabloid scandal when he brought a lawsuit against her and made public the details of their relationship. Gish was consistently rumored to have been involved with D.W. Griffith, but she never confirmed or denied the claim. Politically, Gish became an active member of the controversial America First Committee, which advocated anti-intervention of America in the first years of World War II, as stated by Classic Films.

Hedda Hopper (Left)

Elda Furry (1885-1966) is remembered as the famed gossip columnist Hedda Hopper, but her early career was as a silent screen actress, normally portraying socialite females.

Her acting career began to decline in the early 1930s, and her star did not rise until her gossip column entitled "Hedda Hopper's Hollywood" debuted in the Los Angeles Times on Valentine's Day 1938. Ironically, the column allowed no affectionate forgiveness. For many years, Hopper revealed the gossip and scandals of Hollywood, but her famed feud with rival columnist Louella Parsons became a source of gossip in itself, as stated by Classic Films.

Thomas Harper Ince (Left)
Louella Parsons is rumored to have gained her power as a gossip columnist due to her keeping silent about the circumstances of the death of silent film actor, director, producer, and writer Thomas Ince (1882-1924). Ince, the middle son of the Ince Brothers of the silent screen era, famously died during a weekend party aboard the yacht of William Randolph Hearst. Officially, his death was reported as having been caused by a heart attack, but suspicion has persisted about the actual occurrence. It is often suggested that Hearst murdered Ince. It is sometimes suggested that Hearst suspected Charlie Chaplin, another guest on the yacht, as the lover of Hearst's mistress Marion Davies and Hearst accidentally killed Ince either during a struggle with Chaplin or mistaking Ince for Chaplin.*The Cat's Meow*, starring Kirsten Dunst and Cary Elwes, adapted a version of this rumored story into a modern movie, as reported by Classic Films.

Buck Jones (Left)
Charles Frederick Gebhart (1891-1942) became known as a star of early westerns, but like many movie stars, Buck Jones met with a tragic and early death. In November 1942, Jones became one of the 492 victims of the fire which destroyed Boston nightclub, Cocoanut Grove.
Casualties second only to Chicago's Iroquois Theater fire of 1903, the fire of Cocoanut Grove remains the deadliest nightclub fire of the United States. Legend long held that Jones died from injuries acquired while rescuing others from the blaze, but Jones was actually trapped during the fire, according to Classic Films.

Buster Keaton (Left)
Joseph "Buster" Keaton (1895-1966) was a popular comedian in silent films. Although using physical comedy, his set stoical deadpan facial expression became his trademark. Keaton's career spanned almost forty years, but unfortunate business decisions of plagued his purse. His finances were further affected by costly divorces and the settlements made on his first two wives. Keaton wed three times. His first marriage to Natalie Talmadge ended due to his infidelity.
Talmadge refused Keaton contact with their sons.
Keaton also suffered from alcoholism, supposedly marrying his second wife during an alcoholic blackout, according to Classic Films.

Laurel and Hardy (Left)

One of the most famous and popular comedy teams of motion pictures, Laurel and Hardy were first paired during the silent screen era, starring in twenty-three silent shorts.

They would go on to enjoy even greater success during the sound era. British-born Stan Laurel (1890-1965) caused the comedy pair to be affected by a studio dispute with Hal Roach, which led to a temporary termination of Laurel's contract. Not only being tried for drunk driving, Laurel's personal life also witnessed a carousel of marriages.

First living with Mae Dahlberg, who was paid off to end the relationship, and soon after, Laurel wed his first wife. Continually leaving one wife for the next, Laurel would be married for the next thirty-nine years, but to four different women, one of whom he married twice.

American-born Oliver Norvell "Babe" Hardy (1892-1957) also endured failed marriages, but his health and death are more subject to speculation. Hardy suffered a heart attack in 1954, causing him to consider his health. His weight halved, but in 1956, he still suffered a stroke which left him unable to speak or move for months. In 1957, he suffered two more strokes before his death. Laurel's letters indicate that Hardy had terminal cancer, causing some to think this accounts for Hardy's weight loss and decline, according to Classic Films. Rumours circulated in Hollywood, that Hardy has died from syphilis.

Tom Mix (Left)

As the first screen superstar cowboy, Thomas Mix (1880-1940) is credited with helping to define the genre of film Westerns for the actors who followed. Married five times, Mix went AWOL from the army to wed his first wife. The marriage lasted less than the year, as did his second marriage. His third marriage endured for a decade, but he abandoned his wife and young child to wed his much younger co-star. Over a decade later, Mix divorced his fourth wife and soon married a fifth wife. Following lavish spending, Mix's entire savings were seriously deflated. He continued to work until he was killed in an unusual road accident. Perhaps speeding and driving drunk, Mix was unable to brake before sliding into a gully, causing a large aluminum suitcase from the backseat to fly forward, striking the back of his head, shattering his skull, and breaking his neck. (Source: Classic Films). Mix had several affairs in Hollywood with major stars, as well as underage starlets, but he was never caught. However, he was arrested for stealing horses, and was booked for 2 days.

Oona O'Neill and Charlie Chaplin

Photo: Charlie Chaplin with wife Oona O'Neill.

Although Oona O'Neill (1925-1991) intended to become an actress, she is known as the daughter of Eugene O'Neill, who abandoned the family while Oona was still a toddler, and the wife of Charlie Chaplin, who by himself created some of the most scandalous stories of the silent film era. Charlie Chaplin (1889-1977) is remembered as a comedian of silent films, but scandalous behavior filled his personal life.

He supposedly enjoyed being the first sexual partner of considerably underage girls, who he often mentored professionally.

It has been suggested that his fetish for young teenage girls originated due to his memory of lost teenage love Hetty Kelly. Each of his first two wives, Mildred Harris and Lita Grey, were sixteen when wedding sizably older Chaplin, who only married each due to pregnancy. Both divorces devolved into sensationalist media circuses reporting sexual scandals. Chaplin notoriously had numerous affairs, and thus became linked to the mystery of the 1924 death of Thomas Ince because it was thought that Ince may have been accidentally killed by William Randolph Hearst, who may have intended to murder Chaplin following a suspected affair with Hearst's mistress. Chaplin's reputation was threatened by his living with young actress Paulette Goddard, who was twenty-one years his junior. Years later, another former mistress brought a highly publicized paternity suit against Chaplin.

Chaplin met Oona when she auditioned for him. They married when she was newly eighteen and he was fifty-four. Due to Chaplin being accused of communism, the couple exiled themselves to Switzerland, and Oona renounced her American citizenship, according to the files of Classic Films.

Lillian Russell
Photo: Lillian Russell

Helen Louise Leonard (1860-1922) is most remembered as a stage actress and singer who took the name Lillian Russell.

However, she also starred in a few early silent films, including *Wildfire* (1915) opposite Lionel Barrymore. Russell wed four times. She married her first husband after discovering that she was pregnant, but the baby was accidentally killed by a nanny. After divorcing her first husband, Russell had an illegitimate daughter with composer Edward Solomon, who eventually became her second husband, but unbeknownst to Russell he had committed bigamy by marrying her, causing him to be arrested.

Not only marrying two more times, Russell also became the companion of wealthy businessman Diamond Jim Brady, who financed her lavish lifestyle.

Gloria Swanson

Photo: Gloria Swanson

Gloria Swanson (1899-1983) was prominent as a silent screen star and fashion icon, although she is now most recognized from playing Norma Desmond in *Sunset Boulevard* (1950). Swanson rivaled Henry VIII by also marrying six times. She first married when she was only seventeen, but this marriage to fellow-actor Wallace Beery lasted only two years. Her second husband was the president of Equity Pictures Corporation, and he later owned the Brown Derby restaurant.

The couple had a daughter together, but he eventually divorced Swanson, claiming she had committed adultery with thirteen men including Cecil B. DeMille and Rudolph Valentino. Besides her multiple marriages, one of which was technically bigamy due to Swanson's divorce not being finalized, Swanson also became the longtime mistress of married Joseph P. Kennedy, father of John F. Kennedy. The affair ended when Swanson discovered that Kennedy had mismanaged her finances, bankrupting her.

Talmadge Sisters
Photo: The Talmadge sisters

Norma, Natalie, and Constance Talmadge were silent film actresses, and both Norma and Constance Talmadge were among the very first stars to add their footprints and signatures to the pavement of Grauman's Chinese Theater.

Norma Talmadge (1893-1957) peaked as one of the most popular stars of the early 1920s.

A specialist of melodramatic performance, she became one of the highest stars to fall due to the introduction of sound. Although Norma retired a wealthy woman, she became reclusive and reliant on painkillers to cope with increased arthritic pain. Natalie Talmadge (1896-1969) was never as successful as her two sisters, but she is famed as the first wife of Buster Keaton. It is not entirely

228

clear why the couple wed, but the marriage was tumultuous. Natalie spent money lavishly, while Keaton frequently committed adultery and eventually became an unmanageable alcoholic. Constance Talmadge (1897-1973) was a star in silent films, but few of her movies survive.

Like her sisters, she retired with the introduction of talking pictures, instead investing in real estate and business, but Constance suffered from substance abuse and alcoholism. Although married four times, only her final marriage lasted longer than two years, according to the files of Classic Films. It was rumoured in Hollywood, that she has joined the notorious lesbians' group"
Photo: Rudolph Valentino and Natacha Rambova.

Sewing Circle."

Rudolph Valentino:

Italian actor Rudolph Valentina (1895-1926) became an icon of the silent screen. While living in New York, Valentino was arrested for male prostitution. He is particularly remembered for starring in *The Sheik* (1921). However, his personal life was as eventful as any scripted story. Valentino first wed in 1919, but his bride regretted the marriage immediately, locking him out of her bedroom on their wedding night. Although the marriage went unconsummated, they did not divorce until 1921. Valentino remarried before the finalization, causing him to be arrested for bigamy. Valentino eventually legally married his second wife, Natasha Rambova, who came to be considered controversial. She was sometimes considered controlling, while other times she was praised for her business sense, but the couple divorced bitterly. Not long after the failure of his

second marriage, Valentino became ill and underwent surgery for a perforated ulcer. Only about a week after the operation, he died at the age of thirty-one. His funeral proved to be a circus. His now girlfriend or perhaps fiancé, fellow screen-star Pola Negri became hysterical, crazed fans smashed windows in an attempt to gain admittance, and, as a publicity stunt, actors impersonating soldiers arrived claiming to have been sent by Benito Mussolini, as stated by Classic Films. Read more about Valentino on page 394.

Raoul Walsh (Left)

Raoul Walsh (1887-1980) was an actor and director. During his youth he was the lover of Virginia O'Hanlon, who is the little girl referred to by the line, "Yes, Virginia, there is a Santa Claus." Walsh was successful as a screen actor, but a car accident caused by a jackrabbit jumping onto the windshield caused Walsh to lose his right eye. He refused to have a glass eye, and chose not to continue acting, instead focusing on directing. Supposedly, a few days after the death of John Barrymore, Walsh used the corpse as a practical joke, propping up the suite-dressed body in an armchair of the home of Errol Flynn. This story was told by both Walsh and Flynn, but the event is disputed by others. Walsh managed to squeeze into the lesbians "Sewing Circle", for a short time, and his sexual appetite exploded over the "delicious bodies" of Azinova and Barbara Stanwyck, as he reported to his friend Errol Flynn.

Clara Kimball Young
Photo, left: Clara Kimball Young, right: Drucilla Strain.

Clara Kimball Young (1890-1960) became a successful screen actress playing mainly virtuous female characters. However, the career of the married Young became threatened by her very publicized affair with the also married Lewis J. Selznick, father of David O. Selznick. Young's husband, who was a successful director, sued for

divorce. Selznick and Young became business partners, as well as remaining romantically involved, but the business and personal relationship soon soured. Young asserted that Selznick defrauded her, and before her divorce was complete, she began a new affair with Harry Garson, who also became a temporary business partner.

Billie Burke Ziegfeld (Left)

Mary William Ethelbert Appleton Burke (1884-1970) began life touring with the circus which employed her father Billy Burke as a clown. Herself known as "Billie Burke," she is now most remembered for playing Glinda the Good Witch in *The Wizard of Oz* (1939).

Photo: Flo Ziegfeld

However, she began her career as a stage and silent screen actress. In 1914, Burke became the wife of the famed Florenz Ziegfeld, who was almost twenty years her senior and previously lived with common-law wife, polish actress Anna Held, who had suggested the format for the controversial Ziegfeld Follies.

Florenz first cheated on Anna with actress Lilliane Lorraine, and Drucilla Strain, and when the affair ended he moved on to Billie. Billie and Florenz had one daughter, and led a lavish lifestyle, even keeping a menagerie of animals, including an elephant named "Ziggy." However, the 1929 Stock Market Crash wiped out their money, forcing Burke to return to work for the remainder of her life.

Mary Pickford (Right)
Remembered as America's sweetheart, Mary Pickford (1892-1979) was actually Canadian. Born Gladys Louise Smith, her middle name was soon changed to "Marie."
Pickford experienced a difficult childhood. Her alcoholic father abandoned the family and died while Mary was a very young child. Pickford became a child actress, eventually becoming one of the first mega-movie stars. Pickford wed three times. Her first husband Owen Moore caused

the couple to separate due to his professional jealousy, domestic violence, and alcoholism. It is thought that Pickford became pregnant at some point during the marriage, but due to either a miscarriage or abortion she may have been left unable to have children in the future. Although long separated, Pickford did not divorce Moore until she became romantically involved with Douglas Fairbanks, who became her second husband. The couple were considered "Hollywood Royalty," and they were famous for hosting lavish parties at their home, Pickfair. Strains were placed upon her second marriage with the introduction of talkies. Fairbanks stamped out his restlessness through travel, which Pickford did not enjoy, and the relationship became unsalvagable when Fairbanks embarked on an affair. A string of family deaths and the end of her second marriage upset Pickford, who soon retired from acting. She wished to have all of her films destroyed, but she was persuaded against. She remained married over forty years to her third husband, Charles Rogers, and the couple adopted two children, although it is thought that Pickford continued to miss Fairbanks. At one time, gossipists claimed that Pickord had an intense affair with several members of the "Sewing Circle."

Evelyn Nesbit (Left)

Florence Evelyn Nesbit (1884-1967) was a model, chorus girl, and silent screen actress. She is remembered as the inspiration for the "Gibson Girl" and famed as "The Girl in the Red Velvet Swing." Nesbit was either raped or seduced by the womanizing architect Stanford White, who was forty-seven when she was only sixteen. Following his moving onto other virginal young women, Nesbit embarked on romantic – sexual relationships with several men. Here is her story: Evelyn Nesbit was a showgirl and the world's first supermodel, famous for her entanglement in the 1906 murder of her ex-lover Stanford White by her husband, Harry Thaw. She began modeling for artists like Charles Dana Gibson as a young teen to help support her widowed mother and younger brother at the same time newspapers were first able to reproduce photographs and her anonymous face was reproduced around the globe as the personification of female beauty.

In Canada, Lucy Maude Montgomery pasted Evelyn's portrait on her wall and she served as the inspiration for her *Anne of Green Gables*. Soon, Evelyn had a featured role as a gypsy dancer in the Broadway musical *Florodora*. She attracted a lot of attention from rich New Yorkers, but ultimately it was society architect Stanford White - old enough to be her grandfather - who became her sugar daddy. White, the genius behind some of the most beautiful private homes ever conceived, liked taking young women under his wing and doing a Pygmalion on them. He fixed Evelyn's teeth, showered her with gifts and a roomy apartment on the better side of town, and had regular meetings with her in a narrow NYC loft building that collapsed a few years ago. Inside, he installed a red velvet swing so the naked teenager could sail through the air overhead. As Evelyn later claimed on the witness stand in court, it was during one of those forays that White drugged her with champagne and took her virginity - although it's doubtful he had to drug her. The couple drifted apart, mainly because millionaire White was not going to marry her.

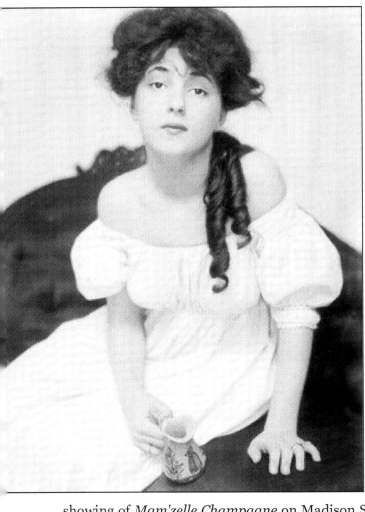

At that point he was nearly bankrupt and had no intention of divorcing his wife of many years.

Evelyn played the field, dating among others, actor John Barrymore, who was smitten enough to impregnate her twice. Both times White intervened, sequestering his former protégée at a convent.

Photo: Evelyn Nesbit in 1903.

The first pregnancy was terminated, and there is speculative evidence that a second child was put up for adoption.

Evelyn's mother didn't approve of actors who knocked up her daughter, but she did okay Pittsburgh millionaire Harry K. Thaw, a true nutjob, a cocaine addict and sadist with a penchant for whipping women and the occasional adolescent boy.

Thaw was obsessed with Stanford White even before his engagement to Evelyn, intensely jealous of the older man's sophistication and style, the easy way he reeled in younger women who wouldn't have given young Harry the time of day.

Thaw took Evelyn on a European jaunt and they holed up in a Bavarian castle, where he beat her into telling him how White had taken her virginity.

On a balmy June night, the Thaws attended a showing of *Mam'zelle Champagne* on Madison Square Garden's rooftop. It was a beautiful night. High overhead a nude statue of Diana the Huntress Evelyn had posed for hung suspended against the starry sky while a chorus of showgirls sang "I Could Love A Million Girls" below. Thaw saw Stanford White in the audience. It was the second sighting that evening, the first at the Café Martin restaurant just a couple of hours earlier. Out of nowhere, as the cliché goes, Harry Thaw pulled out a gun and shot White in the face at close range three times. Two murder trials resulted. The first was deadlocked. In the second, with Evelyn testifying on her husband's behalf, Thaw pled temporary insanity. Thaw's mother promised Evelyn that if she testified that White had raped her and Thaw avenged her honor, she could have a quiet divorce and a million dollar settlement. Evelyn went along with it, and lied to save Thaw from the chair. Thaw -- whose meals in jail were delivered daily by Delmonico's on silver platters -- went into a posh loony bin where he had total freedom to come and go as he pleased. Evelyn got the shaft. No money. The year after his release, Thaw was accused of sexually assaulting and horsewhipping a teen-aged boy, adjudicated insane and again sent to an asylum where he spent seven years. When he died of a heart attack in 1947, he left Evelyn $10,000 -- less than 1% of his fortune. Evelyn used her notoriety to launch new careers as a vaudeville performer, silent film actress, and café owner. Nothing really took off. She was something of a suicidal mess. In 1916, she married her dancing

233

partner Jack Clifford, but by 1918 he'd left her and they were officially divorced in 1933. For years she lived in Northfield, New Jersey.

There were more suicide attempts, and struggles with alcoholism and morphine addiction. Later she taught ceramics classes and moved to Los Angeles after serving as technical adviser when newcomer Joan Collins played her in the film *The Girl in the Red Velvet Swing* (1955). Evelyn died at 82 in a Santa Monica nursing home. Before her death, she said that Stanford White was the only man she had ever loved, stated Claroscureaux.

Nesbit and John Barrymore.

Barrymore, only two years older than Nesbit, wished to marry her, but Nesbit's mother considered the young actor too poor to wed. Against the desires of her ambitious mother, Nesbit continued her relationship with Barrymore, becoming pregnant twice, stated M.L. Costa.

Jobyna Ralston (**Jobyna Lancaster Raulston**):
Photo: Jobyna Ralston

Date and place of birth: November 21, 1899, South Pittsburgh, Tennessee.
Date and place of death: January 22, 1967, in Woodland Hills, California. She died from pneumonia.
Husband: Richard Arlen (Actor, married 1927, divorced 1945), one son, Richard Arlen, Jr. Jobyna Ralston was noted for her appearance in Harold Lloyd comedies. She replaced Mildred Davis, the future wife of Harold Lloyd. Because of her lisp, she could not make a successful transit from silents to talkies. She started her career as a chorus dancer for the legendary George M. Cohan, with whom she had an affair.
She married her future husband Richard Arlen, after she has met him on the set of the Oscar-winning classic "Wings."
From the grapevine, we heard that Jobyna had multiple sexual relations with chorus girls on and off the set.
Ralston was once arrested and convicted in 1930 for indecency.

Jobyna Ralston

Photo: Joan Crawford, a certified nymphomaniac, with a voracious appetite for rough sex.

Joan Crawford

During her long career, Crawford was continually plagued by whispered salacious rumors about her financially strapped early career as a starlet in the 1920s when she danced naked in short arcade peep shows films. When she had achieved initial fame and was still in her twenties, she made gossip column headlines by partying all night longat the legendary Cocoanut Grove at the Ambassador Hotel, where the vodka flowed plentifully her way and helped her win over 100 dance contests.

Scandal continued to follow her throughout her highly successful career. There were stories about the star's legendary relationship with Clark Gable, her countless love affairs, her marriages - three of them to gay men - and her obsession with, and voracious appetite for rough sex. Even at the peak of her career rumors continued to surface about how her loathed mother forced Crawford to work as a prostitute, make blue movies and sleep her way to the top. Bette Davis who had a legendary career-long feud with Crawford, also believed that Joan used sex to advance her career. "She slept with every star at MGM", she alleged later, "of both sexes."

There was some truth in this.

Most of Crawford's leading men had succumbed to her sexual magnetism and she counted several female stars, including Greta Garbo, Marlene Dietrich, Barbara Stanwyck and later Marilyn Monroe, among her lovers.

It was rumored that Crawford would have liked to add Bette to her conquests but was rebuffed by the heterosexual Davis. In Mommie Dearest, published in 1978, the year after Crawford's death, and written by her adopted daughter, Christina Crawford, she was portrayed as a tyrannical, egotistical domestic monster, and this, tragically, is part of the reputation which remains today.

It is a bitter irony that today Joan Crawford is remembered as much for the vitriolic 'Mommie Dearest' and for the scandals of her early years, as for her 18 year reign as the box-office 'Queen of MGM', as stated by Gunsock.

Joan Crawford

237

Jean Harlow

Photo: Jean Harlow; a life full of scandals, sex, and nudity.

Her personal life was perennially the stuff of tabloid gossip, including the suicide of her second husband, producer Paul Bern, her relationships with gangsters, nude photos at the age of 17, problems with a greedy stepfather, and two reported abortions of a child fathered by William Powell, and the second one by Howard Hughes. Humphrey Bogart took her to the aborption clinic on an order from Hughes.

Harlow was the first movie actress to appear on the cover of *Life* magazine (May, 1937). On screen, she caused such a sensation with her easy sensuality that led the Hays Office, the official Hollywood censors, to decree that adultery could not go unpunished, in response to her role in *Red-Headed Woman*. Harlow was first touched by a public scandal that she brought on herself by openly socializing with high profile gangsters Bugsy Siegel and Abner Zwillman.

In 1932, already an established star under contract to MGM, she married MGM producer Paul Bern in what may have been a joint effort by both star and studio to clean up her act. The marriage proved to be a sexual disaster due to Bern's impotence and Harlow threw herself into a torrid affair with her frequent co-star Clark Gable. Just two months after the wedding, Bern was found naked and dead of a gunshot wound in their Beverly Hills home.

MGM did its best to downplay the scandal, but Hollywood and the whole entertainment world was consumed with it.

Bern's mysterious death was officially ruled a suicide but for a time the press openly speculated that Harlow had connived at the murder of her husband. Nevertheless she survived the adverse publicity and after agreeing to the studio's plan for an arranged marriage to cinematographer Harold Rosson, her fame soared to greater heights.

She even found love with debonair leading man William Powell. But Powell, freshly divorced from another firecracker blonde, Carole Lombard, refused to marry her. Five years after Bern's death, Harlow, who had recently been named as a co-defendant in divorce proceedings launched by the wife of boxing champion Max Baer, died suddenly and shockingly of renal failure in 1937. She was only 26, as reported by Gunsock.

Jean Harlow and Paul Bern at their wedding, July 1932.

Little planning went into the nuptials. In fact, Jean Harlow was not even able to purchase a real wedding gown. She simply went into a dress shop that she frequented and bought an off-the-rack white dress and a shawl. They gathered two days after Bern proposed with about 150 friends and relatives at the home of Jean's mother. They were married on July 2, 1932 but had to postpone their honeymoon because of their shooting schedules. They took one day off and then returned to work. According to Jean's friends, she looked "radiant" in the weeks that followed and the couple seemed very happy, as stated in Frances Farmer Revenge.

———————————————

Harlow had affairs with many men, to name a few:
1-Charles McGrew (They fell in love and married in 1927.)
2-Max Baer, with whom she had a torrid affair while he was still married.
3-Clark Gable.
4-William Powell who got her pregnant.
5-Howard Hughes who got her pregnant too.
6-Humphrey Bogart.
7-Harold Rosson, who married her on order by MGM. Seven months later they divorced. (Read more on page 247.)

Jean Harlow, once said, "Men like me because I don't wear a brassiere. Women like me because I don't look like a girl who would steal a husband. At least not for long."

Their Affairs and Lovers

All, had multiple sexual relations, affairs, and numerous lovers. Listed below, the star's name and her/his most recognizable lovers (Just to name a very few, because they are so many to list): The lovers' listing does not include other casual sex affairs, one night stand, and the likes...For instance, in one single night, Clara Bow slept with 17 football players! Alla Nazimova, Tallulah Bankhead et al, participated in orgies gathering dozens of participants, etc. Sex was everywhere, and freely available to Hollywood's stars, on the set, off the set, in cocaine fueled parties, in their homes, and their dressing rooms at the studio! Knock at the door, and it shall be opened...and if you are free "come to see me sometime..."said Mae West.

For the record: The biggest stud was **Howard Hughes,** followed by **Charlie Chaplin. Henry Kissinger** had several affairs with Hollywood's leading ladies, to name a few:

- Candice Bergen,
- Nancy Maginnes,
- Samantha Eggar,
- Joanna Barnes,
- Jill St. John.

Yep! Boom boom, Kissinger got a piece of the action...I should say more than a piece!

Photo: Secretary Henry Kissinger with Dolly Parton. He is looking in the right direction...when he is outside the office.

*** *** ***

240

Hollywood's Stars and Celebrities Who Slept with John F. Kennedy's

Excerpts from Book 2: Hollywood's Most Horrible People, Stars, Times, and Scandals: From The Stars Who Slept With Kennedy To Lavender Marriages And The Casting Couch."

"JFK was pond scum." Wrote Newsweek, on August 19, 1996.

During the early 1960s, journalists and informed observers used to discuss in private the president's casual approach to his marriage vows, and his insatiable sexual appetite, but they nevertheless kept the code of silence that then protected the reputations of politicians (and those of the scribes as well). So Kennedy's extramarital affairs, and his dalliances with women on the fringe of organised crime, went unreported. What the American people were allowed to see were carefully staged occasions, where Kennedy and his wife were seen at their best, displaying their sophistication and good taste. This was how, in the glow of network television, then at the height of its influence, the first truly glamorous presidential couple appeared before the nation. (Source: Professor Lewis L Gould)

In matters of sexual adventure, the Kennedy men have long gone in harm's way. Rose Kennedy's father, Boston Mayor John "Honey Fitz" Fitzgerald, was a known philanderer, but her mother bore it stoically. Rose wished better for herself, but the pattern was replayed. Biographer Doris Kearns Goodwin, in The Fitzgeralds and the Kennedys, quotes a family member's recollection: "Even in the early years of their marriage, Joe had a reputation for being a ladies' man, and some of this gossip must have caught up with Rose."

As time passed, gossip was overtaken by flamboyant fact. Joe brought his women to his Palm Beach and Cape Cod estates and even took film star Gloria Swanson along with Rose on a voyage to Europe. Says Rose's former personal secretary Barbara Gibson: "She never showed any pain about those things." Above all, according to author Garry Wills in The Kennedy Imprisonment, Rose took care "not to embarrass the men of the family, obstruct their careers, dim their accomplishments."

Rose gamely endured her husband's excesses, as did later generations of Kennedy women with the sons and grandsons who carried on the legacy of the founding father. Joe's sons reportedly used to provide their father with female companions when he visited them in Washington, D.C. During the '70s, Rose's grandsons Christopher Lawford and Joseph Kennedy II, as well as the then-married Teddy, would share daiquiris with young women at Rose's Palm Beach lunches, then head for the bedrooms after Rose retired for her nap, according to Gibson, interviewed recently by People magazine.

Jack was a chronic philanderer. Among his reported conquests were Angie Dickinson, Jayne Mansfield and Marilyn Monroe. Bobby also had an affair with Marilyn, as detailed in James Spada's soon to be released Peter Lawford: The Man Who Kept the Secrets. Ted carries on in the family tradition. The brothers' wives, Jackie and Ethel and Joan, had to live with the rumors as best they could. As though fated, Rose's daughters Pat and Jean ended up with faithless husbands as well.

Tolstoy was right, of course: Every unhappy family is unhappy in its own way—and no one can see into the real heart of another's family. Publicly and privately, all of the Kennedy women have had to find a way to cope. Some looked to the bottom of bottles, others upward to God. Some triumphed, others failed. "The Kennedy men expect their sisters and wives to put up with everything as long as the fame and glory are pouring in," says an unkind friend of Jean Kennedy Smith's children who, like many people who discuss this powerful family, declines to be identified. "The fathers set an example for the sons; the mothers set an example for the daughters. It will never cease..." as reported by Paula Chin, Joe Treen, Karen S. Schneider, People Magazine.

*** *** ***

List of names of Hollywood's stars and celebrities who had sexual intercourse with Kennedy:

- JFK did Lee Radziwill, Jackie's sister when Jackie was in hospital with Caroline.
- JFK did Audrey Hepburn.
- JFK did Jayne Mansfield for 3 years.
- JFK did Gene Tierney.
- JFK did Marlene Deitrich.
- Other actresses tied to JFK in the press were Kim Novak, Janet Leigh and Rhonda Flemming, but Fleming denied it.
- Angie Dickinson commenting on JFK's brutal lovemaking style called it "the best 20 seconds of my life."
- Jackie said JFK was a flop as a lover. She told a friend he "just goes too fast and falls asleep" as reported in the book "Grace and Power", by Sally Smith.
- During WWII, JFK was a security risk at the Pentagon for his well-known affair with Nazi spy Ingrid Arvad.
- In 1951, Kennedy had to pay off Alicia Purdom wife of a British actor half a million dollars after making her pregnant and then reneging on his promise to marry her.
- In 1956 Kennedy did Joan Lundberg who says he loved threesomes and was a voyeur. He paid for her abortion and slept with her in Jackie's marriage bed.
- 90 minutes before the first televised debate with Nixon, JFK was with a call-girl. (Reeves p 202) He also had a call-girl inauguration night. The night before the inauguration, he cheated on his wife in their Georgetown house.
- JFK kept an apartment at the Carroll Arms in Washington where he met young women. After a year of marriage a friend said of Jackie, "Jackie was wandering around looking like a survivor of an airplane crash." (Reeves p 116)
- JFK did Mary Pinchot Meyer in about thirty White House visits from Jan '62 to Nov '63. She was mysteriously murdered in 1964 and her diary of their affair ended up at the CIA. Mary and JFK did drugs together.
- JFK did David Niven's wife.
- JFK did Pamela Turnure, 23, a Jackie look-a-like, hired as Jackie's press secretary, in an affair that went on three years in the White House.
- JFK did Fiddle and Faddle, Secret Service code names for 21 and 23 year old staff members hired mostly for sex. JFK tested dangerous drugs on them without their knowledge by putting drugs in their drinks.
- White House intern Marion "Mimi" Beardsley whose married name is Fahnestock was 19 when JFK raped her (statutory rape - the age of consent was 21 in DC at the time). A powerful older man preying on vulnerable young women is what sexual harassment is all about.
- JFK got shots of speed from Dr. Max Jacobson, a.k.a. Dr. Feelgood.

242

- JFK had a penchant for swimming nude with his female guests at wild pool parties.
- JFK & a British female tennis star had a lengthy relationship.
- Bigamist - JFK married socialite Durie Malcolm in Palm Springs in early 1947 and then a few days later had his friend Charles Spalding steal the marriage certificate from the Court House.
- JFK reportedly had an illegitimate child in the late 50s by prostitute Alicia Darr Clark who later tried to blackmail him.
- JFK did Judith Campbell Exner, mob moll, who had some twenty visits starting in May 1961. Exner carried cash bribes to JFK from California defense contractors. When she called JFK and told him that he had made her pregnant, he asked, "What are you going to do about it?" She had an abortion at a Chicago hospital in January 1963. She was never invited back to the White House. Her lover, mob boss Sam Giancana, bragged that he had 'placed' her with the President. Interestingly, both Giancana and another of her mob lovers, Roselli, were given the C.I.A. contract to kill Castro.
- JFK did Ellen Rometsch, an East German spy. When the Profumo affair (a sex scandal with a German spy) was blowing apart the British government, the Kennedys paid her off and had her deported. They abused both the FBI and Congress (by threatening Congressmen with information from their FBI files) to keep this liaison out of the press and the timing strongly suggests that the assassination of South Vietnam's Diem was used to divert press attention from JFK's connection to Rometsch. Kennedy also had had sex both in London and New York with prostitute Suzy Chang who was at the heart of the Profumo affair. Bobby had a hard time covering this up.
- When the Secret Service was asked by local officials in Seattle if Kennedy always had prostitutes brought to him, they answered, "We travel during the day, so this only happens at night." Truckloads of prostitutes were brought to the Whitehouse and admitted without security checks. When JFK inspected military bases, he expected to be supplied with women.
- JFK used Peter Lawford's home in Santa Monica for meeting women.
- JFK kept a large collection of photos of himself with naked women.
- When President, Kennedy blackmailed starlets into servicing him or have their careers destroyed.
- JFK suffered from permanent venereal disease because he had been re-infected so often. He infected his partners with a disease so serious that it causes 35 percent of all infertility in US women.
- Marilyn Monroe told a columnist that JFK would not indulge in foreplay because he lacked the time. They had a one-year affair. Bobby Kennedy also did her and she even aborted his baby which, if she told, would have destroyed his career. The day Monroe died, neighbors saw Robert F. Kennedy and "a man with a doctor's bag" together enter her house. Within four hours she was found dead. Monroe was killed with a barbiturate suppository, but a bottle of oral pills was left at the scene to make it look like a possible suicide. U.S. Attorney General Kennedy was never questioned about his role and his cousin actor Peter Lawford who "cleaned up" the murder scene never explained what happened to Marilyn's incriminating diary. The Kennedys were banned from the funeral. JFK is quoted by Traphes Bryant as saying to a friend, "I'm not through with a girl till I've had her three ways." (Reeves p 241). During a 1961 meeting in Bermuda with British Prime Minister Harold McMillian Kennedy said, "I wonder how it is with you, Harold? If I don't have a woman for three days, I get terrible headaches." There is a much more

vulgar Kennedy quote along the same line in Hersh page 389, as reported on JFK Scandal Page.

Gallery of stars and celebrities who slept with John F. Kennedy, to name a few:

Audrey Hepburn

Jayne Mansfield; he did her for 3 years.

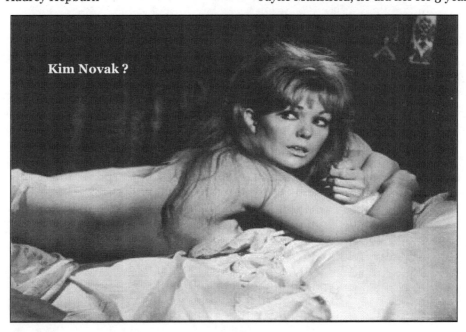

Gene Tierney

Marlene Dietrich

Left: Angie Dickinson, commenting on JFK's brutal lovemaking style called it "the best 20 seconds of my life."
Right: Nazi spy Ingrid Arvad.

Mary Pinchot Meyer (Far right), who was mysteriously murdered in 1964 and her diary of their affair ended up at the CIA. Mary and JFK did drugs together.

Left, Mrs Hjordis Niven, David Niven's wife. Kennedy did her as well.

John Kennedy slept with 26 actresses; stars, starlets and celebrities, the most famous ones (to name a few):

- Mary Biib,
- Ellen Romesch,
- Marilyn Monroe,
- Mary Meyer,
- Judith Exner,
- Angie Dickinson (commenting on JFK's brutal lovemaking style, Dickinson called it "the best 20 seconds of my life."
- Audrey Hepburn,
- Gene Tierney,
- Jayne Mansfield,
- Marlene Deitrich,
- Janet Leigh,
- Hjordis Niven, David Niven's wife.

And those who procured him the goodies, (to name a few) were: Frank Sinatra and Peter Lawford.

(Note: Read more about Kennedy's affairs and the women he slept with in **Book 2:** Hollywood's Most Horrible People, Stars, Times, and Scandals: From The Stars Who Slept With Kennedy To Lavender Marriages And The Casting Couch."

Peter Lawford

Frank Sinatra

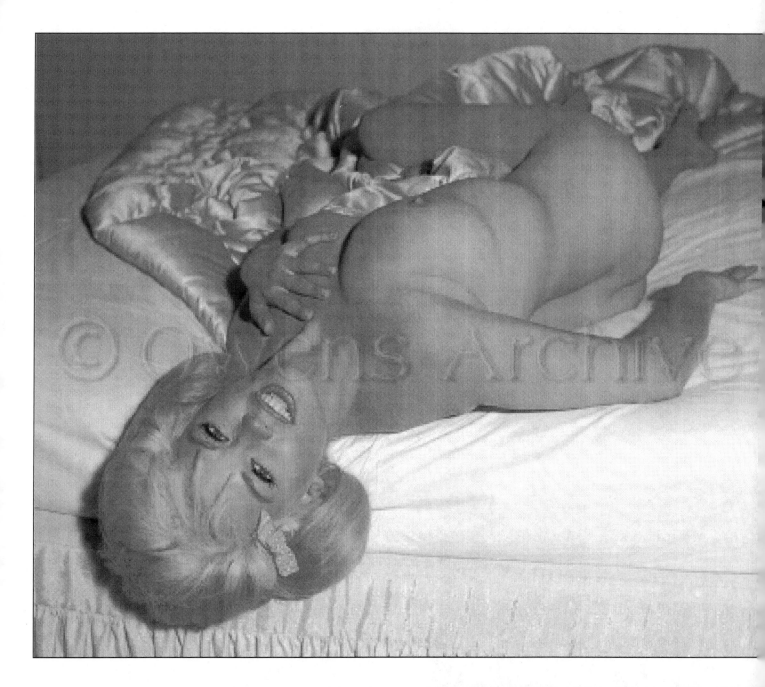

Photo: Jayne Manfield. John F. Kennedy did her for 3 years. (From Owens Archives) Photo, right: Mansfield and Tommy Noonan in the most repeated nude scene of the movie *Promises! Promises!*

Jayne Mansfield ended her career as she began: posing nude and working as a stripper. This reminds me of Madonna, who started as a nude model for several years after she first moved to NYC in 1979. She would became famous for posing nude during the first half of the 1990s and especially in December 1992 with the release of her book, SEX. Madonna is now back at it again as the cover of the latest February 2002 *Pop*

magazine reveals. Madonna, like Mansfield to the very end, continues to capitalize on her natural endowments.

List of their lovers and sexual partners
This is a small, a very small list, folks!

- **Angie Dickinson's lovers:** Johnny Carson, Eddie Fisher, Johnny Grant, John F. Kennedy (A short affair), William Shatner (Oh Yes! Sex trek!), Burt Bacharach.

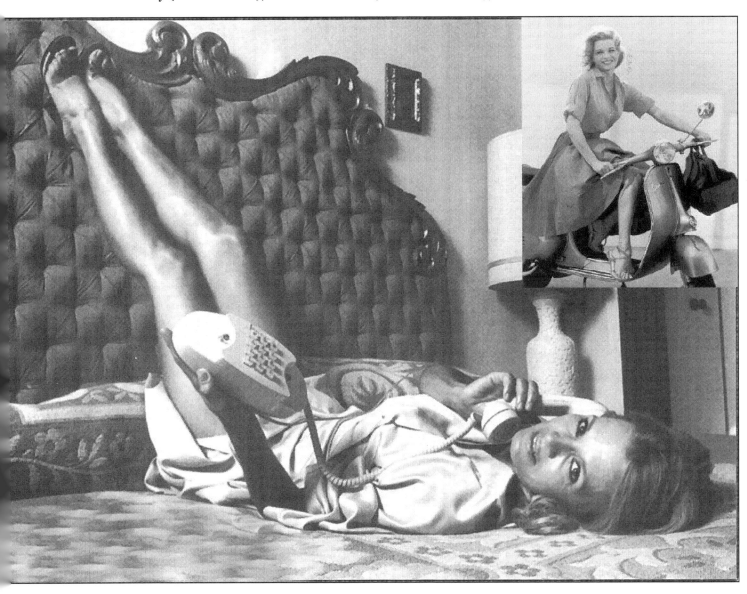

Photo: Angie Dickinson was hot in those days. Angie Dickinson commenting on JFK's brutal lovemaking style called it "the best 20 seconds of my life."

Anita Ekberg's lovers:
Frank Sinatra (He was always ready for big bazookas!),
Rik van Nutter,
Walter Chiari,
Gianni Agnelli,
Fred Buscaglione.

Anita Ekberg in her prime. And below, Anita today.

- **Ann-Margret's lovers:** Elvis Presley (Right away, mamma! It's alright!), Steve McQueen (The cheapest guy in town), Eddie Fisher, Roger Smith, Roger Daltrey (He rocked her saddle!)
- **Audrey Hepburn's lovers:** Cary Grant, Robert Wolders, Peter O'Toole, Ben Gazzara (Slowly and gently, Mazel Tov Ben!), Andrea Botti, and John F. Kennedy.

Photo: Barbara Lamarr was the first silent film star to do a nude bath tub scene.

- **Barbara Lamarr's lovers:** John Guilbert, Jack Dougherty, Ben Deeley, Ernest Hemingway.

- **Barbara Stanwyck's lovers and sexual partners (To name a few):**
- Humphrey Bogart,
- James Cagney,
- Glenn Ford,
- Gene Kelly,
- Anthony Quinn,
- Farley Granger,
- Alla Nazimova,
- Grace Kelly,
- Greta Garbo,
- Marlene Dietrich,
- Tallulah Bankhead,
- Randolph Scott,
- Gary Cooper,
- Cary Grant.
- Note: She was bisexual.
- **Candice Bergen's lovers:** Henry Kissinger, Louis Malle, Marshall Rose, Burt Reynolds, David Nevin.
- **Cary Grant's lovers:** Grace Kelly, Maureen Donaldson, Barbara Harris, Audrey Nepburn, Doris Day, Dyan Cannon, Barbara Stanwyck.
- **Charlie Chaplin's lovers and sexual partners:** I lost count, but here are some:
- Sari Maritza,
- Paulette Goddard (He married her due to pregnancy.),
- Carole Landis,
- Joan Berry,
- Marion Davies,
- Lita Grey (He married her due to pregnancy. She was 16),
- Hetty Kelly, (15 year old)
- Mildred Harris, (He married her due to pregnancy. She was 16),
- Oona Chaplin (He married her, when she was 18. Good!)
- **Clark Gable's lovers: Grace Kelly** (Hollywood notorious nymphomaniac!)Sylvia Ashley, Jean Harlow, Kay Spreckles, Marilyn Maxwell, Slim Hawks.
- **Claudette Colbert's lovers:** Joan Crawford, Clark Gable, Joel Pressman, Kerry Johnson, Joel McCrea. Note: She was bisexual.
- **Cybill Shepherd's lovers:** Elvis Presley, David Ford, Don Johnson, Bruce Oppenheim, Jeff Bridges, Robert Martin.
- **Dean Martin's lovers:** Well, Dean slept with 1.543.000 women, not counting the small change. Sinatra got jealous, Sammy Davis Jr., did not mind, Dean invited him to watch. Perhaps, this is how he lost one eye. He watched too much! Here are some samples: Lana Turner, Janice Lynde, Catherine Hawn, Inger Stevens (Right from the airport), Judy Garland (Under the winebow!)
- **Dolores Del Rio's lovers:** Walt Disney, Cedric Gibbons, Orson Welles, Lew Riley, Baby Pignatari.

- **Don Johnson's lovers:** Cybill Shepherd, Sofia Gucci (Good choice, nice bags!), Jeanne Anderson, Jodi Lyn O'Keefe (No painting!), Yasmine Bleeth, Kelley Phleger, who else? That's enough for now.
- **Doris Day's lovers:** Cary Grant, Barry Comden, Frank Sinatra, Jack Carson, Martin Melcher.
- **Dorothy Lamour's lovers:** Randolph Scott, John Howard, Greg Bautzer, William Ross Howard III, Herbie Kaye.
- **Elvis Presley's lovers:** Ann-Margret, Raquel Welch, (With lots of aerobics!) Kathy Westmoreland, Cybill Shepherd, Ann Pennington, Sheila Caan, Ginger Alden.
- **Ernest Borgnine's lovers:** None ! That's not fair ladies, shame on you!
- **Errol Flynn's lovers:** (Boy Ya Boy! He screwed everything and anything that had a skirt on!), to name a few:
- Maureen O'Sullivan,
- Olivia de Haviland,
- Gita Hall,
- Patrice Wymore,
- Diana Millay,
- Maureen Swanson,
- Lili Damita,
- Beverly Aadland.
- **Frank Sinatra's lovers:**
- Marilyn Monroe,
- Kate Jackson,
- Jacqueline Kennedy Onassis (While she was married to this beast),
- Barbara Max,
- Jill St. John,
- Tiffany Bolling.
- **Gary Coopers' lovers:** (He had the biggest gun in town... a dick like a horse, according to Velez Lupe, wife of Tarzan), so add her to the list, since she knows. The liste of his lovers and sexual partners includes (Just to name a few):
- Barbara Stanwyck,
- Ingrid Bergman,
- Grace Kelly,
- Clara Bow,
- Sandra Shaw,
- Marlene Dietrich,
- Merle Oberon,
- Carole Lombard,
- Barbara Payton,
- Dorothy Di Frasso,
- Rita Hayworth,
- Veronica Lake,
- Paulette Goddard,
- Vera Zorina,
- Arlene Dahl,

- Louise Brooks,
- Tallulah Bankhead,
- Joan Crawford,
- Patricia Neal,
- Barbara Stanwyck.

Gary got the whole stable! A real cowboy!

- **Greta Garbo's lovers:**
- Marlene Dietrich,
- Aristotle Onasis,
- Cecil Beaton,
- George Schlee,
- Gilbert Roland,
- Gaylor Hauser,
- Barbara Stanwyck,
- Tallulah Bankead (And she kept screaming DAAAAAAAAHHHHLING... DAAAAAAAAAHHHHLING!) She was bisexual.
- **Hedy Lamarr's lovers:** Lewis J. Boies, Jay Garon, W. Howard Lee, Teddy Stauffer, Ray Milland.
- **Humphrey Bogart's lovers and sexual partners:**
- Barbara Stanwyck,
- Lauren Bacall (He married her),
- Mary Astor,
- Bette Davis (But! The way she wanted it!),
- Jean Harlow,
- Mayo Methot.
- **Jack Nicholson's lovers:**
- Amber Smith,
- Sylvia Tamsma,
- Lara Flynn Boyle,
- Inger Lise Ebeltoft,
- Kate Moss,
- Cynthia Bassinet.
- **James Dean's lovers:**
- Nicholas Ray,
- Eartha Kitt (Really? Miracles happen),
- Sal Mineo,
- Barbara Hutton,
- Vampira (I don't doubt it!)

Note: He was bisexual.

- **James Stewart's lovers and sexual partners** (Just to name a few):
- Anita Colby,
- Martha Vickers,
- Ellen Ross,
- Gloria Hatrick McLean,
- Myrna Dell,

- Maureen O'Hara,
- Olivia de Haviland,
- Katharine Hepburn. (Yah! Good old Jimmy was busy!)
- **Jean Harlow's lovers and sexual partners** (just to name a few**):**
- Howard Hughes,
- Donald Friede,
- William Powell who got her pregnant,
- Howard Hughes who got her pregnant too.
- Max Baer,
- Jesse Lasky,
- Clark Gable,
- Humphrey Bogart,
- Johnny Weissmuller,
- Charles McGrew,
- Harold Rosson, who married her on order by MGM. Seven months later they divorced.
- **Jill St. John's lovers:**
- Rock Hudson,
- Robert Wagner,
- Jack Jones,
- Tom Mankiewicz,
- Henry Kissinger, Frank Sinatra. (Yah! Kissinger got a piece of the action! In fact, he got more than one piece, Candice Bergen was another one!)
- **Joan Collins' lovers:** Peter Holm (She married him, or he married her, I don't know?), Percy Gibson, Larry Hagman, Ronald S. Kass.
- **Joan Fontaine's lovers:** Brian Aherne, William Dozier, Prince Ali Khan, Collier Young, Alfred Wright, Jr.
- **Johnny Carson's lovers:** Angie Dickinson, Alexis Maas, Joanna Holland, Morgan Fairchild (Really? Don't underestimate him!) Joanne Copeland.
- **Katharine Hepburn's lovers:**
- Spencer Tracey,
- Montgomery Clift,
- Jimmy Stewart,
- Cary Grant,
- Howard Hughes.
- **Lana Turner's lovers:** Dean Martin Charles Evans, Robert Eaton, Ronald Dante, Tylor Pero, Ronald Ziegler (He did lots of ziggi ziggi!)
- **Lili Damita's lovers:**
- Marlene Dietrich,
- Errol Flynn,
- Victor Fleming,
- Michael Curtiz,
- Prince Louis Ferdinand.
Note: She was bisexual.
- **Mabel Normand's lovers:** William Taylor, Mack Sennett, Samuel Goldwyn, Lew Cody.

First issue of "Playboy" Magazine Featuring Marilyn Monroe w/Monroe Nude Spread.

Monroe's lovers (Only the famous ones):
- Frank Sinatra,
- Marlon Brando,
- John F. Kennedy,
- Jose Bolanos,
- Arthur Miller (She married him)
- Clark Gable,
- Humphrey Bogart.

The photo of Marilyn Monroe on the left is from "Playboy" Magazine.

The one on the right (undated publicity photograph,) is the only known autographed nude portrait of Marilyn Monroe, shot by photographer Tom Kelly, the image that helped launch her career. It was auctioned on December 10, 2004 by "Profiles in History" in Los Angeles. The photo, inscribed to costume designer Bill Travilla reads "To Billy, my love Please dress me forever. Love Marilyn." The photograph was sold for $30,000. (Source: Reuters)

Photo, right: Norman Jean Baker (Marilyn Monroe's name at birth) appeared nude on a very famous 1950s calendar as well as being the first *Playboy* Playmate. She was photographed by Tom Kelley in 1949. This 3-D slide is the first nude photo of Marilyn Monroe as well as one of her first photographs as a professional model. The picture was auctioned by Sloans & Kenyon auction house in Chevy Chase, Maryland. Other have said that W.O. Schwartz took these pictures in May 1945, when the 19-year-old model was just beginning her career. The image is totally nude but not full-frontal. Photographer Douglas Kirkland, who photographed the actress in 1961 for *Look* magazine said, "Entirely possible." Kirkland said Monroe survived by modeling at that time, although he had never seen anything like the filmstrip. (Source: 3D Reviews) One slide sold for $455 with 18 bids and the other sold for $282.77 with 22 bids.

- **Marlene Dietrich's lovers and sexual partners** (Just to name a few):
- Greta Garbo,
- Lili Damita,
- Jean Gabin,
- Montgomery Clift,
- Yul Bryner,
- Michael Todd,
- Tallulah Bankhead,
- Edith Piaf,
- Howard Hughes,
- Gary Cooper,
- John Wayne.

Note: She was bisexual.

Marlene Dietrich

- **Marlon Brando's lovers:** Marilyn Monroe, Pina Pellicer, Heidi Feiss, Faye Dunaway, Christina Ruiz, Tarita Teriipia.

Maureen O'Hara

- **Maureen O'Hara's lovers**:
- James Stewart,
- Tyrone Power,
- Gregory Peck,
- Anthony Quinn,
- Charles F. Blair, Jr.

Myrna Loy

- **Myrna Loy's lovers** (Just to name a few):
- Spencer Tracy,
- Arthur Hornblow Jr.,

- John Hertz, Jr.,
- Gene Markey;
- Howland H. Sergeant,
- William Powell,
- Cary Grant.
- **Nancy Reagan's dates** (Let's just be polite!):
- Spencer Tracey,
- Clark Gable,
- Peter Lawford,
- Robert Walker.

Nancy Reagan and actress Claudette Colbert stroll along beach in Barbados.
Nancy Reagan (R) and actress Claudette Colbert take a walk in the surf near Colbert's residence in Bridgetown, Barbados on April 9, 1982. The President and the first lady visited their friend during a day of relaxation on the island, -from the UPI Files.

- **Olivia de Havilland's lovers:**
- Errol Flynn,
- Pierre Galante,
- Jimmy Stewart,
- John Huston,
- Marcus Goodrich,
- Montgomery Clift.

Olivia de Havilland

- **Raquel Welch's lovers:** Elvis Presley, Gary Stretch (He did stretch a lot!), Robert Evans, Andre Weinfeld (He just got lucky!), Richard Palmer.
- **Rita Hayworth's lovers:**
- Prince Ali Khan (She married him),
- Orson Welles (She married him),
- Gary Merrill,
- Dick Haymes,
- Jorge Guinle,
- James Hill,
- George Jessel,
- Gary Cooper.

Rita Hayworth

- **Rock Hudson's lovers:**
- Tom Clark,
- Jill St. John,
- Jack Coates,
- March Christian,
- Armistead Maupin,
- Yvonne De Carlo.
- **Ronald Reagan's lovers:**
- Penny Edwards,
- Ruth Roman,
- Christine Larsen,
- Selene Walters.

Penny Edwards   Ruth Roman

Christine Larsen   Selene Walters

- **Tallulah Bankhead's lovers:** Alla Nazimova, Marlene Dietrich, Beatrice Lillie, Gary Cooper, John Emery, Donald Cook, William Langford. Note: She was bisexual.
- **Warren Beatty's lovers:** Madonna (No sweat!), Halle Berry (Very fruity...tuti frutti!), Annette Benning, Isabelle Adjani (Mais oui Madame, Voila! All yours!), Stephanie Seymour.
- **Yvonne De Carlo's lovers:** Rock Hudson, Bob Morgan, Robert Taylor, Mario Cabre, Carlos Thompson.
- **Zsa Zsa Gabor's lovers:** Michael O'Hara, Joshua S. Cosden, Jr., Jack Ryan, Felipe de Alba, Prince von Anhalt.
- **Susan Hayward's lovers**:
- Howard Hughes (This guy is always on the list of somebody!)
- Robert Wagner,
- Red Barry,
- Richard Egan,
- Floyd Eaton Chalkley.

265

Susan Hayward.

This book continues with Part Two: Book 2.

Table of Contents of Book 2, Part 2.

*** *** ***

Section 2: Modern Hollywood. Scandals in Recent Years...306

269

Chapter 3: Stars'/Celebrities' Mug-Shots and Arrests...335
They are up to no good!

Chapter 4: Sex, and over-sex...361

Chapter 5: What they have said about each other...and themselves...381

Chapter 6: Homeless Stars and Legends...once upon a time...390

Chapter 7: Who were they before they became famous and arrogant?...394

***   ***   ***

The author can be reached at delafayette6@aol.com